To Terry, Max,

THE LIVER DISORDERS AND HEPATITIS SOURCEBOOK

Howard J. Worman, M.D.

McGraw·Hill

New York   Chicago   San Francisco   Lisbon   London   Madrid   Mexico City
Milan   New Delhi   San Juan   Seoul   Singapore   Sydney   Toronto

Library of Congress Cataloging-in-Publication Data

Worman, Howard J.
   [Liver disorders sourcebook]
      The liver disorders and hepatitis sourcebook / Howard J. Worman.
         p.   cm.
      "A completely updated edition of the liver disorders sourcebook."
      Includes bibliographical references.
      ISBN 0-07-147225-8 (book : alk. paper)
      1. Liver—Diseases—Popular works.   I. Title.

   RC845.W67   2006
   616.3'62—dc22   2006002717

2 3 4 5 6 7 8 9 10 11 12 13 14 15   FGR/FGR   0 9 8 7 6

ISBN-13: 978-0-07-147225-8
ISBN-10:   0-07-147225-8

Artwork on pages 2, 3, 31, 212, and 213 by Elizabeth Weadon Massari

McGraw-Hill books are available at special quantity discounts to use as premiums and sales promotions, or for use in corporate training programs. For more information, please write to the Director of Special Sales, Professional Publishing, McGraw-Hill, Two Penn Plaza, New York, NY 10121-2298. Or contact your local bookstore.

The information contained in this book is intended to provide helpful and informative material on the subject addressed. It is not intended to serve as a replacement for professional medical advice. Any use of the information in this book is at the reader's discretion. The author and publisher specifically disclaim any and all liability arising directly or indirectly from the use or application of any information contained in this book. A health care professional should be consulted regarding your specific situation.

This book is printed on acid-free paper.

Contents

Preface

IN 1995, I CREATED the Diseases of the Liver website (http://cpmcnet
.columbia.edu/dept/gi/disliv.html), which was my first attempt to
inform the public about medical conditions. As a result of the interest
in this website, I wrote *The Liver Disorders Sourcebook* in 1999, followed in 2002 by *The Hepatitis C Sourcebook*, which focused on one
relatively "new" disease at that time.

Nothing has changed about the normal liver, its functions, and its
fundamental problems such as acute and chronic liver failure since those
efforts. And, unfortunately, there have not been many major advances
regarding many liver diseases, including alcoholic liver disease. However, there have been significant changes in some areas, particularly the
treatment of chronic hepatitis C, the treatment of chronic hepatitis B,
and how patients are prioritized for liver transplantation. Nonalcoholic
fatty liver disease is also drawing more attention. Many more people
with liver diseases also seem to be interested in "lifestyle" issues these
days. Since many of the changes in the treatment of viral hepatitis have
occurred since the first edition of *The Hepatitis C Sourcebook* and *The
Liver Disorders Sourcebook*, these books are now being combined into
this new edition: *The Liver Disorders and Hepatitis Sourcebook*.

While the material in this book is primarily for patients and family, some allied health professionals involved in the care of patients with

liver disorders also will find it very useful. It also should be a useful resource for individuals in other professions who do work that relates to liver disorders. *The Liver Disorders and Hepatitis Sourcebook* is written to help the reader develop an understanding of what the liver does, what goes wrong in various diseases, what a doctor thinks about when seeing patients with liver diseases, and what treatments are available as well as how to live with liver disease. *This book is not a substitute for professional medical care; specific diagnostic and treatment recommendations can only be made by an experienced physician who knows a patient's complete history.*

This book is not meant to be a comprehensive or exhaustive description of liver diseases. Some liver diseases are remarkably complex and, out of necessity, the information has been simplified for easy comprehension. However, because of the complexity of some liver diseases, brief discussions of virology, immunology, and genetics are included. I have tried my best to make these discussions as uncomplicated as possible. Readers who want to can probably skip them and still obtain some understanding of the various liver diseases. Other readers, who are fascinated by these basic aspects of disease, will hopefully be stimulated to look elsewhere to learn even more.

Several individuals have been helpful in the writing of this book from start to finish. My mother and father, Dora and Louis Worman, encouraged me to obtain the education that made everything possible. Dr. Fenton Schaffner, the late George Baher Professor of Medicine at the Mount Sinai School of Medicine, taught me how to be a liver specialist. I thank Edwin Baum for providing some legal advice and Arlene M. Sklar and Louis Worman for help with some business matters. My frequent discussions with Dr. Howard P. Reynolds while revising this book were also, as always, very interesting. I also thank Michele Matrisciani and Julia Anderson Bauer at McGraw-Hill for their support on this project, and last, but not least, I thank my wife, Terry, my son, Max, and my daughter, Naomi.

1

The Normal Liver

VIRTUALLY EVERYONE KNOWS that the liver is an organ essential to life, but most people do not really know what it does. Many will say that the liver plays some role in "purifying," or "cleansing," the blood. Some will know that it is the site of metabolism for many different drugs. Others will know that the liver is involved in the formation of bile.

The liver has many different functions, indeed. A thorough understanding of the three critical aspects of normal liver structure and function is essential to understanding what has gone wrong in a diseased liver. The first critical aspect is the liver's overall anatomy and, in particular, its blood supply. The second aspect is the synthetic biochemical functioning of the hepatocytes, the predominant cells in the liver. The third critical aspect is the central role of the liver in the metabolism and secretion of bilirubin.

Anatomy and Blood Supply

The liver is located in the right upper quadrant of the abdomen (Figure 1.1). If you place your fingers under your rib cage on the right side, you should be able to feel the edge of your liver when you take a deep breath. The liver itself is divided into the right and left lobes. A portion of the right lobe is subdivided into the caudate and quadrate lobes. Various ligaments separate the lobes from each other. Most of the liver's mass is found in the right lobe. Most of the liver's surface is covered by a capsule that contains nerves that can sense pain. The gallbladder is located under the liver.

Familiarity with the blood supply of the liver is essential to understanding its function as well as some of the major complications of cir-

Figure 1.1 Location of the Liver

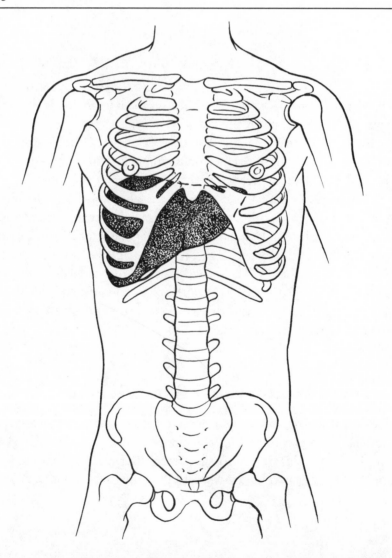

rhosis. About one-quarter of a person's blood volume passes through the liver every minute. How this blood supply is delivered to the liver is shown in Figure 1.2.

The liver receives most of its blood from the portal vein. This blood does not reach the liver directly from the heart but first passes through

Figure 1.2 Liver's Blood Supply

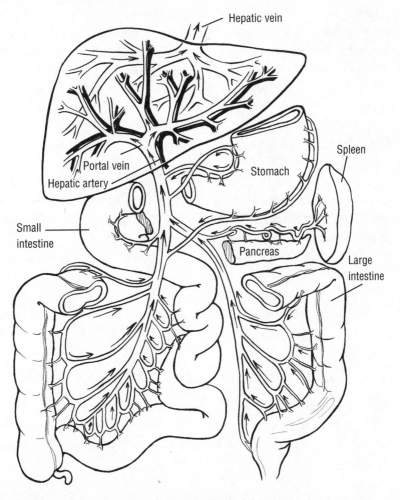

Blood enters the liver via the hepatic artery and portal vein. The blood from the hepatic artery is oxygen-rich and comes directly from the heart, whereas the blood in the portal vein has already absorbed nutrients and other substances from the gastrointestinal tract. Within the liver, the blood supplies from these two vessels mix. Blood leaves the liver via the hepatic vein, draining into the vena cava, which returns the blood to the heart.

the gut. Because of this, the liver is the first organ to gain nutrients, drugs, and toxins that are absorbed from the stomach and intestine. Consequently, the liver plays a primary role in the metabolism of these nutrients, drugs, and toxins. The portal vein also connects with the splenic vein, which drains the spleen. This connection is important because if the blood flow to, within, or exiting the liver is impeded for any reason, it will back up into the spleen.

The liver also receives blood from the hepatic artery. This blood reaches the liver directly from the heart after passing through the lungs and is higher in oxygen content than the blood in the portal vein. When entering the liver, the blood from the portal vein and hepatic artery mix. This dual blood supply to the liver makes the probability of suffering an infarction (or death of tissue due to loss of blood supply from a clot as occurs in the heart during a myocardial infarction, or heart attack) low.

Within the liver itself, blood flows through specialized capillaries called *sinusoids*. The sinusoids are quite permeable and allow compounds in the blood to have direct access to hepatocytes, which are the major cells of the liver. Many nutrients, drugs, and toxins in the blood readily pass through the walls of the sinusoids and are taken up by the hepatocytes, where they are metabolized.

Blood exits the liver via the hepatic vein. From the hepatic vein, the blood enters the body's largest vein, the vena cava, and returns to the heart. A small amount of blood flow to the liver may never have access to the hepatocytes, returning directly to the heart via the hepatic vein.

Biochemical Functions of Liver Cells

The liver performs numerous biochemical functions. These functions take place primarily in the hepatocytes, which are the predominant cells in the liver. Some of the most important biochemical functions of the liver are:

- Synthesis of blood clotting factors
- Metabolism of alcohol and many drugs
- Detoxification of various harmful substances

- Conjugation and secretion of bilirubin
- Synthesis of bile salts
- Metabolism of glucose (simple sugar) and carbohydrate (complex sugar)
- Metabolism of cholesterol and fatty acid
- Metabolism of protein

The liver synthesizes several factors involved in blood clotting, and normal function is necessary to prevent bleeding. Another function is synthesis and secretion of albumin, the major protein present in the blood. Albumin is necessary for maintaining proper fluid balance; decreases in blood albumin concentration can contribute to abnormal accumulation of fluid in the body. The synthesis of clotting factors and albumin are two of the most important biochemical functions of the liver, and they are frequently assessed when diagnosing and treating patients with liver disorders.

The liver is the site of metabolism of many nutrients. Carbohydrates, fats, and proteins are both broken down and synthesized there. Normal liver function is critical for maintaining adequate blood sugar concentrations. The liver is also the major site of ammonia metabolism. Ammonia is a nitrogen compound that primarily results from the metabolism of proteins. Abnormal liver function can cause poor mental functioning because ammonia (and probably other nitrogen compounds) is not being adequately metabolized.

Because most compounds absorbed from the gastrointestinal tract pass through the liver first before reaching the systemic circulation, the liver is the organ of "first pass" metabolism of many drugs. Many compounds present in the environment, some of which are toxins, are also first metabolized in the liver. Metabolism in the liver usually leads to detoxification of environmental compounds, hence the concept that the liver "purifies," or "cleanses," the blood. The detoxified metabolites are then eliminated from the body by either kidney secretion into the urine or secretion into the bile by the liver. Sometimes, liver metabolism can lead to the production of metabolites that are more toxic than the parent drug or environmental toxin itself. One example is carbon tetrachloride, which is metabolized in the liver and becomes an extremely toxic compound that kills liver cells.

Bilirubin Formation and Secretion

Bilirubin derives primarily from the breakdown of old red blood cells (a small fraction also comes from the breakdown of proteins in other organs). Dying red blood cells (the life span of a normal red blood cell is approximately 120 days) are taken up by specialized cells—primarily in the spleen—where they are destroyed. The major red blood cell protein hemoglobin, which is the protein that carries oxygen in the blood, is then chemically converted to bilirubin, which is greenish-yellow in color.

Bilirubin is extremely insoluble in water and circulates in the bloodstream bound to albumin. Albumin-bound bilirubin is taken up from the blood by hepatocytes. In hepatocytes, bilirubin is chemically converted by a process called *conjugation* into an increased water-soluble form. In conjugation, bilirubin undergoes a chemical reaction with a water-soluble compound called *glucuronic acid*. As a result of this chemical reaction, two glucuronic acid molecules are usually attached to one bilirubin molecule. The result is a compound known as *bilirubin diglucuronide*. Bilirubin diglucuronide is generally referred to as *conjugated bilirubin*. (Actually, a rather small amount of conjugated bilirubin has only one glucuronic acid molecule attached and is known as *bilirubin monoglucuronide*.) The bilirubin conjugation reaction normally proceeds extremely slowly, but in the liver it is catalyzed (sped up) due to an enzyme known as *UDP-glucuronosyltransferase*. Without this enzyme, bilirubin conjugation does not occur to any appreciable degree.

Conjugated bilirubin is secreted from the hepatocytes into the very tiny bile ducts within the liver. These tiny ducts merge into larger bile ducts that eventually form the common bile duct that empties into the small intestine. In the healthy liver, almost all of the conjugated bilirubin is secreted into the common bile duct and only a very small amount leaks out of hepatocytes and back into the bloodstream. As a result of conjugation in the liver and secretion into the bile, the total blood bilirubin concentration in normal individuals is usually less than 1 milligram per deciliter. The steps in bilirubin metabolism and secretion are outlined in Figure 1.3.

When bilirubin in the blood is measured in the clinical laboratory, values for direct and total bilirubin are usually reported. The direct

Figure 1.3 Metabolism of Bilirubin in the Liver

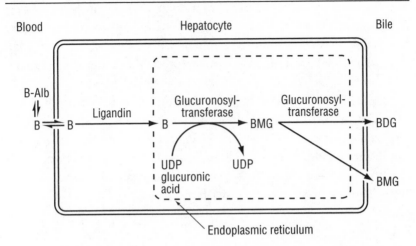

Albumin-bound bilirubin (B-Alb) is taken by hepatocytes from the blood. In hepatocytes, bilirubin (B) may be transiently bound to a compound called ligandin. The bilirubin is conjugated to glucuronic acid within the endoplasmic reticulum of the hepatocyte. The enzyme UDP-glucuronosyltransferase helps this chemical reaction take place. The conjugated bilirubin (primarily bilirubin diglucuronide [BDG] and a small amount of bilirubin monoglucuronide [BMG]) are secreted from the hepatocytes into the bile.

bilirubin represents roughly the more water-soluble conjugated bilirubin. The direct bilirubin measured in the clinical laboratory is normally only one-third or less of total bilirubin in the blood. Actually, there is much less conjugated bilirubin in the blood than the amount of direct bilirubin measured in the clinical laboratory. Because of the methodology routinely applied, the concentration of conjugated or direct bilirubin in the blood is usually overestimated. This is not significant as this overestimation is always accounted for in the normal values. Most of the total bilirubin in the blood is the unconjugated bilirubin produced from hemoglobin and other proteins prior to being conjugated in the liver. The unconjugated bilirubin measured either in the clinical laboratory or calculated as total bilirubin minus direct bilirubin is called *indirect bilirubin*.

The conversion of compounds to more water-soluble forms by conjugation in the liver is a general process that also plays a role in metabolism of compounds other than bilirubin. Drugs and toxins are frequently conjugated to glucuronic acid and become more water soluble, thus facilitating elimination from the body. Several slightly different forms of the enzyme UDP-glucuronosyltransferase are responsible for conjugation of different compounds with glucuronic acid. In addition, some drugs and toxins are conjugated to other water-soluble chemical moieties, such as sulfate, for secretion from the body.

Generally, conjugated bilirubin or other conjugated compounds, that leak from the liver into the blood are filtered readily by the kidneys and secreted in the urine. If the concentration of conjugated bilirubin in the blood becomes too high, it can be detected in the urine. If the liver for some reason fails to secrete conjugated bilirubin into the bile, the urine may appear yellowish or brown.

Critical Things to Remember About Liver Structure and Function

Before reading further, it is essential to keep in mind the following aspects of normal liver structure and function:

- The liver receives most of its blood from the portal vein. This blood passes first through the gut and is rich in materials absorbed from the stomach and intestine. The portal vein is also connected to the splenic vein.
- The liver is the first site of metabolism of many nutrients, drugs, and toxins.
- Hepatocytes, the predominant cells in the liver, perform many biochemical functions that are essential for normal life. Two critical biochemical functions of the liver that are assessed in diagnosing and following patients with liver diseases are the synthesis of blood clotting factors and the synthesis of albumin.
- The liver takes unconjugated bilirubin from the blood and conjugates it to a more water-soluble form that is secreted into the bile. The amount of bilirubin in the blood normally does not exceed 1 milligram per deciliter.

2

The Diseased Liver

LIVER DISEASE CAN AFFECT the normal functions of the liver. However, abnormalities in liver function are usually not apparent in most individuals with chronic liver disease until the disease is rather advanced. Clinical and laboratory evidence of abnormal function is usually not present unless the liver is significantly compromised. Patients with clinically abnormal liver function usually have advanced cirrhosis or significant acute destruction of liver cells, as discussed in Chapter 3. Nevertheless, there are clinical findings and laboratory tests that can detect liver disease prior to significant deterioration in liver function. Before discussing these clinical findings and laboratory tests, however, it is important to distinguish acute versus chronic liver disease.

Acute Versus Chronic Disease

A critical distinction in liver disease is to establish whether it is acute or chronic. Acute diseases occur suddenly and are usually relatively short in duration. Chronic diseases are typically long-term and their onset may be insidious. A general definition of a chronic liver disease is one lasting more than six months.

The concerns in acute and chronic liver disease are different to some extent. An acute liver disease resolves itself, becomes chronic, or kills the patient. Some acute liver diseases can cause a severe type of liver failure known as *fulminant hepatic failure*. (See Chapter 3.) The therapeutic goal in acute liver disease is to keep the patient alive and, in some cases, to prevent the disease from becoming chronic. This involves either curing the acute disease or supporting the patient until it spontaneously resolves.

By contrast, the therapeutic goal in chronic liver disease is to cure the disorder, prevent it from advancing, or control the complications. Preventing advancement of a chronic liver disease usually means stopping it from becoming cirrhosis. In an individual who already has cirrhosis, preventing further deterioration of liver function and controlling the resulting complications are the treatment goals.

Causes of Acute and Chronic Liver Disease

Several agents cause only acute liver disease:

- Hepatitis A virus
- Hepatitis E virus
- Other viral infections
- Overdose of some drugs
- Short-term exposure to some drugs and toxins
- Shock

Hepatitis A virus and hepatitis E virus are important examples. Infections with these viruses never become chronic. Other viruses, such as yellow fever or dengue, can cause acute liver disease. Single or brief exposures to certain toxic substances, or single overdoses of some drugs, can also cause acute liver disease.

Some liver diseases are chronic by definition. There are chronic congenital disorders resulting from the inheritance of abnormal genes such as hemochromatosis, Wilson disease, and alpha-1-antitrypsin deficiency. Primary biliary cirrhosis and sclerosing cholangitis are also chronic diseases. Autoimmune hepatitis is always a chronic disease. Cirrhosis, which is identified by scarring and nodules in the liver, is a chronic disease and occurs after long-term damage to the liver from inflammation or other insults, such as persistent bile duct obstruction or heart failure.

Several agents cause both acute and chronic hepatitis:

- Alcohol
- Many drugs
- Hepatitis B virus
- Hepatitis C virus
- Hepatitis D virus (only in individuals with hepatitis B)
- Circulatory problems (e.g., heart failure)

Drinking alcohol heavily for several weeks, for example, can cause acute fatty liver or hepatitis that will resolve if the individual stops drinking. However, most alcohol-induced liver disease is chronic as most alcohol abusers drink for years. There are several other drugs and toxins in addition to alcohol that can cause both acute and chronic liver disease.

The hepatitis B virus can cause both acute and chronic hepatitis. About 95 percent of adults infected with hepatitis B virus develop acute liver disease that resolves or, in about 2 percent of these cases, kills the patient if a liver transplant is not performed. About 5 percent of adults acutely infected with hepatitis B virus develop chronic hepatitis (hepatitis that lasts longer than six months). In newborn babies, the situation is virtually opposite that of adults, as about 90 percent of infants acutely infected with hepatitis B virus at or near birth become infected for life.

About 85 percent of individuals infected with hepatitis C virus develop chronic hepatitis. In rare cases, the hepatitis C virus can cause acute liver disease. In most cases, however, the acute infection is asymptomatic.

Problems in Distinguishing Acute from Chronic Liver Disease

Although seemingly obvious on the surface, the distinction between acute and chronic liver disease is not always straightforward. A patient with a chronic liver disease that has not been diagnosed at an earlier stage may come to the doctor with worsening, or newly apparent, symptoms or laboratory abnormalities. Examples could be Wilson disease, autoimmune hepatitis, or hemochromatosis. In other instances, patients with cirrhosis can have acute worsening of liver function if, for example, they develop an infectious illness. Such a case can be considered an acute exacerbation, or acute presentation, of a chronic disease.

Patients with acute liver diseases can often be misdiagnosed as having chronic liver diseases. Patients with severe, acute alcoholic or viral hepatitis, for example, sometimes have the same signs and symptoms as patients with end-stage cirrhosis and can be misdiagnosed as having cirrhosis. In these cases, the illness and symptoms can resolve completely. An acute liver disease can also occur superimposed on a chronic liver disease. In these cases, individuals with cirrhosis—a chronic disease—can develop acute hepatitis on top of the existing cirrhosis. A classic example is the alcoholic with cirrhosis whose condition suddenly worsens when developing acute alcoholic hepatitis from binge drinking. The doctor must keep all of these possibilities in mind when approaching a patient with a liver disease, especially one seeking medical treatment for the first time.

When Patients with Liver Disease Visit the Doctor

The diagnosis of liver diseases depends upon a combination of patient history, physical examination, laboratory tests, radiological tests (usually), and, frequently, a liver biopsy. It is hazardous to accurately diagnose a liver disease without knowing all of this information. Individuals often call or send me e-mail messages with one or two test results and ask, "What's wrong?" My answer always is, "Only a doctor who obtains a complete history, examines the patient, reviews all of the laboratory test results, knows the results of relevant radiological tests, and, in some cases, examines the liver biopsy can make an accurate diagnosis of liver disease." Having emphasized this fact, I will review the aspects of history, physical examination, blood tests, radiological tests, and liver biopsy relevant to the diagnosis of individuals with liver diseases. This information should provide patients with a general idea about what to expect when they see their doctors.

History

As in any medical specialty or subspecialty, a cornerstone of the diagnosis of liver disease is the patient's history. There are certain historical facts that are of primary importance. Patients should be willing to openly and honestly discuss the following issues with their doctors:

- Alcohol consumption
- Prescription and over-the-counter drug use
- Intravenous drug use, even if the use was only once long ago
- Sexual activities
- Blood transfusions
- Travel to or emigration from certain areas of the world
- Exposure to possible environmental toxins
- Ingestion of contaminated foods
- Liver disease in family members

Drug and alcohol use, in particular, must be carefully evaluated in a patient with liver disease. Alcohol abuse is the leading cause of acquired liver disease in the United States and most Western countries. Patients should not hide information from or lie to their doctors about the amount of alcohol they drink (nonetheless, virtually all individuals with alcohol abuse or dependence disorders significantly underreport alcohol consumption). The quantity of alcohol that individuals must consume to acquire liver disease varies tremendously; the reasons for these differences are unknown. Some individuals can drink half a gallon of alcohol a day and never develop liver disease (they will likely develop several other medical problems!) while others may develop liver disease from drinking as little as three drinks per day over many years. In general, alcohol should always be considered as a possible contributing factor to liver disease in individuals who regularly consume more than two drinks per day.

Both prescription and over-the-counter drugs can cause liver disease. It is essential for an examining doctor to obtain a thorough drug history from individuals with suspected liver disease and for patients to discuss all drug use in detail with their doctors. Even if drugs are not the cause of liver disease, drugs may be metabolized differently in patients with liver disease and can contribute to an underlying problem. Toxins and even unusual food products, such as Jamaican bush tea or *Amanita phalloides* mushrooms, also can cause liver disease.

Viruses that cause acute and chronic hepatitis are spread by various routes, and information about possible exposure is of vital importance to any medical history. Hepatitis B, C, and D viruses are spread by blood and blood products, and important patient information includes knowledge of past blood transfusions and past or present intravenous drug use. Even someone who used intravenous drugs just once in the remote past could be infected with the hepatitis B or C virus; thus, patients should openly discuss any prior drug use with their doctors. Questions about sex can be embarrassing, but a careful history of sexual practices is also important as hepatitis viruses, especially hepatitis B virus, can be transmitted by homosexual and heterosexual relations.

Hepatitis A is generally transmitted by contaminated foods—usually seafood—or unsanitary conditions of waste disposal. If a patient comes to the doctor with acute liver disease, it is important to rule out this virus as a cause and obtain a careful history of food consumption. A travel history is also important to detect travel to countries where hepatitis A is common or to parts of the world where infection due to hepatitis E virus occurs. Similarly, a history of living in certain countries in Asia, or parts of Africa where hepatitis B infection is endemic, should be ascertained. Past or present occupational exposure to blood products, such as employment or volunteer work in the health care field, also should be investigated.

Several liver diseases are inherited. For this reason, it is important to ask a patient with suspected liver disease about family history. A family history may also be relevant to liver diseases that are not inherited. For example, a careful family history may identify a household contact with viral hepatitis that could prove contagious.

Many individuals with liver disease will have no symptoms or only nonspecific complaints such as fatigue or depression; other symptoms, however, are very suggestive of liver disease. A history of current or past jaundice (yellow skin and eyes) would be suggestive of liver disease. Itching, generally all over the body, could also be suggestive of liver dysfunction. Swelling in the abdomen and/or legs caused by fluid retention could be from cirrhosis. In addition, mental confusion, from mild to severe, can occur due to cirrhosis or acute liver failure. Bruising easily and bleeding upon even slight contact with objects also may indicate abnormal liver function. A doctor should question any patient with suspected liver disease about such symptoms.

Physical Examination

All patients with suspected liver disease should undergo a complete physical. Many, or even perhaps most, patients with liver disease will have a normal physical examination. However, there are several physical signs that can indicate the presence of liver disease or the severity of liver dysfunction. The physical examination begins with "inspection." Signs of liver disease may be apparent to the examining doctor just by looking at a patient. Jaundice may be obvious. Evidence of muscle wasting or weight loss may be obvious in the patient with cirrhosis. Severe fluid retention in the abdomen may also be readily visible in patients with advanced cirrhosis or severe, more recent liver damage.

Every patient with liver disease should be weighed. Obese individuals are at increased risk for fatty liver. Fluid retention in cirrhosis can lead to weight gain, and weight should be regularly followed in individuals with cirrhosis. Weight loss also may occur in individuals who suffer from chronic liver abnormalities.

The doctor should also pay careful attention to specific parts of the physical examination that may indicate the presence of liver disease. The patient's hands should be examined for Depuytren's contracture, shortening and thickening of a tendon under the skin of the palm that can cause the middle fingers to be bent. Some individuals with cirrhosis or alcohol liver disease may have this. Patients with liver disease also may have what is known as *liver palms*, palms that are abnormally red in color.

Examining the skin is critical in the evaluation of a patient with suspected liver disease. Jaundice, a yellowing of the skin and whites of the eyes, is caused by a high concentration of bilirubin in the blood and is a hallmark of liver disease. It can also occur, however, in non-liver diseases, such as those caused by increased red blood cell destruction. At high blood bilirubin concentrations, the skin may appear obviously yellow. Jaundice is sometimes more readily observed under the nails or in the gums than in the skin, especially in individuals with dark skin. The skin should also be examined for bruises. Some individuals with chronic or severe liver disease have small vascular skin lesions called *spiders*, or more correctly, *spider angiomata*. These are usually found on the arms, shoulders, chest, and back (they are virtually never found below the waistline). Spider angiomata are small red dots with "legs" that radiate from the center (hence the name). They blanch when compressed and turn red again when pressure is released.

The head and eyes also should be examined carefully. Jaundice may first be apparent in the whites of the eyes before yellowing of the skin is detectable. Some individuals with liver disease, especially those with alcoholic cirrhosis, may have enlarged parotid glands (the salivary glands on the side of the face).

In patients with liver disease, examining the abdomen is very important. Protrusion of the abdomen may result from fluid retention. Some individuals with cirrhosis will have an umbilical hernia that sticks out of the belly button and can be temporarily pushed in by the doctor. The doctor should feel for the edge of the liver on the upper right side of the abdomen under the ribs as the liver may be enlarged or abnormal in texture. Similarly, the doctor should feel for the spleen on the left upper portion of the abdomen. The spleen should not be felt in normal individuals but may be swollen in patients with liver disease. The doctor should also "percuss" the liver, that is, drum on the abdomen. Percussion allows the size of the liver to be estimated.

The liver may be enlarged (hepatomegaly) in some diseases and shrunken in others. The doctor should feel around the abdomen for the presence of retained fluid, which can also be detected by percussion of the flanks, and look at the legs and ankles for evidence of fluid retention.

The nervous system also should be examined. Patients with severe acute liver disease or cirrhosis may have hepatic encephalopathy, which can cause mental changes. These mental changes can range from very subtle changes in mental status to deep coma. The first mental status change that usually occurs is the inability to construct simple objects, such as a six-point star. Patients with early hepatic encephalopathy may also have difficulty with "connect the dots" drawings similar to those that children do. In cases of severe hepatic encephalopathy, marked confusion can occur and patients may have a "liver flap" (asterexis) in which the hand drops when held up by the patient like the hand of a policeman stopping traffic.

Having reviewed these physical signs, it again must be emphasized that most individuals with liver disease will have a normal physical examination. Nevertheless, a careful physical examination is mandatory, and a doctor really cannot know what's going on without performing one.

Blood Tests

Blood testing plays an important role in the diagnosis of liver disease and in following patients with various liver disorders. Blood tests comprise only a part of the picture, however, and must be considered along with the patient's history and physical examination. Isolated laboratory test results usually have very little meaning outside of the entire clinical picture. Despite this fact, patients with liver disease (and sometimes doctors) too often focus a tremendous amount of concern—usually too much—on the meaning of isolated, abnormal laboratory test results. Most patients, and even some doctors, have a difficult time understanding the significance of laboratory tests in liver disease. Very frequently, too much weight is given to the absolute values and random fluctuations of laboratory test results. After cautioning again that a particular laboratory test result means little outside of the complete history, I will explain the relevance of various blood tests commonly used to assess patients with liver disease. Some of the relevant tests that usually comprise part of "routine" blood biochemistry panels are summarized in Table 2.1.

Aminotransferases (ALT and AST)

Aminotransferases are enzymes that facilitate certain chemical reactions within cells. Two major aminotransferases are present in hepatocytes, the primary liver cells. These are alanine aminotransferase (ALT) and aspartate aminotransferase (AST). (The older names for these enzymes, still used by some doctors and clinical laboratories, are SGPT and SGOT, respectively.) ALT is present almost exclusively in hepatocytes while AST is present in cells of some other tissues, such as heart and skeletal muscle. ALT and AST leak from dead or damaged cells into the bloodstream. As a result, their activities (*activity* is a unit of measurement used by biochemists that is roughly proportional to amount) in the blood can be

Table 2.1 Routine Blood Tests Relevant to Individuals with Liver Diseases

Test	What's Measured	Significance
ALT (SGPT)	Enzyme activity	Elevated in many liver diseases. Rough estimate for hepatocyte death from inflammation or other causes.
AST (SGOT)	Enzyme activity	Same as ALT, but also may be elevated in heart or muscle cell death. Usually two or more times higher than ALT in alcoholic hepatitis.
Alkaline phosphatase	Enzyme activity	Elevation suggests abnormality of large bile ducts outside of liver or tiny ones within. May be elevated in nonliver diseases, especially disorders of tumors or bone.
GGTP	Enzyme activity	Same as alkaline phosphatase but specific for bile ducts. May be elevated in normal individuals or individuals who drink excessive alcohol without structural liver disease.
Bilirubin	Concentration	Elevated in many liver diseases, but mostly bile duct obstruction, severe acute liver damage, or advanced cirrhosis. May be elevated in nonliver diseases such as those of red blood cells.
Albumin	Concentration	Decreased in severe liver disease. Usually decreased in end-stage cirrhosis. Can also be decreased in some kidney diseases, intestinal disorders, malnourishment, or any serious chronic disease.
Prothrombin	Time/INR	Increased in advanced cirrhosis or severe acute liver damage. May be time elevated in blood clotting disorders that are not related to the liver.

measured. In healthy individuals, the activities (amounts) of ALT and AST in the blood fall into normal ranges that vary slightly from one laboratory to another. When hepatocyte death is increased, as in hepatitis, ALT and AST leak from dying cells at greater rates and their activities in the blood are increased. Elevations in blood ALT and AST activities, therefore, suggest increased hepatocyte death.

ALT and AST activities are measured on routine blood testing panels as indicators of possible liver disease. Some doctors, nurses, and patients refer to ALT and AST as "liver enzymes," a very imprecise term I try to avoid. ALT and AST also have come to be known as "liver function tests." This is unfortunate because blood ALT and AST activities do not relate to the liver's function. I constantly have to remind many of the medical students, interns, residents, and fellows at Columbia and New York–Presbyterian Hospital that ALT and AST are *not* "liver function tests." The activities of these enzymes in the blood correlate roughly to the degree of ongoing liver cell death or damage, but *not* liver function.

In most cases of hepatocyte death, blood ALT and AST activities are elevated to approximately equal levels. One notable exception is alcoholic hepatitis, where for reasons that are unclear, the blood AST activity is frequently more highly elevated than the ALT activity. Blood AST activity, and usually to a lesser extent ALT activity, can also be elevated in nonliver diseases such as heart attack and skeletal muscle damage as these enzymes are present in heart and muscle cells as well as in hepatocytes. Sometimes, only the blood ALT activity will be elevated in liver disease while AST activity remains normal. Sometimes the opposite can occur.

Blood aminotransferase activities are elevated in many different liver diseases. In chronic hepatitis from any cause (e.g., viruses, drugs, alcohol), they are usually less than ten times normal. ALT and AST are also elevated in cases of acute liver cell necrosis (death) caused by shock, drugs, toxins, viral hepatitis, or other insults. In cases of massive liver cell death, in shock, for example, or after an overdose of a drug toxic to the liver, blood aminotransferase activities can be several hundred times normal immediately after the injury and then rapidly return to near normal in a few days.

The degree of elevation of blood AST and ALT activities roughly approximates the amount of liver cell death from inflammation or other causes. Some individuals with hepatitis can have significant inflammation on biopsy and only mild elevations of blood aminotransferase activities, however. In rare cases, some individuals will exhibit very high blood aminotransferase activities and only mild inflammation on liver biopsy. This is one reason why liver biopsy is usually essential to the evaluation of patients with chronic hepatitis.

The five most important points to remember about blood AST and ALT activities are:

1. Blood AST and ALT activities are elevated in many different liver diseases where liver cell death from inflammation or other causes occurs. Elevations in blood ALT and AST activities are not specific for any particular diagnosis and further evaluation is necessary.
2. AST and ALT activities are not "liver function tests" despite common jargon used by doctors and patients. ALT and AST activities can be very high in someone with acute liver cell death and reasonably good liver function who will completely recover. On the other hand, they can be normal in someone with end-stage cirrhosis and virtually no remaining liver function.
3. Elevations of blood aminotransferase activities strongly suggest the presence of liver disease and should be evaluated by a doctor.
4. In individuals with known chronic liver disease, such as viral hepatitis, blood ALT and AST should be periodically followed as approximate markers of the amount of liver inflammation or liver cell death.
5. ALT and AST activities should be tested in people at risk for liver disease. Examples of people at risk include those taking certain drugs that can affect the liver and those with a past history of injection drug use.

Alkaline Phosphatase and Gamma-Glutamyltranspeptidase

Two other enzyme activities measured routinely in the blood are important to diagnosing liver disease. These are the alkaline phosphatase and gamma-glutamyltranspeptidase (GGTP) activities. (Perhaps you can begin to appreciate why "liver enzymes" is not a good term to describe any blood test related to the liver.) Alkaline phosphatase is found in many different cells including those lining the large bile ducts and very tiny bile ducts in the liver. Alkaline phosphatase is also present in cells of the kidney, intestine, bone, and placenta. Blood alkaline phosphatase activity can be elevated in disorders involving any of these tissues. GGTP, on the other hand, is present almost exclusively in the parts of the hepatocytes that secrete bile plus the bile duct cells.

Elevations in blood alkaline phosphatase and GGTP activities, especially in the setting of normal or only modestly elevated ALT and AST activities, suggest bile duct disease or abnormal bile flow. These can be diseases of either the large bile ducts outside the liver (e.g., obstruction by a gallstone or cancer) or of the tiny bile ducts within the liver. Many drugs also cause stagnation of bile flow, or cholestasis, resulting in elevated blood alkaline phosphatase and GGTP activities.

In liver diseases not directly affecting the bile ducts, such as hepatitis or cirrhosis, blood alkaline phosphatase and GGTP activities may also be elevated. In these diseases, however, elevations are usually more modest, and ALT and AST activities become elevated to a more significant degree when hepatocyte death predominates.

In contrast, liver diseases that primarily affect the bile ducts are characterized by more marked elevations in blood alkaline phosphatase and GGTP activities and only modestly elevated or normal blood ALT and AST activities.

Abnormally high blood alkaline phosphatase may also be seen in a patient with bone disease. In addition, blood alkaline phosphatase activity may be elevated in pregnancy as it is produced by the placenta. In these instances, blood GGTP activity should be normal. If blood alkaline phosphatase activity is elevated together with serum GGTP activity, bile duct or liver disease is the likely cause.

Elevations in only blood GGTP activity can be problematic to evaluate. GGTP activity is an extremely sensitive and variable test and may be elevated to some degree in virtually any liver disease. It can also be elevated in some normal individuals and people with very subtle and clinically insignificant liver abnormalities. GGTP is also induced by many drugs, including alcohol, and its activity in the blood may be increased in heavy drinkers. Isolated elevations in blood GGTP activity suggest early bile duct disorders, liver diseases, heavy alcohol use, or drug use. However, GGTP also can be elevated in the absence of meaningful liver disease. Only an experienced physician who knows a patient's entire history can determine if and how an isolated elevation in blood GGTP activity needs to be evaluated further.

As is the case with aminotransferase activities, elevations in blood alkaline phosphatase or GGTP activities are not diagnostic for any specific disease. Their elevations suggest disorders of the bile ducts or bile flow. They may also be elevated to a lesser degree than ALT and AST in liver diseases that primarily affect hepatocytes.

Bilirubin

An elevated concentration of bilirubin in the blood is known as *hyperbilirubinemia*. Hyperbilirubinemia occurs as a result of four problems: (1) increased production; (2) decreased uptake by the liver; (3) decreased conjugation; or (4) decreased secretion from the liver. The normal bilirubin concentration in the blood is approximately less than 1 milligram per deciliter. When the blood bilirubin exceeds about 2 milligrams per deciliter, jaundice becomes apparent.

In disorders causing increased production of bilirubin, the indirect bilirubin concentration in the blood will be elevated. Increased bilirubin production results from conditions that cause increased destruction of red blood cells and not from liver diseases. In such conditions, the direct bilirubin concentration in the blood will be normal as long as liver function is not compromised.

Indirect bilirubin concentration in the blood is also primarily increased in conditions that cause decreased bilirubin uptake by the liver or decreased conjugation within the liver. Decreased bilirubin uptake by hepatocytes can be caused by some drugs, fasting, and infections. Serious problems with bilirubin conjugation almost always appear in childhood. These conditions include hereditary diseases in which the enzyme that conjugates bilirubin is lacking or abnormal, and jaundice of premature babies in which conjugation of bilirubin is impaired.

Most acquired liver diseases in adults cause impairment in bilirubin secretion from liver cells that results in elevations primarily in the direct bilirubin concentration in the blood. In most chronic acquired liver diseases, the blood bilirubin concentration is usually normal until a significant amount of liver damage has occurred and cirrhosis is present. The rise in blood bilirubin concentration is roughly proportional to the amount of liver dysfunction. In acute liver diseases, the serum bilirubin concentration usually rises in proportion to the severity of liver damage.

Disorders that cause obstruction of the small and large bile ducts also cause elevations in the direct bilirubin concentration in the blood. Some drugs also impede bile flow in the liver and cause elevations in direct bilirubin concentration. In these disorders, the blood alkaline phosphatase and GGTP activities are usually elevated concurrently.

When the concentration of direct bilirubin in the blood becomes high, some of it is filtered by the kidneys. This excreted bilirubin turns the urine yellowish to brown in color. Bilirubin can also be detected by urinalysis.

Albumin

Albumin is the most abundant protein in the bloodstream. It is synthesized in the liver and secreted into the blood. If liver function is abnormal, the blood albumin concentration may fall. This usually occurs in patients with cirrhosis who have moderate or advanced liver dysfunction. The albumin concentration in the blood also can be low in conditions other than liver diseases including serious malnutrition, kidney diseases, and rare forms of intestinal dysfunction. Low albumin concentration in the blood is sometimes referred to as *hypoalbuminemia*.

Prothrombin Time

When liver function is compromised, the synthesis of several blood clotting factors may be decreased. The prothrombin time (PT) is a blood clotting test that measures the function of several blood clotting factors. The PT is sometimes reported in time (seconds) compared to control. Another way to report the PT is using the International Normalized Ratio, or INR. The World Health Organization created the INR because PT results may vary depending on the reagent used in a particular laboratory. INR is a conversion that takes into account the different sensitivities of the laboratory reagent and is mostly widely used today as the standard to report the value of the PT.

The PT is prolonged when blood concentrations of some of the clotting factors made by the liver are low. In chronic liver diseases, the PT is usually not significantly prolonged until cirrhosis has developed and the amount of liver damage is significant. In acute liver diseases, the PT can be prolonged due to severe liver damage and then return to normal as the patient recovers. The PT can also be prolonged in other conditions besides liver diseases, such as vitamin K deficiency (which can occur from malabsorption in some bile duct diseases) and inherited or acquired blood clotting disorders. Drugs, such as warfarin

(Coumadin), which is used therapeutically as an anticoagulant, can also prolong PT.

Complete Blood Count and Platelet Count

The complete blood count (CBC) is an important laboratory test in patients with liver diseases. Although not specific for liver problems, abnormalities may be seen on the CBC in patients with liver diseases. Individuals with chronic liver disease, especially cirrhosis, can be anemic and have low serum hemoglobin concentrations and hematocrits, which are roughly proportional to the number of red blood cells. Patients with cirrhosis can also have decreased white blood cell counts (white blood cells fight infection). On the other hand, the white blood cell count can be increased in individuals with acute inflammatory liver diseases such as viral or alcoholic hepatitis.

An important part of the CBC in individuals with liver disease is the platelet count. Platelets are the smallest of the blood cells and are involved in blood clotting. In individuals with cirrhosis or very severe, acute liver disease, the spleen can become enlarged as blood flow through the liver is impeded. Platelets may become trapped in the enlarged spleen and, as a result, the platelet count can fall. A low platelet count (thrombocytopenia) in a patient with chronic liver disease suggests the presence of cirrhosis. Low platelet counts are not specific for liver diseases, however, and can be observed in many different conditions.

Serum Protein Electrophoresis

Serum protein electrophoresis is an informative blood test for patients with liver disease; however, it is not routinely done by most physicians. In this test, the blood's major proteins are separated in an electric field and their concentrations measured. The serum proteins measured in this test are albumin, alpha-globulins, beta-globulins, and gamma-globulins. The result can provide clues to several diagnostic possibilities and also about the liver's function.

Ammonia

Blood ammonia concentrations can increase when the liver fails. Ammonia is absorbed from the intestine, where it is generated by the breakdown of proteins by bacteria that live in the colon. Since ammonia is not effectively removed from the blood by the failing liver or the liver with advanced cirrhosis, the concentration of ammonia in the blood increases.

Elevations in blood ammonia concentration very roughly correlate to the degree of hepatic encephalopathy. However, hepatic encephalopathy should be followed by physical signs and symptoms and not by serial determinations of the blood ammonia. Onetime determination of blood ammonia concentration will suggest that the liver may not be properly functioning if it is elevated. Blood ammonia concentrations can be elevated in conditions other than liver failure, including rare metabolic disorders.

Laboratory Tests for Specific Liver Diseases

Several blood tests are performed for the diagnosis of specific liver diseases. Specific tests for viral components in serum and antibodies against viruses are used to diagnose viral hepatitis. Tests for certain autoantibodies (abnormal antibodies that recognize constituents of a person's own cells) are useful in the diagnosis of autoimmune liver diseases. Measurements of various metabolic products or minerals are helpful in the diagnosis of inherited liver diseases. Some of the various laboratory tests for specific viral, autoimmune, and congenital liver diseases are listed in Table 2.2. These tests are discussed in greater detail in subsequent chapters on the specific liver diseases.

Radiological Tests

Radiological procedures may be used to evaluate patients with liver diseases. Each of these tests has certain strengths and all have limitations. The most common radiological procedures used in the evaluation of liver diseases are:

- Ultrasound or sonography
- Computerized axial tomography (CAT or CT) scan
- Magnetic resonance imaging (MRI) scan
- Liver-spleen scan
- Tagged red blood cell scan
- Magnetic resonance cholangiopancreatography (MRCP)
- Endoscopic retrograde cholangiopancreatography (ERCP)

Table 2.2 Laboratory Tests for Viral, Autoimmune, and Congenital Liver Diseases*

Condition	Test
Viral Hepatitis	
Hepatitis A	Antibodies against viral proteins for past or current infection
Hepatitis B	Antibodies against viral proteins for evidence of past or current infection; test for viral protein or DNA in blood for current infection
Hepatitis C	Antibodies against viral proteins and presence of viral RNA in blood for current infection
Hepatitis D	Antibodies against viral proteins for current infection
Hepatitis E	Antibodies against viral proteins for past or current infection
Autoimmune Diseases	
Autoimmune hepatitis	Autoantibodies against proteins from cell nuclei (antinuclear antibodies) and smooth muscle cells (antismooth muscle antibodies)
Primary biliary cirrhosis	Autoantibodies against proteins from mitochondria (antimitochondrial antibodies) and certain antinuclear antibodies
Primary sclerosing cholangitis	Autoantibodies known as "atypical ANCA"
Congenital Diseases	
Hemochromatosis	Iron, transferrin, and ferritin
Wilson disease	Ceruloplasmin, urine copper
Alpha-1-antitrypsin deficiency	Alpha-1-antitrypsin concentration

*More information can be found in subsequent chapters on the specific diseases.

The methodology of performing each of these tests as well as the indications for and the limitations of each are discussed in the following sections.

Ultrasound or Sonography

The ultrasound examination or sonogram is the most widely used radiological procedure to evaluate patients with liver diseases. The test is noninvasive and relatively cheap. To perform the test, probes that emit and detect sound waves are placed against the surface of the abdomen.

An image based on the deflection and penetration of sound waves is then generated. There are virtually no risks to performing an ultrasound of the liver.

Ultrasound is an excellent test for the detection of liver masses such as tumors or cysts. It is also a very powerful method to determine widening of the bile ducts that can result from obstruction due to a stone or tumor. Ultrasound also provides a clear image of the gallbladder and is very sensitive for detecting gallstones. Combined with another type of sound wave analysis that detects Doppler shifts (a change in the pitch of a sound wave emanating or reflected from a moving object, such as the pitch of a train whistle when the train is moving toward or away from you), ultrasound can provide information about blood flow in the major veins and arteries of the liver.

Although often used on patients with acute and chronic hepatitis, an ultrasound provides very little to no useful information in such cases. Ultrasound cannot diagnose hepatitis (inflammation of the liver) or accurately assess the degree of inflammation or scar tissue (fibrosis) in the liver. Drug, alcoholic, or viral hepatitis cannot be diagnosed by ultrasound. Cirrhosis cannot be diagnosed reliably unless it is advanced and the liver is shrunken and nodular. The results of ultrasound scanning provide no information about liver function. Although an ultrasound can provide some clues as to the presence of fat in the liver, it is not by itself adequate to diagnose the condition known as *fatty liver*.

In sum, ultrasound is an excellent test for the detection of liver masses and gallstones and the assessment of bile ducts and gallbladder. It is not capable of assessing liver function or the degree of inflammation or fibrosis in hepatitis. It cannot diagnose cirrhosis unless it is advanced and the liver is shrunken or nodular. Ultrasound is noninvasive, and there are no real risks associated with the procedure, except risks associated with additional testing due to inconclusive scans.

Computerized Axial Tomography Scan

Computerized axial tomography, better known as *CAT* or *CT scanning*, generates an image based upon X-rays taken from multiple angles. To perform a CAT scan, the patient lies in a scanner shaped like a giant doughnut and X-rays are emitted and detected from multiple locations around the body. A computer reconstructs an image based upon the penetration and scattering of X-rays. A CAT scan is generally a safe procedure with one of its few possible side effects being an allergic reaction to the intravenous contrast dyes sometimes administered prior to the test. Intravenous contrast agents can also cause acute kidney failure in individuals with kidney problems.

CAT scanning of the liver has many of the same attributes as ultrasound. It is an excellent way to detect masses and gallstones and to image the gallbladder and bile ducts. It is one of the best tests to assess the extent of liver tumors and image the entire abdomen. It also can be used to accurately measure the size of the liver. CAT scans of the liver have most of the same limitations as ultrasound. Like ultrasound, CAT scans can diagnose cirrhosis only if it is advanced and the liver is shrunken and nodular. CAT scans cannot be used to diagnose hepatitis or estimate the degree of inflammation or scarring in the liver. Finally, CAT scans reveal nothing about liver function.

CAT scans are more expensive than ultrasound and more difficult to perform. It is not a routine test for individuals with liver diseases. In most cases, it should not be used in individuals with chronic liver disease unless tumors, other masses, bile duct disorders, or gallbladder disorders are suspected.

Magnetic Resonance Imaging Scan

Magnetic resonance imaging (MRI) scans use nuclear magnetic resonance to produce images. The patient is placed in a very strong magnetic field to align the spins of the protons in the atoms in the patient's body. "Spin relaxation times" (the time it takes protons to change rotation when the body is pulsed with radio waves, which varies in different chemical environments) are measured and used to generate images of the internal organs. To perform an MRI scan, the patient is usually placed in a small "tunnel" that is surrounded by giant magnets. MRI is similar to CAT scan in its strengths and limitations. It may be slightly more sensitive for the evaluation of certain tumors.

Liver-Spleen Scan

The liver-spleen scan is a nuclear medicine test that can occasionally detect the presence of cirrhosis. In this test, a radioactive compound is injected into the patient and a picture taken with a camera that detects the emitted radiation. If blood flow to the liver is "backed up," as it might be in cirrhosis, the test will detect a "colloid shift" in which more of the radioactive material is taken up by the bone marrow as opposed to the liver. The liver-spleen scan is used less and less today and provides useful information only occasionally. It cannot diagnose cirrhosis in its early stages.

Tagged Red Blood Cell Scan

In a tagged red blood cell scan, a radioactive material is attached to red blood cells that are then injected into the patient's vein. A picture of the liver is taken with a camera that detects the emitted radioactivity. This test is excellent for one particular purpose: detection of hemangioma, a benign tumor of the liver. Because hemangioma has a very rich blood supply, the radioactive tagged red blood cells accumulate in it and the camera can visualize the hemangioma. As ultrasound and CT scan have become more sophisticated in recent years and very often can reliably be used to diagnose liver hemangioma, the tagged red blood cell scan is being used less frequently.

Magnetic Resonance Cholangiopancreatography

Magnetic resonance cholangiopancreatography (MRCP) is a relatively new type of MRI that allows for evaluation of the bile ducts, pancreatic duct, and gallbladder. It is very useful in the evaluation of bile duct stones, obstruction of the bile ducts by tumors, and chronic pancreatitis. In most instances, MRCP can be completed in approximately ten minutes.

Endoscopic Retrograde Cholangiopancreatography

Endoscopic retrograde cholangiopancreatography (ERCP) is used to visualize the bile ducts and gallbladder. In ERCP, a fiber-optic tube (endoscope) is inserted into the patient's esophagus and passed to the small intestine. The patient is lightly sedated during this procedure. A smaller tube is then inserted into the end of the common bile duct that empties into the small intestine. Dye is injected into the bile duct to fill the smaller bile ducts within the liver and the ducts from the pancreas and gallbladder. After dye injection, X-ray images are taken of the upper abdomen. As the injected dye does not permit X-rays to pass through it, the filled structures appear white on a dark background. ERCP is the most sensitive procedure used to visualize the bile ducts. Subtle abnormalities or very small gallstones not seen on ultrasound or CT scanning can be detected. A major advantage of ERCP is that it can be modified to perform procedures such as removing gallstones stuck in the bile duct or placing a stent through a bile duct obstruction. It also can be used to obtain tissue samples from the bile ducts, for example, to biopsy a mass to determine if it is a tumor.

Liver Biopsy

Despite the availability of numerous blood tests and radiological procedures to assess the liver, biopsy provides critical information that none of the other tests can. In most chronic liver diseases, adequate diagnosis and treatment plans can be made only after a biopsy is performed. In short, in the absence of contraindications, liver biopsy is usually an important diagnostic test for all patients with chronic, but usually not acute, liver diseases.

Most liver biopsies are performed percutaneously (through the skin) with a needle. The patient is awake and not sedated. A percutaneous liver biopsy does not hurt that much. While the patient lies on his or her back, a spot in the right mid-axillary line (a line drawn roughly from the armpit to the hip) between two ribs is identified by the doctor, as shown in Figure 2.1. The area is cleaned with an antiseptic solution and numbed with lidocaine (similar to how the dentist numbs the mouth before filling a cavity). The doctor then breaks the tough surface skin with a sharp metal stick. A needle at the end of a syringe is placed lightly into the small hole in the skin. While the patient is breathing calmly, the doctor rapidly sticks the needle into the liver and withdraws it in one swift motion that takes less than one second. In the process, a tiny piece of liver is sucked into the needle attached to the syringe. Most liver biopsies are preformed "blindly," with the doctor knowing where to stick the needle because of the normal position of the liver, a large organ. Sometimes, a radiologist will perform the biopsy with ultrasound or CT imagining.

After the biopsy, the patient remains in bed for a period of time before being sent home. During this time, a nurse should periodically check the patient's pulse and blood pressure to ensure that there is no

Figure 2.1 Percutaneous Needle Biopsy of the Liver

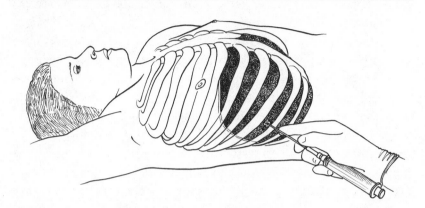

As the patient lies on his back, a spot in the right mid-axillary line between two ribs (as shown by the location of the needle in the diagram) is identified. The area is cleaned with antiseptic and numbed with lidocaine. The doctor then breaks the tough surface skin with a sharp metal stick. A needle at the end of a syringe is placed lightly into the small hole in the skin. While the patient is breathing calmly, the doctor rapidly sticks the needle into the liver and withdraws it in one swift motion that takes less than one second.

serious bleeding. Usually I perform liver biopsies around 8 A.M. or 9 A.M., let the patient have lunch in bed around noon, and send him or her home around 1 P.M. or 2 P.M.

The thought of a liver biopsy often provokes considerable anxiety in the patient (and some doctors, too). However, if patients relax throughout the procedure, there is very little pain. The sensation associated with the actual biopsy (sticking a needle into the liver) has been described by many patients as feeling like being punched in the ribs. There may also be some dull pain in the right shoulder after the biopsy as irritation of the capsule of the liver is often referred as pain to that area. There is usually a little bleeding at the site of the biopsy but often not more than can be routinely washed away with a couple of pieces of cotton.

In patients who do not have low platelet counts, elevated PTs, or other evidence of abnormal blood clotting, percutaneous biopsy is a safe procedure. The major complication is bleeding that may very rarely require blood transfusion in less than one in one hundred cases. Although deaths from percutaneous biopsy do occur, they are extremely rare in patients with normal platelet counts and PTs who demonstrate absence of advanced liver disease, of fluid in the abdomen, or of bleeding tendencies.

If the platelet count is too low, the PT is too high, or significant ascites (fluid in the abdomen) is present, percutaneous liver biopsy should probably not be performed. In these cases, liver tissue can be obtained using other approaches. One alternative approach is to insert a catheter into the jugular vein in the neck. Another approach is with a laparoscope, an instrument inserted into the abdomen through which the doctor can see and cauterize bleeding areas. An open surgical liver biopsy can be performed as a last resort. Blind, percutaneous biopsy is also usually not appropriate if the aim is to obtain tissue from a liver tumor. In such cases, biopsy should be performed by a radiologist under ultrasound or CT guidance, with a laparoscope, or by a surgeon in an open procedure.

Why perform a liver biopsy? Several biopsy findings are diagnostic for particular diseases. Others confirm the diagnosis suspected from clinical and laboratory data. Even if the diagnosis is relatively certain based on a patient's medical history, physical examination, and blood tests, a liver biopsy is usually the only way to know exactly what's going on in the liver. By looking at a piece of liver tissue under a microscope, the pathologist can determine the precise degree of inflammation and scar tissue in cases of chronic hepatitis. Usually biopsy can establish if chronic hepatitis is due to alcohol, viruses, or a combination of both. It is the only accurate way to diagnose fatty liver or hepatitis caused by fat. And unless cirrhosis is advanced, liver biopsy is the only way to establish its presence or absence.

Special studies can also be performed on liver tissue obtained at biopsy to definitively diagnose some diseases. For example, tissue iron content can be measured in suspected cases of hereditary hemochromatosis, in which case iron would be elevated. Copper content can be measured in Wilson disease, in which case copper would be high. Special tests can be performed on liver tissue and used to diagnose rare metabolic disorders such as glycogen storage diseases. Special stains of biopsy material can be used to detect accumulation of alpha-1-antitrypsin in cases of alpha-1-antitrypsin deficiency. Other special stains can be used to demonstrate the presence of viruses, other infectious agents, and certain types of cancer cells.

In sum, liver biopsy often provides data critical to the overall assessment of many patients with liver diseases. It is usually not necessary in acute liver diseases that resolve and in which a diagnosis can be established without it. In patients with chronic liver disease, however, liver biopsy is often the only way to clearly assess the status of the liver. It is also frequently the only way to determine the patient's prognosis, in particular the presence of cirrhosis.

3

The Failing Liver

LIVER FAILURE OCCURS when a large portion of hepatocytes (the major cells in the liver) die or cease to function. The liver can fail with sudden or acute loss of liver cell function in an otherwise healthy body. The presentation in such cases of sudden liver failure is dramatic. Liver failure can also occur gradually in patients with cirrhosis who slowly lose liver function over time. Patients with cirrhosis can also suddenly suffer from liver failure as a result of a new source of damage to an organ that is functioning only marginally.

As with liver diseases in general, liver failure can be broken down into two categories: acute and chronic. Although many signs and symptoms overlap, there are important differences. The first part of this chapter discusses acute, or sudden, liver failure in individuals who do not have underlying liver disease. In particular, it will focus on the most severe type of acute liver failure, known as *fulminant hepatic failure*. The rest of this chapter looks at chronic liver failure, which in virtually all cases occurs as a result of cirrhosis. Some complications from cirrhosis, however, do not result from loss of hepatocytes per se, but from abnormal architecture of the cirrhotic liver.

Fulminant Hepatic Failure

Fulminant hepatic failure is acute liver failure with hepatic encephalopathy. Hepatic encephalopathy is abnormal mental functioning that results from failure of the liver to remove ammonia and other toxins from the blood. Several medical researchers have proposed slightly different definitions for fulminant hepatic failure. Common to all of these definitions is the acute onset of liver failure with hepatic encephalopathy. The term *fulminant hepatic failure* should not be used for patients with underlying chronic liver disease. In fulminant hepatic failure, encephalopathy must result directly from, and occur concurrently or within a short time after, acute liver injury. Fulminant hepatic failure should not be used unless liver failure is acute and accompanied by encephalopathy. If encephalopathy is not present but other signs and symptoms of liver dysfunction are, the condition should be described as acute liver failure.

The patient with fulminant hepatic failure will have other indications of liver failure besides hepatic encephalopathy. These indications usually include jaundice and may, after some time, include ascites and edema. Blood alanine aminotransferase (ALT) and aspartate aminotransferase (AST) activities will often be markedly elevated as a result of the massive hepatocyte necrosis that causes fulminant hepatic failure. Blood AST and ALT activities may be elevated for only a few days, however, and then rapidly return to normal or near normal. Remember, ALT and AST activities are not liver function tests. Right after an acute, massive injury to the liver, the blood ALT and AST activities will be extremely high—even thousands of times above normal—because all of the liver hepatocytes die suddenly. Blood AST and ALT activities will then return to normal in a few days as virtually no more hepatocytes remain to die. Despite having normal aminotransferase activities at this time, a patient's liver may not be functioning.

Fulminant hepatic failure is almost always associated with elevated bilirubin concentration in the blood and prolonged prothrombin time. When hepatocytes die, bilirubin is no longer metabolized sufficiently in the liver and the serum concentration rises. As the conjugating ability of the liver is very high, the few remaining hepatocytes may conjugate bilirubin but it will not be secreted into bile and return into the blood. As a result, both direct and, to some extent, indirect bilirubin concentrations in the blood can rise in fulminant hepatic failure. Similarly, production of clotting factors normally made in hepatocytes is reduced significantly and prothrombin time increases. In fact, the degree of prolongation of prothrombin time is a fairly good predictor of the severity of liver failure. If liver function does not return to normal, then albumin concentration in the blood will also begin to fall over a period of several days to weeks as its synthesis also decreases.

In fulminant hepatic failure, encephalopathy can progress to coma if liver function does not return. Brain edema or swelling, which also can result from fulminant hepatic failure, can lead to irreversible brain damage and death. The kidneys and lungs may also fail, allowing the patient to become susceptible to massive infections. Bleeding complications occur because clotting factors are no longer adequately synthesized and the platelet count gradually falls.

Causes of Fulminant Hepatic Failure

Many of the agents that cause acute liver disease can cause fulminant hepatic failure. In addition, shock caused by hemorrhage, severe dehydration, heatstroke, or overwhelming infection (sepsis) can cause the liver to fail. In many patients admitted to hospitals with fulminant hepatic failure, the cause is never determined. This may be because the patient deteriorates too rapidly or is too sick for appropriate diagnostic tests to be performed. Sometimes the cause, such as ingestion of a toxin, is never witnessed or reported by the patient. Table 3.1 lists some causes of fulminant hepatic failure.

Wilson disease and autoimmune hepatitis are marked with asterisks in Table 3.1. Individuals with these diseases can present with sudden onset liver failure with encephalopathy that appears identical to fulminant hepatic failure. These diseases are chronic but can present as acute liver failure. Therefore, precisely speaking, the term *fulminant hepatic failure* does not apply to a patient with a chronic liver disease, even if the disease presents as sudden liver failure with encephalopathy.

Table 3.1 Causes of Fulminant Hepatic Failure

Acute Viral Hepatitis	Drugs and Toxins	Shock to Liver	Other Causes
Hepatitis A	Overdose of acetaminophen (over-the-counter pain reliever)	Hemorrhage	Fatty liver of pregnancy
Hepatitis B	Halothane (rarely used)	Sepsis (overwhelming infection)	Wilson disease*
Hepatitis C (rarely)	Isoniazid (used to treat tuberculosis)	Heatstroke	Autoimmune hepatitis*
Hepatitis D	*Amanita phalloides* (poisonous mushrooms)	Heart failure	
Hepatitis E	Carbon tetrachloride	Severe dehydration	
Yellow fever	Others		
Others (very rare)			

*Although patients with these disorders can present with signs and symptoms identical to fulminant hepatic failure, both are technically chronic diseases.

Treatment

Patients with fulminant hepatic failure are among the sickest in any hospital. The major goal of treatment is to keep the patient alive and free of serious complications until liver function spontaneously recovers or emergency liver transplantation can be performed. In some patients, hepatocytes regenerate and liver function returns to normal. Until liver function returns, however, the patient may be comatose and suffer from numerous complications. In other cases, liver function never returns and the patient dies unless a liver transplant is performed. One of the major challenges in caring for patients with fulminant hepatic failure is to try to predict in which cases liver function will return with supportive care only, and in which instances emergency liver transplantation will be absolutely necessary to save the patient's life. This is not always an easy decision.

Patients with fulminant hepatic failure should be admitted to an intensive care unit. Treatment is directed at supporting the patient and preventing and dealing with complications. Patients must often be put on ventilators to assist with breathing, and dialysis may be necessary if kidney failure occurs. Intravenous fluid support is required, and antibiotics are frequently necessary to fight infections. Transfusions of blood and blood products are often required to treat bleeding complications. If the patient goes into a deep coma, a monitor to measure central nervous system pressure is inserted through the skull. The pressure in the patient's brain is carefully monitored because a sudden increase in brain swelling can lead to rapid death. If significant brain swelling occurs, rapid liver transplantation may be needed to prevent death. Once brain swelling becomes severe, nothing can be done to save the patient.

A patient with fulminant hepatic failure ideally should be transferred to a center where a liver transplant can be performed. Doctors at transplant centers have the most experience in determining which patients will not recover and which ones will require a transplant to survive. Liver transplants can be done only at these medical centers.

Cirrhosis and Its Complications

Many people associate cirrhosis only with excessive alcohol consumption. Although long-term alcohol drinking is the leading cause of cirrhosis in the United States, any chronic liver disease can cause cirrhosis. People who have chronic liver diseases can develop cirrhosis even if they have never consumed alcohol. Generally, cirrhosis occurs after having a chronic liver disease (which could be from consuming excess alcohol) over decades.

Cirrhosis is defined as widespread nodules in the liver and fibrosis. Fibrosis is the deposition of scar tissue that results from ongoing inflammation and liver cell death. Nodules, abnormal spherical areas of cells, form as dying liver cells are replaced by regenerating cells. Unfortunately, this regeneration results in abnormal liver architecture.

Cirrhosis can be clinically silent. In its early stages, the nodules and fibrosis of cirrhosis may be detected only by examination of tissue obtained by liver biopsy. The patient may have no symptoms and live a normal, sometimes very active life. Ultimately, the fibrosis and nodule formation in cirrhosis can cause distortion of the liver architecture that interferes with blood flow through the organ. Cirrhosis can also lead to an inability of the liver to perform its biochemical functions. As cirrhosis becomes advanced, the abnormalities in the liver's blood flow and biochemical functions lead to several potentially serious complications such as:

- Splenomegaly (enlarged spleen)
- Bleeding from esophageal and gastric varices (varicose veins)
- Edema (generalized fluid retention)
- Ascites (fluid retention, specifically in the abdomen)
- Jaundice (yellow discoloration of the skin from bilirubin retention)
- Hepatic encephalopathy (mental changes from mild confusion to coma)
- Spontaneous bacterial peritonitis (infected fluid in the abdomen)
- Increased susceptibility to infections
- Cachexia (wasting)
- Bleeding tendencies
- Electrolyte abnormalities such as hyponatremia (low blood sodium concentration)
- Kidney abnormalities
- Low or high blood sugars

Portal Hypertension

In cirrhosis, blood flow through the liver is impeded because of the abnormal architecture. As a result, blood backs up in the portal vein and portal circulation. This leads to elevated blood pressure in the portal circulation, which is known as *portal hypertension*. Portal hypertension can also sometimes occur in severe cases of acute hepatitis and other forms of liver damage. Cirrhosis is by far the leading cause, however. Portal hypertension can cause several serious problems, including splenomegaly and bleeding from esophageal and gastric varices.

- **Splenomegaly.** Because the portal vein is connected to the splenic vein, portal hypertension can cause blood to back up in the spleen. This, in turn, causes the spleen to become enlarged (splenomegaly) and trap blood cells. Sequestration of platelets in an abnormally enlarged spleen can result in a drop in the platelet count and abnormal bleeding tendencies.

- **Bleeding from esophageal and gastric varices.** As the pressure in the portal circulation increases, blood can flow backward from the portal circulation into the systemic venous circulation at certain points where they are connected. Prominent connections between the portal and systemic venous circulations occur in the esophagus and stomach. Portal hypertension can, therefore, lead to varicose veins in the stomach and esophagus. Varicose veins in the stomach and esophagus are known as gastric and esophageal *varices*, respectively. Portal and systemic circulations are also connected in the rectum, and increased portal pressure can cause hemorrhoids. The two circulations also connect under the skin on the abdomen, and increased pressure can cause prominent visible veins and a swollen collection of congested veins known as a *caput medusa*.

    Gastric and esophageal varices are one of the most serious complications of portal hypertension because they can rupture and bleed. Internal bleeding from esophageal and gastric varices can be massive and life-threatening. Often the patient will experience nausea and vomiting when gastric or esophageal varices bleed. The vomitus usually has a "coffee grounds" appearance that results from the action of stomach acid on blood, which causes clumps of normally soluble material to denature and fall out of solution, making the blood look like coffee grounds. Bleeding gastric or esophageal varices also can cause black, tarry stools, known as *melana*, if partially digested blood passes through the digestive tract. Patients with either coffee grounds emesis (vomit) or melana (black stools) should head immediately to the emergency room, as these symptoms are usually a result of brisk internal bleeding into the upper gastrointestinal tract.

- **Edema and ascites.** Hypertension in the portal circulation, along with complex hormonal, metabolic, and possibly kidney abnormalities in cirrhosis, can lead to fluid accumulation. *Edema* is the general term for fluid retention in the body. In cirrhosis, there is a tendency for fluid to be retained in the abdomen. This is referred to as *ascites*. In cirrhosis, ascites may not be present or may be massive (gallons of fluid). It is not uncommon for a patient with cirrhosis to first seek medical attention because he or she can no longer fit into a dress or pair of pants. Because of the tendency to retain fluid, patients with cirrhosis should have their weight checked periodically.

Jaundice

Bilirubin is taken up by the healthy liver, conjugated to a more water-soluble form, and secreted into the bile. (See Chapter 1.) In cirrhosis, there is decreased bilirubin secretion from hepatocytes. This leads to a backup of bilirubin in the blood, elevated blood bilirubin concentrations (usually mostly direct bilirubin as described in Chapter 2), and jaundice. As the conjugated form of bilirubin backs up, bilirubin can spill into the urine, giving it a yellowish to brown color.

Hepatic Encephalopathy

Hepatic encephalopathy is abnormal brain function that can range from subtle mental status changes to deep coma. Hepatic encephalopathy occurs in both fulminant hepatic failure and advanced cirrhosis. In cirrhosis, some toxin-laden blood leaving the gut bypasses the liver hepatocytes as a result of the abnormal architecture. Metabolism of certain toxic compounds absorbed in the gut may also be decreased within the liver as biochemical function deteriorates. Both of these derangements can lead to hepatic encephalopathy as toxic metabolites, normally removed from the blood by the liver, reach the brain.

In its early stages, hepatic encephalopathy is characterized by subtle mental changes such as poor concentration or irritability. One of the first problems in hepatic encephalopathy is the inability to construct simple objects such as a six-point star out of toothpicks. Various degrees of confusion and sleepiness occur in more advanced cases. In severe cases, hepatic encephalopathy is manifested as stupor or coma.

Infectious Complications

Individuals with cirrhosis may have depressed immune systems and are at higher risk for more types of infections than healthy individuals. One infectious complication unique to individuals with ascites is spontaneous bacterial peritonitis (SBP). In SBP, the abnormally retained fluid in the abdomen becomes spontaneously infected by the bacteria present in the colon. If not adequately treated with antibiotics, SBP can lead to sepsis, an overwhelming infection of the blood.

Other Complications

Because the liver plays a central or participating role in many aspects of whole-body metabolism, other problems affecting various systems may occur in patients with cirrhosis.

Cachexia

Patients with cirrhosis have generalized wasting, which is known as *cachexia*. In advanced cirrhosis, there is significant loss of muscle mass even if nutrient intake is maintained. This is usually most noticeable in the temporal muscles on the sides of the head just in front of the ears. Patients with end-stage cirrhosis and ascites often look like balloons with toothpicks for arms and legs as fluid accumulates in the abdomen and muscle mass is lost in the extremities.

It is not entirely understood why muscle wasting occurs in patients with cirrhosis or other chronic diseases. It may result, in part, from the abnormal secretion of various cytokines (compounds secreted into the blood that alter body metabolism). As a result, patients develop an overall metabolic state in which muscle proteins are degraded more rapidly than they are synthesized. Patients with cirrhosis usually have high circulating levels of the cytokine tumor necrosis factor, which used to be known as *cachexin*, because it causes wasting when injected into animals.

Bleeding Tendencies

In cirrhosis, the platelet counts fall secondary to abnormal trapping of platelets in an enlarged spleen. The prothrombin time is also increased as a result of decreased synthesis of certain blood clotting factors in the failing liver. As a result of both of these alterations, individuals with cirrhosis have an increased chance of bleeding. Decreased blood clotting capability can be a major aggravating factor in patients with gastric or esophageal varices that rupture and bleed. The odds of stopping the bleeding lessen as well.

Electrolyte Abnormalities

Abnormalities in total body fluid balance and altered kidney and hormone function in cirrhosis can lead to problems with blood electrolytes. Electrolytes are soluble elements in the form of ions in the blood. The most abundant electrolytes in the blood are sodium and chloride (table salt). Bicarbonate and potassium are also important blood electrolytes. Significant abnormalities in their concentrations can result in numerous problems.

The electrolyte abnormality most often seen in advanced cirrhosis, especially in patients with edema and ascites, is hyponatremia or an abnormally low blood sodium concentration. Severe hyponatremia (very low blood sodium concentrations) can cause seizures and other brain abnormalities. Although sodium concentration in the blood may be low, total body sodium paradoxically increases in patients with cirrhosis and hyponatremia. Administration of excess sodium only worsens the problem by increasing the amount of ascites and edema. Because patients with cirrhosis and ascites may have subtle kidney abnormalities and are often thirsty secondary to hormonal changes, drinking of excess water contributes to hyponatremia. Therefore, hyponatremia will generally improve with restriction of free water intake. In very severe cases of hyponatremia, intravenous administration of concentrated sodium solutions may be necessary to prevent seizures, even though this may worsen ascites and edema. This must be done slowly and carefully.

Kidney Abnormalities

Cirrhosis also leads to abnormalities in kidney function that range from mild to complete kidney shutdown. Subtle alterations in kidney function and consequent hormonal changes contribute to the formation of ascites and edema and the development of hyponatremia. In advanced cases of cirrhosis, a type of kidney failure known as *hepatorenal syndrome* can occur. In hepatorenal syndrome, the kidneys fail to function in the cirrhotic body for reasons that are unclear. Surprisingly, the same kidneys work fine if they are put in a normal body. Therefore, there is something about advanced cirrhosis that makes them shut down. Hepatorenal syndrome can be treated with dialysis for a short time; however, it is virtually always fatal unless liver transplantation is performed. When the liver is replaced in a patient with hepatorenal syndrome, kidney function returns to normal.

Other Metabolic Complications

There are several other metabolic complications associated with cirrhosis.

- Low blood albumin concentration occurs, which can enhance formation of ascites and edema.
- The metabolism of many drugs is decreased, and the dosages of some medications must be adjusted appropriately.
- In men, breast enlargement or gynecomastia sometimes occurs because metabolism of estrogens by the liver is decreased. Atrophy of the testicles can also occur.
- Derangements in the metabolism of triglycerides and cholesterol can occur. Blood cholesterol concentration is usually very low, except in cases of cirrhosis caused by bile duct obstruction where it can be abnormally elevated.
- Abnormalities arise in sugar metabolism including, in earlier stages, insulin resistance that leads to high blood sugars. In advanced stages of cirrhosis, however, blood sugar may be dangerously low because it cannot be synthesized from glycogen, fats, or proteins in the failing liver.

Diagnosis of Cirrhosis

Cirrhosis is usually an easy diagnosis when some or all of the above complications are present in a chronically ill individual with a history of liver disease. Virtually any chronic liver disease can cause cirrhosis. The underlying cause of cirrhosis can be identified in most cases though sometimes it remains elusive. Such cases are called *cryptogenic cirrhosis*, which is not really a diagnosis but a term signifying that the disease that caused cirrhosis cannot be determined. Conditions such as metastatic cancer, clots in the hepatic vein, severe acute hepatitis, or acute bile duct obstruction can cause some of the same abnormalities observed in patients with cirrhosis. A careful history, combined with special diagnostic tests, will usually identify these conditions.

As emphasized in previous chapters, some individuals with cirrhosis, especially early in the course of the disease, will have no overt clinical signs or symptoms. Radiological and nuclear medicine tests suggest the presence of cirrhosis in only a few of these cases. In most patients without clinical complications, a diagnosis of cirrhosis usually requires liver biopsy.

Treatment of Patients with Cirrhosis

Cirrhosis of the liver is irreversible. Scarring and nodules cannot revert to normal liver architecture. Treatment of the underlying liver disease may slow or stop the progression of cirrhosis by preventing the accumulation of additional scar tissue and formation of new nodules. This may avert the development of complications and serious liver dysfunction. For example, termination of alcohol intake may stop the progression of alcoholic cirrhosis. Treatment of metabolic liver diseases may also slow the progression of cirrhosis. Chronic viral hepatitis B and C may respond to treatment with interferon or other medications, and autoimmune hepatitis may improve with immunosuppressive drugs.

As shown in Table 3.2, current treatments of cirrhosis are directed at reversing or preventing complications; unfortunately, no current treatment can significantly reverse the scar tissue and nodule formation. When cirrhosis is advanced, some complications become nearly impossible to treat or prevent. This condition is commonly referred to as *end-stage liver disease*. In end-stage liver disease, transplantation is the only option. Hence, careful periodic follow-up by a doctor knowledgeable in liver diseases is an important aspect in the care of patients with cirrhosis. If the complications of cirrhosis become uncontrollable, or when an experienced physician realizes that they will soon become uncontrollable, referral to a liver transplantation center is essential. Fortunately, in many cases, complications of cirrhosis respond to the various interventions described below.

Bleeding from Esophageal or Gastric Varices

Bleeding from esophageal or gastric varices is treated immediately using intravenous fluids and blood transfusions as necessary. Fluid and blood should be given immediately if the patient is not stable. The diagnosis

Table 3.2 Treatments for Some Complications of Cirrhosis

Bleeding from Esophageal Varices	Endoscopic sclerotherapy
	Endoscopic rubber band ligation
	Beta-blockers and possibly nitrates
	Vasopressin and somatostatin analogue (emergencies only)
	Balloon compression (emergencies only)
	Transjugular intrahepatic portosystemic shunt (TIPS)
	Surgical portosystemic shunts
Edema and Ascites	Low-sodium diet (very important)
	Diuretics (spironolactone usually first choice)
	Paracentesis (removal of ascites with needle)
Hepatic Encephalopathy	Low-protein diet
	Lactulose
	Neomycin
Bleeding Tendencies	Vitamin K
	Fresh frozen plasma (emergencies only)
Spontaneous Bacterial Peritonitis	Antibiotics
Hyponatremia (Low Blood Sodium Concentration)	Restriction of free water intake

is generally made by endoscopy, giving the doctor a direct view of the bleeding varices (or other possible sources of bleeding).

If bleeding esophageal varices are identified, sclerotherapy and rubber band ligation are usually first-line treatments. Both of these procedures are done through the endoscope. Sclerotherapy is accomplished by injection of a caustic substance into the varicose vein. In rubber band ligation, rubber bands are ligated (tied) around varices to stop the bleeding and obliterate them. Gastric varices cannot be treated by sclerotherapy because the caustic chemical can irritate the stomach and cause it to rupture. Gastric varices can sometimes be treated by rubber band ligation.

Sclerotherapy or rubber band ligation should be performed only on patients who have varices that are actively bleeding or have been previously documented to bleed. If varices are detected incidentally but have never bled, these treatments are not indicated. If sclerotherapy or rubber band ligation stops variceal bleeding, follow-up endoscopy should be performed on a regular schedule and repeat courses of sclerotherapy or rubber band ligation should be performed until all visible esophageal varices are obliterated.

Beta-blockers and nitrates are oral drugs used to prevent bleeding from esophageal and gastric varices. Several studies have shown that these medications can decrease the incidence of bleeding or re-bleeding from esophageal varices. For this reason, individuals with cirrhosis should have an upper gastrointestinal endoscopy to look for varices and, if they are present, probably be started on beta-blockers. Individuals who present with bleeding from varices should also receive beta-blockers and possibly nitrates.

Sometimes, endoscopic sclerotherapy or rubber band ligation cannot stop acute bleeding from esophageal or gastric varices. In other cases, bleeding may result from a condition known as *portal gastropathy* in which the pressure is increased diffusely in the veins of the stomach but there is no single prominent varicose vein to ligate. In this case, the patient should be admitted to an intensive care unit where medical therapy with vasopression or somatostatin may be attempted. These medications constrict some blood vessels and/or lower portal pressures.

If acute bleeding from esophageal varices does not stop despite attempted endoscopic and medical treatment, balloon compression may be used as a lifesaving option. A tube with a large balloon at the end is inserted into the esophagus and the balloon is inflated. The inflated balloon may stop bleeding by direct compression. This method is rarely used these days as shunts placed by radiologists can often be done emergently and are probably more effective in stopping the bleeding.

Shunts are surgical connections that are made between the portal circulation—which has increased pressure in cirrhosis—and the systemic circulation. Shunts can stop bleeding from gastric or esophageal varices in individuals with cirrhosis and portal hypertension because they lower the blood pressure in the portal system. In classical open surgical shunt procedures, a major vein of the portal circulation is directly connected to a major vein of the lower-pressure systemic circulation. For example, the portal vein may be connected directly to the vena cava, or the splenic vein (which is connected to the portal vein) can be connected to a vein leading to a kidney. These connections allow some portal blood to bypass the cirrhotic liver, causing pressure in the portal system to be lower. The major complication of surgical shunts is worsening of hepatic encephalopathy as a larger portion of portal blood bypasses the liver and cannot be detoxified.

Surgical shunt procedures are rarely performed today. More recently, a less invasive shunt procedure has been developed and is generally performed by interventional radiologists. This procedure is known as a *transjugular intrahepatic portosystemic shunt* (TIPS). In TIPS, a hollow tube is placed directly into the liver from an approach through the jugular vein in the neck. The tube is placed so as to connect the portal vein and hepatic vein directly through the liver, thus allowing some of the blood to bypass the cirrhotic architecture and relieve pressure in the portal circulation. Patients undergoing TIPS are at increased risk for developing worsening hepatic encephalopathy afterward. In addition, the shunt may clot with time, again increasing the risk of bleeding from gastric or esophageal varices. Despite these complications, TIPS can be lifesaving.

Edema and Ascites

The most important initial therapeutic intervention to prevent edema and ascites in cirrhosis is a strict, low-salt diet. In individuals with significant ascites and/or edema, a daily allowance of only 500 milligrams of sodium chloride is ideal; however, most patients find this kind of diet terribly unpalatable. Nonetheless, it is important that the patient do everything possible to significantly restrict salt consumption. Virtually all canned and processed foods should be avoided. Meat and fish should be consumed only in small quantities as they contain significant amounts of salt. A patient with cirrhosis and ascites should (generally) stick to a mostly vegetarian diet with low-salt fruits, grains, pastas, and vegetables providing most of the calories. An occasional egg and, on an infrequent basis, small portions of meat (but no cured or processed meats such as salami or pastrami) may be consumed. The bottom line is that the patient's diet should be as salt-free as possible with every effort necessary to reduce the intake of foods, including meats, which contain a high salt content. If a cirrhotic patient with ascites and edema also has hyponatremia (low blood sodium concentration), free water intake should also be restricted. Water is restricted to usually one quart per day or less until blood sodium concentrations return to near normal.

If diet alone does not control edema and ascites, the next step is to add a diuretic. Diuretics are not substitutes for a low-salt diet but are complementary. The first-choice diuretic is usually spironolactone (Aldactone). Spironolactone works by countering the effects of aldosterone, a hormone that acts on kidneys whose blood levels are abnormally increased in cirrhotic individuals with ascites and edema. If spironolactone and diet do not control ascites and edema, a second diuretic medication with a different mechanism of action is cautiously added. Either hydrochlorothiazide, or a so-called "loop diuretic" such as furosemide (Lasix), is added next. Patients with cirrhosis who are taking diuretics should be monitored closely by their doctors for (possible) excessive intravascular dehydration, and their kidney function should be checked periodically.

If diet and diuretics do not relieve ascites and abdominal swelling becomes so intense that it is painful, or the patient has difficulty breathing due to compression on the diaphragm, large-volume paracentesis is an option. In this procedure, a needle is inserted into the abdomen through the skin and fluid is drained gradually. About four to six liters (one liter is approximately one quart) can be drained at a time. Sometimes, an infusion of albumin will be given at the time paracentesis is performed. In some patients with advanced cirrhosis, repeated large-volume paracenteses are required.

A type of surgical procedure is available in refractory ascites that cannot be managed by recurrent large-volume paracentesis treatments. The surgical procedure, known as a *Denver* or a *Laveen shunt*, places a tube with a one-way valve between the intra-abdominal space and a large vein. As a result of this shunting, the ascites fluid drains directly into the patient's bloodstream. Although theoretically appealing, serious complications, such as infection, clotting of the shunt, and disseminated intravascular coagulation (abnormal clotting of the blood), are common after this procedure. Denver or Laveen shunts are usually reserved as last-resort comfort measures for individuals who have massive ascites and are not eligible for liver transplantation. Some doctors also recommend TIPS for refractory ascites, but there are arguments in favor of and against this procedure for this purpose.

Spontaneous Bacterial Peritonitis (SBP)

Patients with ascites are at risk for SBP. This infection should be considered in any patient with ascites who develops fever or abdominal pain. Sometimes, SBP will appear as a general deterioration in overall condition or worsening hepatic encephalopathy in the absence of fever. The diagnostic procedure for SBP is paracentesis. Usually, only a small volume of ascites fluid needs to be removed with a needle and syringe. The diagnosis of SBP is made if the white blood cell count in the ascites fluid is elevated. Treatment with antibiotics is essential and usually done intravenously in the hospital. Some studies have suggested that long-term oral antibiotics may be useful to prevent subsequent infections in individuals with recurrent episodes of SBP.

Hepatic Encephalopathy

The first step in the treatment of hepatic encephalopathy is a low-protein diet. Proteins are high in nitrogen content. Ammonia and other nitrogen-containing compounds, which are toxic to the brain when not removed by the cirrhotic liver, are produced by the metabolism of proteins by bacteria in the colon. Therefore, meats, nuts, and other high-protein foods should be consumed only in very low quantities by individuals with hepatic encephalopathy. Vegetables, fruits, grains, and pastas should be substituted. This diet is in many aspects similar to the low-salt diet for ascites and edema.

The first-line drug treatment is usually lactulose, a sugar that is not absorbed from the gut. In part, it acts as a laxative to expel nitrogen-containing compounds from the colon before bacteria can metabolize them into substances toxic to an individual with a liver that cannot adequately clear them from the blood. Lactulose also causes the inside of the gut to be increasingly acidic, making it less favorable for nitrogen-containing toxins and ammonia to be absorbed. Another drug treatment for encephalopathy is neomycin, an antibiotic not absorbed from the gut, which kills bacteria in the colon that produce ammonia and other nitrogen-containing toxic compounds.

Bleeding Tendencies

Administration of vitamin K can sometimes help the decreased production of clotting factors in patients with cirrhosis. In emergency bleeding situations, or prior to invasive medical procedures that may be necessary, fresh frozen plasma can be transfused intravenously. Fresh frozen plasma is the component of blood from which red and white cells have been removed; it contains clotting factors and other proteins. Platelet transfusions may also be given to patients with low platelet counts to help stop or prevent bleeding.

Liver Transplantation

In some patients, the complications of cirrhosis become refractory to all medical therapies. As the liver continues to fail, hepatic encephalopathy worsens, ascites continue to accumulate, and other complications worsen. These complications may no longer be responsive to medical interventions. Cachexia and muscle wasting cannot be halted no matter how many nutrients the patient receives. Kidney function may gradually fail and hepatorenal syndrome may develop. In these advanced cases of cirrhosis—also known as *end-stage liver disease*—only a liver transplant can save the patient's life. The general goal of liver transplantation is to replace the patient's liver just before complications of cirrhosis become refractory to medical treatment. In ideal cases, this can be estimated. In many cases, as previously mentioned however, there is considerable uncertainty as to how soon the complications of cirrhosis and liver failure will become life-threatening. Patients with cirrhosis and one or more of its complications should probably be evaluated at a center for liver transplantation at least two years before the doctor anticipates that the condition will deteriorate and medical treatment will no longer suffice to control the complications. Liver transplantation is discussed in more detail in Chapter 12.

4

The A, B, C, D, E's of
Viral Hepatitis

HEPATITIS MEANS "inflammation of the liver." By now, it should be obvious that there are many causes of hepatitis, including drugs and alcohol. However, most people equate hepatitis with the liver disease caused by several different viruses. Hepatitis caused by a virus is more precisely called *viral hepatitis*.

After alcohol, viral hepatitis is the leading cause of chronic liver disease in the United States. It is estimated that, at the present time, about one million Americans are chronically infected with the hepatitis B virus and three to four million with the hepatitis C virus. Worldwide, viral hepatitis surpasses alcohol as the number one cause of chronic liver disease. Approximately 350 million people, mostly in Southeast Asia and sub-Saharan Africa, are chronically infected with hepatitis B virus. The hepatitis C virus chronically infects about 170 million people worldwide. These numbers are staggering, especially since hepatitis B and hepatitis C are infectious diseases whose transmission can be prevented by avoiding certain behaviors and using some commonsense precautions. Hepatitis B can also be prevented by vaccination.

Because of advances in basic molecular biology and the large numbers of affected individuals, diagnosis and treatment of viral hepatitis is currently the most active area of medicine related to diseases of the liver. The different forms of viral hepatitis are also the liver diseases most patients seem to have questions about. Our knowledge of viral hepatitis is still expanding, especially regarding hepatitis C, which was identified only about fifteen years ago. However, currently available information makes it possible to understand a good deal about the major hepatitis viruses and the diseases that each causes.

What Is a Virus?

Before discussing the various types of viral hepatitis, it is important to have some understanding of what a virus is. This will hopefully provide some insight as to why viral diseases are formidable problems. So sit tight and try to bear with a little basic biochemistry and cell biology.

Some people define viruses as the simplest forms of life. It is really a matter of philosophical debate—and not science—to decide if viruses are "alive." Like other life-forms, viruses reproduce and mutate (randomly change their genetic material). However, viruses do not have an independent metabolism and can replicate only within another organism's cells. You can decide for yourself if this constitutes life.

Viruses are small and range in size from about 15 nanometers to 250 nanometers in their longest dimension. There are a billion nanometers in a meter, which is roughly equal to one yard. The human red blood cell, one of the smallest cells in the body, is about thirty times the size of the largest virus. Hepatocytes, the predominant liver cells, are much larger than the various hepatitis viruses. Particles as small as viruses cannot be observed under a light microscope. Electron microscopy is necessary to see virus particles.

Viruses contain either ribonucleic acid (RNA) or deoxyribonucleic acid (DNA) as their genetic material (animals and plants have DNA as their genetic material). Viruses also contain proteins. Most viruses have core or capsid proteins that form a nucleocapsid around which the viral RNA or DNA winds. Some viruses are enveloped in that they contain a lipid (fat) outer layer that derives from the cells in which they replicate. The envelope usually contains specific viral proteins. In addition to the proteins that comprise the viral particle, most viruses also produce proteins that perform essential biochemical functions necessary for their replication. These proteins may be expressed and function only within the cells that the virus infects and not be present in the mature viral particles.

An important property of viruses is cellular tropism. Tropism indicates a virus's ability to infect a particular type of cell or cells. Viruses that cause hepatitis are referred to as primarily *hepatotropic* because they preferentially infect hepatocytes, the major cells of the liver. Primarily hepatotropic viruses may also infect cells other than hepatocytes. Various viruses have different cellular tropisms. For example, the human immunodeficiency virus (HIV) primarily infects certain cells of the immune system.

Another important property of viruses is their ability to mutate. Because the genomes of viruses are small and replicate rapidly, the mutation rates of viruses are usually high. This ability to mutate is of critical importance in the ability of viruses to cause disease. Constant mutation allows viruses to escape detection by the host's immune system. For this reason, it is sometimes not possible for the body to clear a viral infection. Mutation may be an important way that hepatitis C virus escapes detection by the immune system. Mutation also makes it difficult to design drugs against viruses as they can cause changes in the viral proteins that are targets for drugs.

Latency is another property of viruses of major significance for treatment of human diseases. Viruses may stop replicating and integrate their DNA, or a DNA copy of their RNA, into the host cell DNA. The virus then can be propagated as the host cell divides. However, viral particles will not be made and the immune system will usually not kill the cells in which viral genetic material is integrated. A latent or integrated virus can later be activated for various reasons and begin to replicate and make infectious viral particles. This is an important property of the hepatitis B virus, which can either replicate in infected individuals at high levels or integrate into the cell's DNA.

Viruses do not have their own independent metabolism, utilizing instead the energy, chemical compounds, and protein synthesis machinery of the cells they infect. For this reason, it has been an extremely difficult task to design antiviral drugs. Antibiotics that kill bacteria are often targeted against the bacterial proteins involved in protein synthesis or energy metabolism. Since viruses use host cell metabolites and protein synthesis machinery, drugs directed against these targets would not only inhibit viral replication but also kill host cells. Fortunately, some viruses make a few proteins that are uniquely essential for their own replication that can be targets for antiviral drugs. An example that has received a lot of attention in recent years is the protease of HIV, which is a viral protein essential for replication of the virus that is the target of drugs known as *protease inhibitors.*

In summary, viruses can be considered as tiny cellular parasites (whether they are alive or not is not really an issue). Viruses infect cells and utilize their energy sources, chemical compounds, and protein synthesis machinery to replicate. Many viruses can live quietly inside cells for many years without replicating and can be activated at any time. They use various tricks, including rapid mutation, to evade the host's immune system so that they can live in the host for a long time (ideally for the virus, a lifetime). The relationship between most viruses and hosts is not mutual, however. Virus infection in humans often leads to disease and sometimes death because either the virus itself, or the immune response directed against infected cells, kills all cells infected with a virus.

Major Human Hepatotropic Viruses

There are five major human hepatotropic viruses: hepatitis A virus, hepatitis B virus, hepatitis C virus, hepatitis D virus, and hepatitis E virus. (See Table 4.1.) The diseases they cause are known as *hepatitis A*, *hepatitis B*, *hepatitis C*, *hepatitis D*, and *hepatitis E*, respectively. Papers published in 1995 and 1996 reported discovery of a virus known as *hepatitis G virus* that is commonly present in the blood supply and has been detected in individuals with acute and chronic hepatitis. Most medical researchers believe that hepatitis G virus does *not* cause hepatitis. There is no "hepatitis F" virus.

The various human hepatitis viruses are actually very different. They cause different types of liver disease, and there are several possible ways to classify them. Virologists may classify them based on the sequences of their DNA and RNA or based upon the families of related viruses to which they belong. Clinicians, on the other hand, may prefer to classify them by the types of hepatitis they cause. Epidemiologists may be more interested in the ways hepatitis viruses are transmitted.

Table 4.1 Major Human Hepatitis Viruses

Virus	Genetic Material	Family	Disease	Major Modes of Transmission
Hepatitis A	RNA	*Picornaviridae*	Acute	Contaminated food and water
Hepatitis B	DNA	*Hepadnaviridae*	Acute and chronic	Blood; mother to infant; sex
Hepatitis C	RNA	*Flaviviridae*	Acute and chronic	Blood; mother to infant; sex less efficiently
Hepatitis D	RNA	*Deltaviridae*	Acute and chronic	Blood (only infection along with hepatitis B)
Hepatitis E	RNA	*Caliciviridea*	Acute	Contaminated food and water

Hepatitis A

The illness caused by infection from the hepatitis A virus is called *hepatitis A*. In the past, several different terms were used to describe this illness, including *infectious hepatitis*, *epidemic hepatitis*, *epidemic jaundice*, *catarrhal jaundice*, and *infectious icterus*. These terms are generally no longer used.

The hepatitis A virus causes only acute liver disease. This is critical to understand as many patients, and even some doctors, consider hepatitis A as a possible cause of chronic liver disease. Individuals with other chronic liver diseases, as might any susceptible individual, can be infected with hepatitis A virus and develop acute hepatitis. However, hepatitis A virus does *not* cause chronic liver disease. Hepatitis A always resolves itself or, in rare cases, kills the patient.

In most patients, hepatitis A is either a relatively mild disease or no apparent disease at all. Many children who get infected do not develop clinically apparent liver disease. There is a correlation between age and disease severity. Most cases of fulminant hepatic failure from hepatitis A virus infection occur in older individuals, usually over age fifty. Patients with a relatively mild form of the disease may suffer from nausea, vomiting, fever, fatigue, and loss of appetite. Blood tests usually reveal elevations in aminotransferase activities and possible elevations in bilirubin concentration. Patients with a more severe hepatitis A condition develop jaundice and laboratory examination reveals significant elevation in blood bilirubin concentration. In more severe cases, prothrombin time may be prolonged. In instances of massive hepatocyte death, blood alanine aminotransferase (ALT) and aspartate aminotransferase (AST) activities can be very highly elevated.

The large majority of patients with hepatitis A recover without complications. Hospitalization and supportive care may be necessary for very ill patients who are unable to eat or drink fluids. Occasionally, patients may suffer from fatigue and malaise for several months after the disease resolves. About 1 percent of individuals with hepatitis A, usually those over age fifty, develop serious liver failure, sometimes fulminant. These patients require hospitalization and supportive care. In the United States, about one in three hundred cases of hepatitis A results in death or emergency liver transplantation.

Transmission

Hepatitis A virus is spread primarily by the fecal-oral route. The virus is excreted in feces of infected people and infects susceptible individuals who consume contaminated water or foods. Water, shellfish, and salads are the most frequently implicated sources of transmission. Cold cuts, fruits, fruit juices, milk, and vegetables also have been implicated in various outbreaks. Hepatitis A is more common in underdeveloped parts of the world with poor sanitary conditions, and travelers to these regions are at an increased risk for infection.

The time from infection with hepatitis A virus to onset of symptoms varies from ten to fifty days. Thirty days is the average. The greatest danger of infecting others occurs during the middle of the incubation period and before presentation of symptoms. The patient remains potentially infectious up until a week or more after the onset of symptoms.

Although ingestion of contaminated food and water is the most common route of transmission, hepatitis A virus can be transmitted in other ways. Infected individuals can spread the virus to others who live in the same household or with whom they have sexual contact. In particular, hepatitis A virus may be spread by sexual practices in which the mouth comes in direct contact with the anal area of an infected individual. Homosexual men are at an increased risk for hepatitis A. Casual contact at work or in social settings usually does not spread the virus. Hepatitis A virus infection, however, can be spread among children and employees in child-care centers where a child or employee is infected. Residents and staff workers in institutions for developmentally disabled persons are at a particularly increased risk for being infected with hepatitis A virus. There also have been reports of transmission by sharing contaminated materials among intravenous drug users.

In industrialized countries such as the United States, hepatitis A often occurs in isolated outbreaks or epidemics. These outbreaks can usually be traced to contaminated foods. Foods implicated in hepatitis A outbreaks in the United States have included lettuce, raw oysters, other shellfish, and frozen strawberries.

Diagnosis

The diagnosis of hepatitis A is suspected when sudden onset of clinical liver disease is observed ten to fifty days after exposure to the hepatitis A virus. Diagnosis is confirmed by blood tests. The laboratory diagnosis of hepatitis A virus is made by detection of antibodies against the virus in the blood; interpretation of blood test results is often tricky and requires some explanation. Patients who have been infected with hepatitis A develop two different types of antibodies against the virus. IgG antibodies are found in individuals who have been exposed at any time in the past. Hence the presence of IgG antibodies against hepatitis A is not diagnostic for acute infection and indicates past infection or exposure that may or may not have been accompanied by a recognized illness. Successful vaccination also induces IgG antibodies. Patients possessing IgG antibodies against the hepatitis A virus, therefore, become immune. IgM antibodies against hepatitis A virus are present only in acute hepatitis A, usually appearing within ten days of infection. The presence of IgM antibodies against the hepatitis A virus in someone with sudden-onset liver disease is nearly 100 percent specific for the diagnosis of hepatitis A.

Prevention

The most important issue regarding hepatitis A is prevention. There are three primary ways to prevent hepatitis A—hygiene, passive immunity, and vaccination.

Hygienic measures to prevent hepatitis A infection include preventing the contamination of food and water and avoiding contact with contaminated foods. In many developing countries, widespread sewage systems have not been constructed, especially in rural areas. Water from lakes and rivers into which people defecate may be used for drinking, washing, or preparing foods. Living conditions are often crowded. Only overall improvement in the socioeconomic structure can remedy these problems. Visitors to such areas should avoid drinking from the local water supply and eating fresh fruits or vegetables that may have been washed with water from local rivers, lakes, or reservoirs. Locally caught shellfish also should not be consumed. If local water must be consumed, it should be boiled first.

People living in the same household as an individual with hepatitis A, or individuals working in situations where the disease is common, should follow commonsense rules. Hand washing should be strictly observed, especially when using the bathroom and before preparing or eating food. People working in child-care centers or institutions for developmentally disabled individuals should wash their hands after changing diapers or sheets, before eating, or after any close contact with residents.

Passive immunization with immune globulin is recommended for short-term protection against hepatitis A and for persons who have been exposed to the hepatitis A virus. Immune globulin is a concentration of antibodies pooled from the blood of individuals with IgG antibodies against the hepatitis A virus. Immune globulin should be administered to individuals who will be traveling to endemic areas that have not received vaccination far enough in advance of departure (about four weeks) for it to be effective. The U.S. Centers for Disease Control and Prevention (cdc.gov) provides recommendations for travelers going to various parts of the world. Immune globulin should also be given to individuals who may have been exposed to hepatitis A virus within two weeks of suspected exposure.

Hepatitis A vaccines provide long-term protection against hepatitis A. Two shots administered in six- to twelve-month intervals are given. Vaccination is recommended for individuals who will travel to or work in areas where hepatitis A is endemic. Again, the U.S. Centers for Disease Control and Prevention provides recommendations for travelers to various parts of the world. The first dose of vaccine should be given at least four weeks before travel. This usually provides protection for a short trip, but a booster is necessary six to twelve months later for long-term protection.

Children in communities with high rates of hepatitis A should also be vaccinated. These communities include Alaska Native villages, Native American reservations, and some religious communities, for example, the Kiryas Joel Hassidic community in New York. Homosexual men should also be vaccinated, as should people who use street drugs. Individuals with chronic liver diseases should be vaccinated as hepatitis A virus infection may be more severe in individuals with another underlying liver disease. This may be particularly true for individuals with chronic hepatitis C. People with some other chronic diseases, such as inherited clotting factor deficiencies like hemophilia, should also be vaccinated. Hepatitis A vaccination is not recommended for all health care workers; however, those working in high-risk environments, such as institutions for the developmentally disabled, should receive the hepatitis A vaccine. Individuals who work with hepatitis A virus-infected animals or with the hepatitis A virus in a research laboratory should also be vaccinated.

People who have been previously infected with hepatitis A virus are generally immune to another infection and episode of hepatitis A. Immune individuals have serum IgG antibodies against the hepatitis A virus. Such people do not need to be vaccinated. However, it remains unclear whether it is more cost-effective to screen the blood of an at-risk individual for the presence of IgG antibodies or to just administer the vaccine.

Treatment

There is no specific treatment for hepatitis A. In most cases, the disease is mild and self-limiting. As long as the patient is drinking and eating, hospitalization is generally not necessary. If the patient is so sick that he or she is vomiting extensively and cannot eat or drink, hospitalization may be necessary for administration of intravenous fluids. The patient can be discharged once he or she has adequate oral intake. In very serious cases, such as those causing fulminant hepatic failure, hospitalization and intensive care are required. Preferably, patients with fulminant hepatic failure should be hospitalized in medical centers where liver transplantation can be performed should it become necessary.

Hepatitis B

A little background on the virus that causes hepatitis B is essential for understanding the disease, its symptoms, and especially its diagnosis. The existence of hepatitis B virus was discovered by accident in the 1960s. In 1965, Dr. Baruch Blumberg and collaborators discovered a protein of the hepatitis B virus in the blood of an Australian aborigine. This protein was called the *Australia antigen*. At the time of its discovery, the Australia antigen was not thought to be a viral protein. Over the next few years, however, Dr. Blumberg, his collaborators, and other groups proved that the Australia antigen was associated with hepatitis, specifically a form that was then known as *serum hepatitis* and was transmitted by blood. Dr. Blumberg was awarded the Nobel Prize in Physiology or Medicine in 1976 for this discovery.

In subsequent years, the hepatitis B virus was photographed under an electron microscope and was propagated in cell culture. Its genetic material was analyzed. A schematic diagram of hepatitis B virus is shown in Figure 4.1. The hepatitis B virus is a member of the *Hepadnaviridae* family; other very similar viruses in this family cause liver disease in woodchucks, ground squirrels, and ducks. These animals have served as experimental models for research on hepatitis B.

The genetic material of hepatitis B virus is a circular strand of DNA. This circular DNA encodes four viral proteins, two of which are structural proteins of the viral particle. (See Table 4.2.) It is important to be familiar with these proteins, especially the hepatitis B surface and core proteins, because detection of these proteins in the blood, or detection of antibodies against them, plays a critical role in diagnosis.

Figure 4.1 Hepatitis B Virus

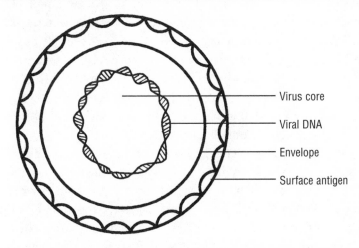

Virus core
Viral DNA
Envelope
Surface antigen

Hepatitis B virus contains a core, or nucleocapsid, with which viral DNA is associated. This core is surrounded by an envelope that contains the surface antigen.

The hepatitis B virus surface antigen (HBsAg) is the "Australia antigen" discovered by Dr. Blumberg. HBsAg is a major structural component of the viral particle that is present on its surface. Testing a patient's blood for circulating hepatitis B surface antigen is presently the single most important test for infection with the hepatitis B virus.

Table 4.2 Proteins of Hepatitis B Virus

Protein	Function
Surface antigen (HBsAg)	Structural protein on the surface of the virus. Also circulates as spherical and filamentous aggregates in the blood of infected individuals.
Core antigen (HBcAg)	Structural protein forming the core, or nucleocapsid, of the virus. A shorter form of HBcAg, known as *Be antigen* (HBeAg), is found in the blood of individuals when the virus is rapidly replicating.
DNA polymerase (pol)	A virally encoded enzyme essential for viral DNA replication.
Protein X	A protein of unclear function; may be involved in carcinogenesis.

Hepatitis B core antigen (HBcAg) is a protein that forms the nucleocapsid, or core, of the viral particle and is associated with the viral DNA. Hepatitis B core antigen is not readily detectable in the blood of infected individuals but can be seen in the liver cells. If the virus is rapidly replicating in the liver, a smaller form of the hepatitis B core antigen can be detected in the infected patient's blood. This form is known as *hepatitis Be antigen* (HBeAg). Detection of HBeAg in the blood has important clinical significance in the diagnosis of more serious and more highly contagious disease.

Infection with the hepatitis B virus causes both acute and chronic hepatitis. The symptoms and courses of the illness are very different. The most important determinant for whether hepatitis B virus infection will become chronic is the age at which the individual is infected. About 90 percent of infected newborn babies become chronically infected with hepatitis B virus. About 50 percent of young children who are infected become chronically infected. In adults, only about 5 percent of newly infected individuals become chronically infected.

Some hypothetical case histories are illustrative before discussing acute and chronic hepatitis B and the various ways in which patients can present.

• **Case 1.** A forty-five-year-old active intravenous heroin user comes to the emergency room complaining of nausea, vomiting, abdominal pain, and yellow eyes. Blood tests show both ALT and AST activity and bilirubin concentration to be elevated. Another blood test detects HBsAg. The patient is admitted to a drug rehabilitation program and over the next few weeks feels much better. A month later, he is no longer jaundiced and laboratory tests are normal. A repeat test for blood HBsAg is negative.

• **Case 2.** Another forty-five-year-old intravenous heroin user is brought to the emergency room by ambulance after being found comatose on the street. He is jaundiced. Blood tests indicate elevated ALT and AST activities, elevated bilirubin concentration, prolonged prothrombin time, and detectable HBsAg and IgM antibodies against HBcAg. He is admitted to the intensive care unit and put on a mechanical ventilator. The coma deepens and he dies.

• **Case 3.** A twenty-five-year-old woman who was born in China and emigrated to the United States has been healthy her entire life. She graduated from college and business school and now works as a securities analyst. She is married and pregnant for the first time. A routine blood test performed by her obstetrician detects HBsAg in her blood. All other blood tests are normal and she feels fine.

- **Case 4.** A thirty-nine-year-old homosexual man sees his doctor because he feels tired all the time. Blood tests show elevations in ALT and AST activities. A test for HBsAg is positive. Six months later, blood ALT and AST activities are again elevated and HBsAg is again detected. A blood test for HBeAg is also positive. A liver biopsy shows chronic hepatitis, fibrosis, and cirrhotic nodules.

- **Case 5.** A sixty-nine-year-old man who was born in Korea has been in good health all his life. He sees a doctor for the first time in more than fifty years because of an inability to fit into his pants and mild abdominal pain. A blood test detects HBsAg. An ultrasound examination shows a shrunken, nodular liver with a mass. Biopsy of the liver mass reveals hepatocellular carcinoma.

Acute infection with the hepatitis B virus can cause a wide range of initial conditions, from no symptoms to fulminant hepatic failure. In newborn babies, acute infection, usually transmitted from the mother at the time of delivery, generally does not cause clinical disease. In younger children, acute infection with hepatitis B virus also does not usually cause clinically apparent disease. In adults, most acutely infected individuals develop acute clinical hepatitis that varies in severity.

In most adult cases, acute infection with the hepatitis B virus causes moderate illness that spontaneously resolves, as in Case 1 above. Symptoms of hepatitis typically occur within six to fifteen weeks after infection. Symptoms include nausea, vomiting, fever, right upper quadrant abdominal pain, and jaundice. Blood ALT and AST activities are elevated roughly in proportion to the degree of acute inflammation and liver cell death. Elevations in blood bilirubin concentration and, in more severe cases, prolongation of PT may also occur. About 2 percent of acutely infected adults develop fulminant hepatic failure. This is what happened to the patient described in Case 2. Most of these individuals either die or require emergency liver transplantation. The vast majority of acutely infected adults, as seen in Case 1, have spontaneous resolution of acute hepatitis. About 5 percent of individuals infected as adults go on to develop chronic hepatitis B, as did the patient in Case 4.

Hepatitis B virus infection is the leading cause of chronic liver disease in the world. Most chronically infected individuals are infected as infants or children. Chronic infection can cause various problems. Some chronically infected individuals are clinically classified as chronic carriers. Chronic carriers have no clinically apparent liver disease; however, this may be an inaccurate term as some so-called chronic carriers exhibit evidence of hepatitis on liver biopsy. Other individuals chronically infected with hepatitis B virus have clinically apparent chronic hepatitis. Long-standing chronic hepatitis resulting from hepatitis B can lead to cirrhosis. Long-standing hepatitis B infection is also a major risk factor for the development of hepatocellular carcinoma or primary liver cancer, which is the number one or two (along with lung cancer) cause of cancer death worldwide.

Chronic carriers are considered to be individuals persistently infected with the hepatitis B virus who do not have clinical evidence of hepatitis. The woman described in Case 3 is an example of a chronic carrier. Chronic carriers have detectable HBsAg in their blood but no signs or symptoms of hepatitis or liver disease. The diagnosis is often made during routine screening of pregnant women, as in Case 3, or of blood donors. Typically, blood ALT and AST activities are normal and there is no laboratory evidence of liver damage or dysfunction. The term *chronic carrier* derives from the fact that these individuals have laboratory evidence of hepatitis B virus infection but no clinical or laboratory evidence of liver disease. About 75 percent of chronic carriers will have no evidence of inflammation on liver biopsy and can truly be called carriers who do not have evidence of chronic hepatitis. About 25 percent of chronic carriers, however, are not really only carriers and will have evidence of inflammation on liver biopsy. These individuals have chronic hepatitis despite normal laboratory tests and no exhibition of symptoms. Some so-called chronic carriers may even have cirrhosis if liver biopsy is performed. Therefore, although almost universally used to describe patients chronically infected with hepatitis B virus and no evidence of liver disease, *chronic carrier* may not technically be a correct description of all such patients. Furthermore, individuals who are defined as chronic carriers can sometimes develop clinically apparent hepatitis at a later time.

Chronic hepatitis that is clinically apparent, as in the patient described in Case 4, occurs in many individuals chronically infected with the hepatitis B virus. These individuals have detectable serum HBsAg. They may have symptoms of chronic hepatitis including fatigue, depression, loss of appetite, and other nonspecific complaints. Sometimes, the disease is clinically silent and the patient will not have symptoms. Blood tests will usually reveal elevated ALT and AST activities. Sometimes, chronic hepatitis will be diagnosed only by liver biopsy in an individual who is diagnosed clinically as a chronic carrier.

Individuals with chronic hepatitis B infection, especially those with evidence of ongoing liver inflammation, are at risk of developing cirrhosis over time. Signs and symptoms of cirrhosis may not be apparent, and the diagnosis may be made only on liver biopsy. Case 4 describes such an example. Some patients with long-standing chronic hepatitis B may not even seek medical attention until they are suffering from complications of cirrhosis (see, for example, Case 5).

Individuals with chronic hepatitis B infection, especially those with cirrhosis, are at increased risk for development of hepatocellular carcinoma (primary liver cancer), as in Case 5. As noted previously, while relatively rare in the United States, hepatocellular carcinoma is the number one or number two cause of cancer death in the world, especially in certain Asian and African countries. Individuals with hepatitis B and cirrhosis bear the greatest risk for development of hepatocellular carcinoma. Individuals with hepatitis and no cirrhosis are also at increased risk compared to the general population.

Chronic hepatitis B infection is separated into two distinguishable "states." The best way to distinguish these two states of hepatitis B virus infection is by the presence or absence of hepatitis Be antigen (HBeAg) in blood. In instances where the hepatitis B virus is rapidly replicating, a short form of the hepatitis B core antigen, called *HBeAg*, is usually detected in the blood. HBeAg is detected in the blood during acute infection, when the virus rapidly replicates, and becomes undetectable as the acute infection resolves. In most cases of chronic infection, HBeAg is not detected because the virus enters a state of low replication and its genetic material integrates into the DNA of infected cells. In some cases of chronic infection, however, the virus maintains a highly replicative "lifestyle" (*are viruses alive?*) and, in most of these cases, HBeAg will be detected in the blood. In individuals chronically infected with hepatitis B virus, the state of infection can switch from HBeAg-positive (high replication) to HBeAg-negative (low replication) at any time.

The distinction between HBeAg-positive and HBeAg-negative chronic hepatitis B is critical regarding disease severity, prognosis, contagiousness, and treatment. Patients who have HBeAg in their blood usually have more severe clinical disease with a greater amount of inflammation in the liver. They are usually sicker and have more symptoms. The chances of progression to cirrhosis and hepatocellular carcinoma are greater. In addition, individuals with detectable HBeAg in their blood are highly infectious as high viral replication is associated with the presence of more viral particles in the blood. A major goal of treatment for chronic hepatitis B is to convert a patient who has detectable HBeAg in the blood (a state of high virus replication) to one who does not have detectable HBeAg in the blood (a state of low-level virus replication). This change after treatment is associated with a better long-term prognosis.

Individuals with chronic hepatitis B virus infection can spontaneously convert from HBeAg-negative to HBeAg-positive. This is associated with worsening disease severity and prognosis. Paradoxically, conversion from HBeAg-positive to HBeAg-negative, which is associated with a better long-term outlook, is associated with a transient worsening of hepatitis and higher elevations in blood ALT and AST activities. This probably occurs because the immune system attacks the hepatocytes in which the virus is rapidly replicating, causing increased liver inflammation and cell death as infected cells are killed. The "flare" in hepatitis associated with conversion from HBeAg-positive to HBeAg-negative usually resolves with improvement in condition.

An exception to the rule that HBeAg is detectable in the blood of individuals infected with the hepatitis B virus when the virus is rapidly replicating occurs when there is infection with mutant forms of hepatitis B virus known as *precore mutants*. Precore mutants of the hepatitis B virus have mutations in their core proteins. As a result, they do not make HBeAg, even when they are rapidly replicating. Therefore, in precore mutant infection, the presence or absence of HBeAg in the blood is not a determinant of prognosis. It may be suspected when patients do not have detectable HBeAg but do have high concentrations of hepatitis B virus DNA in the blood. Precore mutants are definitively identified only by isolating the virus from the patient and examining its DNA sequence.

Transmission

Approximately 350 million individuals throughout the world are chronically infected with the hepatitis B virus, making it the number one worldwide cause of liver disease. The geographic distribution of cases varies tremendously from one part of the world to another. Hepatitis B virus infection is relatively uncommon in the United States and other Western countries. In the United States, just over one million individuals are chronically infected with hepatitis B virus. On the other hand, hepatitis B virus infection is endemic in Southeast Asia and sub-Saharan Africa. In countries such as Senegal, Thailand, and parts of China, as many as 25 percent of the population may become infected with hepatitis B virus by early childhood. The prevalence of infection due to hepatitis B virus in different regions around the world is shown in Figure 4.2.

Figure 4.2 Worldwide Prevalence of Hepatitis B Virus Infection

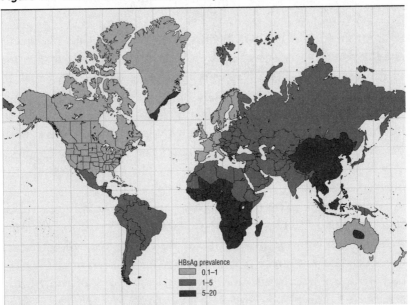

The prevalence of infection is extremely high in parts of Asia and Africa.

Hepatitis B virus is transmitted by blood and blood products. It is also transmitted by sex. The virus can be transmitted from mother to newborn baby. The major routes of transmission vary in different parts of the world. In Western countries, including the United States, intravenous drug use and sex are very important modes of transmission. In other parts of the world where infection is endemic, transmission from mother to newborn is the most important mode of transmission. The major risk factors for transmission of hepatitis B virus are:

- Transmission from infected mother to newborn baby
- Blood transfusions (prior to 1970 in developed countries)
- Intravenous drug use
- Homosexual sex
- Heterosexual sex
- Exposure to blood by health care workers
- Transmission from infected health care workers to patients (rare)
- Hemodialysis
- Staff of institutions for the developmentally challenged
- Incarceration in prison (most likely male homosexual sex)
- Household contacts of infected individuals

Transmission of hepatitis B virus from mother to baby may occur either before delivery or by exposure to the mother's blood at the time of delivery. The hepatitis B virus is also present in the breast milk of infected mothers, but a large study has shown that breast-feeding is not a major source of transmission of hepatitis B. Some babies of infected mothers who are not infected with the hepatitis B virus at birth become infected during the first few months or first year of life—probably by household exposure to the mother's blood or that of infected brothers or sisters.

A major route of transmission of hepatitis B in the West was transfusion of blood and blood products. Since the association of the Australia antigen with serum hepatitis in the 1960s, tremendous efforts have been taken to screen the blood supply and keep it free of hepatitis B virus. In most industrialized countries, the risk of contracting hepatitis B from a blood transfusion is extremely low as donated blood is screened for the virus. In addition, intravenous drug users and other individuals at high risk for hepatitis B are excluded from donating blood if they are identified. Although the blood supply is remarkably safe, no screening test is perfect, and the risk of contracting hepatitis B from a transfusion of one unit of blood in the United States is approximately one in sixty thousand to one in one hundred thousand. The hepatitis B virus can also be transmitted by organ transplantation, but the organ donor's blood is generally tested for hepatitis B virus infection before an organ is used.

Hepatitis B virus can be transmitted by sharing needles. Intravenous drug users frequently share needles to inject heroin or cocaine, and blood is transmitted from one individual to the other via needle. In inner cities in the United States, intravenous drug use is a major risk factor for hepatitis B. Hepatitis B virus can also be transmitted by tattooing, acupuncture, ear piercing, and piercing of other body parts if unsterilized needles are used.

Sexual contact is another way to transmit the hepatitis B virus. Individuals with multiple sexual partners are at significantly increased risk for hepatitis B. Male homosexuals and female professional sex workers have much higher rates of hepatitis B virus infection than the general population. Patients at sexually transmitted disease clinics also have higher incidences of hepatitis B. Male prisoners are at increased risk for hepatitis B, most likely due to increased rates of unprotected homosexual activities among inmates and also because many are intravenous drug users. In households with an infected individual, the sexual partner runs a higher risk of contracting hepatitis B than from other household contact. Sexual transmission of hepatitis B virus most often occurs by intercourse, either anal or vaginal, as hepatitis B virus can be isolated from semen. The sexual transmission rate from infected women to men is probably less than that from men to women or men to men. Sexual transmission from women to men does occur, however.

Health care workers who are regularly exposed to blood are at increased risk for hepatitis B virus infection. The most likely route of infection is by accidental sticks with needles and other sharp equipment used on infected patients. The hepatitis B virus may also be transmitted by various other pieces of hospital equipment that can contain small quantities of blood, such as unsterilized endoscopes and mechanical ventilators. Hemodialysis is an important route of transmission. Patients with chronic kidney failure who receive hemodialysis are at significantly increased risk for hepatitis B virus infection. There have been sporadic case reports of hepatitis B virus transmission from health care workers to patients, but, fortunately, transmission by this route is rare. Most cases have been traced to persistently infected surgeons, dentists, or physicians who perform invasive procedures. Health care workers who transmit the hepatitis B virus to patients are almost always found to be HBeAg-positive upon blood testing.

Staff workers at institutions for the developmentally disabled are also at increased risk for hepatitis B. Hepatitis B virus can most likely be transmitted by biting. This is not uncommon among residents of such institutions. Inapparent exposure to infected blood is probably also relatively common at such institutions.

Household contacts with common objects by infected individuals also increase the risk of contracting hepatitis B. Transmission by blood that is not always obvious can occur among household members; possible household instruments of transmission include shared razors, toothbrushes, baby bottles, and children's toys. Transmission of hepatitis B virus does *not* occur by touching, holding hands, kissing, or hugging.

Diagnosis

The first step in diagnosing hepatitis B virus infection, either acute or chronic, is blood testing. Blood tests are used to detect various viral proteins or antibodies against viral proteins. Various blood tests used to diagnosis hepatitis B infection are listed in Table 4.3.

Diagnosis of Acute Hepatitis B

The most commonly used marker to detect the presence of hepatitis B virus infection in the blood is HBsAg. Its detection is a relatively simple procedure in the clinical laboratory. HBsAg is present in the blood early in the course of infection and remains present in the blood during chronic infection. HBsAg disappears from the blood when infection resolves; its loss means that the patient is cured.

Antibodies of the IgM class against the hepatitis B core antigen (IgM anti-HBc) are detected in acute infection. They become detectable in the blood shortly after the appearance of HBsAg and remain detectable for a few weeks after HBsAg is lost while the disease is resolving. Testing for IgM anti-HBc is, therefore, important in a patient

Table 4.3 Blood Tests for Hepatitis B Virus Infection

Test	Characteristics
HBsAg	Present early in infection, remains in chronic infection (if absent, the patient does not have chronic infection). Disappears with resolution of infection.
IgM anti-HBc	Present in acute infection and disappears with resolution.
IgG anti-HBc	Present in individuals chronically infected or in those previously infected. Hence, detection in the absence of HBsAg does not indicate chronic infection.
anti-HBs	Present in previously infected individuals who have cleared the virus from their bodies. Protective against reinfection. Not present in chronically infected individuals. Also induced by vaccination.
HBeAg	Present in patients with very active viral replication. Individuals with chronic infection who are HBeAg-positive are highly infectious and generally have a poorer prognosis.
IgG anti-HBe	Present in patients without high viral replication.

who presents late in the course of acute hepatitis B. If IgM anti-HBc is detectable, but HBsAg is not, it indicates that the patient is in the resolution stage of acute hepatitis B.

Antibodies of the IgG class against the hepatitis B core antigen (IgG anti-HBc) are present in the blood of almost all individuals who have been infected with, or possibly exposed to, the virus. These antibodies become detectable in the blood a few months after acute infection, usually after the IgM class antibodies disappear. IgG anti-HBc persists in the blood after infection resolves, sometimes for the patient's lifetime. It may be detected in someone with acute infection that is nearly resolved. IgG anti-HBc is not protective against subsequent hepatitis B virus infection.

Individuals with hepatitis B virus infection who clear the virus from their bodies develop antibodies against hepatitis B surface antigen (anti-HBs). If present, these antibodies indicate protection against reinfection. Anti-HBs antibodies are virtually never present in chronically infected individuals who have HBsAg. They are also the type of antibodies induced by vaccination.

The significance of hepatitis Be antigen (HBeAg) has been discussed previously in reference to states of high viral replication versus low viral replication. HBeAg is detectable in the blood of patients with high levels of viral replication. It is present in the blood of individuals with acute infection because, in acute infection, the virus replicates at a high level. Antibodies against HBeAg (IgG anti-HBe) are usually present in the blood of individuals with hepatitis B who do not have HBeAg, that is, those who have low-level viral replication.

In individuals with suspected acute hepatitis B virus infection, blood testing for HBsAg, IgM anti-HBc, and anti-HBs should be performed. Acute hepatitis B virus infection is usually suspected in the patient with new-onset jaundice and other symptoms including fatigue, right upper quadrant abdominal pain, fever, loss of appetite, nausea, and vomiting. A risk factor for infection may be elicited from the patient's history, for example, intravenous drug use, an accidental needle stick (in a health care worker), or exposure to an infected contact within the past several weeks or months. The presence of HBsAg in blood will indicate acute infection or the continued presence of the virus. The detection of IgM anti-HBc, in the absence of HBsAg, will suggest resolving infection. The presence of anti-HBs will indicate resolution of the disease and that the patient is now immune to future infection. In rare cases, HBsAg and antibodies against it (anti-HBs) can be present at the same time. Such individuals can have complications if these two types of antibodies react with each other in the bloodstream and deposit in the small blood vessels of various organs.

A patient in whom acute hepatitis B virus infection is diagnosed by the presence of HBsAg in the blood should be followed for loss of HBsAg and the development of anti-HBs. In about 95 percent of acutely infected adults, HBsAg will be lost. Most of them will develop anti-HBs. In about 5 percent, however, HBsAg will persist. If HBsAg persists for more than six months after acute infection, the illness is then considered chronic hepatitis B.

Diagnosis of Chronic Hepatitis B

Chronic hepatitis B is defined as infection with the hepatitis B virus for more than six months. Chronic hepatitis B infection should be suspected in individuals with known risk factors and individuals from parts of the world where the disease is endemic. Most patients from parts of the world where hepatitis B is endemic were infected as newborn babies or in childhood. A smaller percentage was infected as adults. Most chronically infected individuals in Western countries acquired the disease as adults.

Individuals with chronic hepatitis B infection may have no symptoms (chronic carriers) or have symptoms and clinical evidence of chronic hepatitis, cirrhosis, or even hepatocellular carcinoma. Sometimes, the disease is suspected when elevated ALT and AST activities are detected on routine blood tests or testing for other purposes. The most important test to establish or exclude chronic hepatitis B is blood testing for HBsAg.

If HBsAg is detected in the blood, and presumably has been present for more than six months if no recent history of acute hepatitis can be ascertained, chronic hepatitis B virus infection is established. If HBsAg is not detected in the blood, the individual does not have chronic hepatitis B. It must be emphasized that, in the absence of HBsAg, the detection of IgG anti-HBc in the blood does not indicate a diagnosis of chronic hepatitis B. This is critical to realize and is a mistake that I have seen many doctors make. HBsAg must be detected in the blood—or the individual does not have chronic hepatitis B. In individuals who have clinical evidence of chronic hepatitis but do not have detectable blood HBsAg, a search for another cause of hepatitis (for example, hepatitis C, alcohol, drugs) should be initiated.

For individuals in whom chronic hepatitis B virus infection is established, that is, those who have had HBsAg in their blood for more than six months, further evaluation is indicated. The blood AST and ALT activities should be checked, as should biochemical tests related to liver function, such as albumin concentration, bilirubin concentration, and prothrombin time. If all of these are normal, then the patient is generally considered to be a chronic carrier. Abnormalities suggest chronic hepatitis and possibly cirrhosis.

Individuals with chronic hepatitis B virus infection and HBsAg should be tested for HBeAg. The presence of serum HBeAg indicates high viral replication, a highly infectious state, and possible indication for treatment. The absence of serum HBeAg and/or the presence of anti-HBe suggest a low state of viral replication and a generally better prognosis. The individuals should also be tested for the presence of viral DNA in the blood. Detection of viral DNA suggests viral replication, even in the absence of HBeAg.

What is the role of liver biopsy in a patient with chronic hepatitis B infection? If any controversy exists, it is probably in individuals who are clinically diagnosed as chronic carriers. These are patients who have HBsAg in the blood but have no symptoms and have normal ALT and AST activities. Many liver specialists would say that such individuals do not need liver biopsies. Their argument would be that, at the present time, there is no treatment for such individuals and they most likely will have minimal or no liver inflammation. This is true. However, many liver specialists will advocate liver biopsy for such patients. Although most chronic carriers will have normal liver biopsies, about 25 percent of chronic carriers will have inflammation on liver biopsy and a few will even have cirrhosis. Even if you knew this, there are no recommended treatment interventions at the present time for those individuals who do not have detectable blood HBeAg or viral DNA.

In the end, the decision to perform a liver biopsy on a patient diagnosed as a hepatitis B virus chronic carrier probably should depend upon the desire of the patient (and doctor) to want to better assess the state of the patient's liver. Some patients will want to know if they have cirrhosis or ongoing inflammation, which would be correlated with a poorer prognosis than no inflammation or cirrhosis. Some patients do not want to know. Therefore, the final decision to perform liver biopsy on these patients depends upon the desire to know as much as possible about prognosis.

Most liver specialists will probably agree that their patients with chronic hepatitis B who exhibit laboratory evidence of liver inflammation should have liver biopsies if there are no contraindications. Nonetheless, there are no treatment options for those without evidence of viral replication, detected by the presence of HBeAg and/or viral DNA in the blood. The chance of having cirrhosis is much greater in a patient with hepatitis B virus infection and ongoing hepatitis than in a chronic carrier without evidence of hepatitis, however. And in many cases, only a liver biopsy can definitely establish the presence of cirrhosis.

Patients with chronic hepatitis B and detectable HBeAg and/or viral DNA in the blood should have liver biopsies if there are no contraindications. Most of these patients will have clinical and/or laboratory evidence of hepatitis. The degree of inflammation and, in most cases, the presence or absence of cirrhosis can be established only by examination of the liver biopsy. These patients are also candidates for treatment and, before any treatment is considered, a diagnosis should be confirmed.

Prevention

Hepatitis B is a contagious disease. All individuals infected with hepatitis B virus are potentially contagious. Those who have detectable HBeAg in the blood are especially contagious.

Certain commonsense preventive measures can be used to curtail the spread of hepatitis B among individuals who are not immune. Sexually promiscuous individuals—as well as individuals who do not know much about their single sex partner—should use condoms. Condoms should also be used in sexual relationships if one partner is known to be infected with the hepatitis B virus and the other is not immune. Those living in a household with a hepatitis B virus-infected individual should avoid contacts with blood, some of which may not be readily apparent. For example, they should not share razors, toothbrushes, or similar items. Caution should be used in tending to injured individuals who are bleeding. In hospitals and doctor's offices, extreme caution should be used in drawing blood and in properly disposing of needles and surgical instruments.

Individuals not immune to hepatitis B infection (those who do not have anti-HBs) who are accidentally exposed to contaminated blood, or have sex with an infected individual, can receive passive immunization with hepatitis B immune globulin (HBIG). HBIG is a preparation of antibodies pooled from the blood of many individuals who are immune to hepatitis B. The antibodies are sterilized so that infectious viruses are not spread with the immune globulin preparations. HBIG should be given by injection soon after contact, at most within thirty days, to prevent hepatitis B in exposed individuals.

Since hepatitis B virus can be transmitted from a pregnant woman to her newborn baby, all pregnant women should be screened for HBsAg in their blood. If it is detected, the newborn should be given HBIG followed by a vaccination series beginning one week after birth. Several studies suggest that this will significantly decrease the chance of the baby becoming chronically infected with hepatitis B virus.

Effective vaccines against hepatitis B virus are available. Most current preparations are of recombinant hepatitis B surface antigen manufactured using recombinant DNA technology. Three shots are needed in most individuals to assure long-term immunity. After the initial vaccine shot, a second shot is given one month later and a third six months later. The large majority of individuals respond to three shots with the development of anti-HBs. Elderly individuals or individuals with chronic diseases are less likely to respond.

Who should be vaccinated for hepatitis B? At the present time, universal vaccination is recommended for all children in the United States. Adults who are at high risk of exposure to hepatitis B virus also should be vaccinated. This would include health care workers, household members living with an individual with hepatitis B, sexual partners of individuals with chronic hepatitis B, and, perhaps, all sexually promiscuous individuals. People from Western countries who will reside for extended periods of time in parts of the world where hepatitis B virus infection is endemic should also be vaccinated.

All available scientific data indicate that the hepatitis B vaccines presently in use are extremely safe. Some press reports have focused on a few individuals claiming to have developed "autoimmune disorders" after receiving hepatitis B vaccines. There is no valid scientific evidence that people who have received hepatitis B vaccines have a higher incidence of any diseases compared to those not vaccinated. Such studies, in fact, indicate that vaccinated individuals have fewer diseases, namely hepatitis B and primary liver cancer. So far, all of the claims that have appeared in the press stating that hepatitis B vaccine may cause autoimmune disorders are based on isolated, retrospective (backward-looking) reports that may be coincidental and do not demonstrate cause and effect. Claims such as these should not be considered as scientific evidence.

Theoretically, hepatitis B should be a very rare disease and ultimately eradicated from the world because effective vaccines are available. In a landmark study in Taiwan, it was demonstrated that universal vaccination against hepatitis B virus led to a reduction in primary liver cancer. Imagine a vaccine that prevents one of the most common causes of cancer death in the world! Well, it really is here! However, socioeconomic and political realities make it difficult to provide hepatitis B vaccines to individuals in the parts of the world where it is needed most. Sadly, hepatitis B will likely exist for a long time and primary liver cancer will continue to be a leading cause of cancer death worldwide.

Treatment

The treatment of acute hepatitis B is supportive. Most patients can probably rest at home and see their doctors as outpatients. Patients who cannot eat or drink fluids may have to be admitted to the hospital until these symptoms resolve. Patients with signs and symptoms of liver failure also have to be admitted to the hospital. As discussed previously, acute hepatitis B in adults is a self-limited illness that resolves in approximately 90 to 95 percent of cases and does not become chronic. These patients do not need medical follow-up for the illness once it has resolved. Treatment and long-term care of patients with chronic hepatitis B virus infection are discussed in Chapter 5.

Hepatitis C

The discovery of hepatitis C virus in 1989 revolutionized the approach to many patients suffering with chronic liver disease. Around the same time that the virus was discovered, interferon alpha was shown to be an effective treatment in some individuals with hepatitis C, which was formerly called *non-A, non-B hepatitis*. As a result of this research, millions of people with liver disease are given a diagnosis and offered treatment for a condition that previously did not even have an actual name. In addition, numerous gastroenterologists and other physicians decided that they would now be hepatologists (liver specialists).

Before discussing hepatitis C, it is worthwhile to provide a description of the virus that causes it. Only the issues essential to understanding the hepatitis C virus, such as viral structure and function, are discussed; additional details are included in figures for completeness.

Workers at the biotechnology company Chiron Corporation reported the discovery of the hepatitis C virus in 1989. Its discovery relied on the discipline of molecular biology, which made the cloning of its genetic material possible. The virus is extremely difficult to culture, and even fifteen years after its discovery, only a few laboratories have done so successfully.

Individuals with non-A, non-B hepatitis had clinical or laboratory evidence of hepatitis without evidence of hepatitis A or hepatitis B virus infection. Evidence based on transmission patterns suggested that non-A, non-B hepatitis was caused by an unidentified virus. Non-A, non-B hepatitis was observed in patients after they had received blood transfusions. It was also commonly seen in intravenous drug users. Furthermore, blood from individuals with non-A, non-B hepatitis caused hepatitis if injected into chimpanzees, and blood from one infected chimpanzee could transmit hepatitis to another chimpanzee. These findings indicated that another human hepatotropic virus (or viruses) was a significant cause of liver disease.

The creative approach used by workers at Chiron that led to the identification of a new human hepatitis is outlined in Figure 4.3. After identifying the virus using techniques from molecular biology, these investigators and their collaborators demonstrated what was responsible for at least 85 percent of what was then diagnosed as non-A, non-B hepatitis. Their results were published in two papers in the journal *Science* in 1989. The following year, Chiron investigators as well as several other groups of scientists used the partial genetic sequence information to isolate and sequence the complete genetic material (actually a DNA copy of the virus's RNA genome) of the then-novel hepatitis C virus.

The genetic material of hepatitis C is RNA. Based on sequence similarity, it is a member of the *Flaviviridae* family of viruses. Viral RNA encodes a large protein that is processed in infected host cells into several smaller structural and nonstructural proteins, as represented in Figure 4.4.

It is not important to remember the names and functions of all the hepatitis C viral proteins. For those who are interested, they are briefly described in Table 4.4. What is important to remember is that detection of antibodies against these proteins in the blood of infected individuals plays a critical role in diagnosis and screening of the common blood supply. Some of these proteins are also targets of attack for novel drugs that are in development to treat hepatitis C.

Nobody has with certainty seen the hepatitis C virus with an electron microscope. The presumed structure of hepatitis C is inferred from

Figure 4.3 Strategy to Identify Hepatitis C Virus

Infect chimpanzees with blood from patients with post-transfusion non-A, non-B hepatitis

↓

Extract DNA and RNA, some presumably of the putative hepatitis C virus, from serum of infected chimpanzees

↓

Construct DNA library from DNA and RNA reverse transcribed to complementary DNA

↓

Express proteins encoded by DNA in library in bacteria, some of which are encoded by viral DNA or complementary DNA

↓

Screen bacteria expressing proteins with antibodies from blood of a patient with non-A, non-B hepatitis that presumably contains antibodies against the putative hepatitis C virus

↓

Purify DNA clones from bacteria expressing proteins recognized by antibodies of the patient's blood

↓

Isolate and sequence DNA that corresponds to a portion of the putative hepatitis virus gene (actually complementary DNA copy of a portion of the viral RNA genome)

↓

Use this fragment to isolate the rest of the viral genome

structures of proteins encoded by its genetic material and comparison to other related viruses. The size of the virus is also estimated by passing infectious blood through filters before it is injected into chimpanzees to determine if they develop hepatitis. A schematic diagram of the presumed structure of the hepatitis C virus is shown in Figure 4.5.

Two important issues in hepatitis C virology are those of genotype and quasispecies. Many liver specialists are determining the genotype of the infecting hepatitis C virus as a matter of routine, and many patients have questions about this. In brief, hepatitis C viruses isolated from different patients show differences in their genetic material. These differences may cause changes in the structures of the encoded pro-

Figure 4.4 Large Protein Encoded by Hepatitis C Viral RNA Molecule Is Processed into Smaller Proteins in Infected Cells

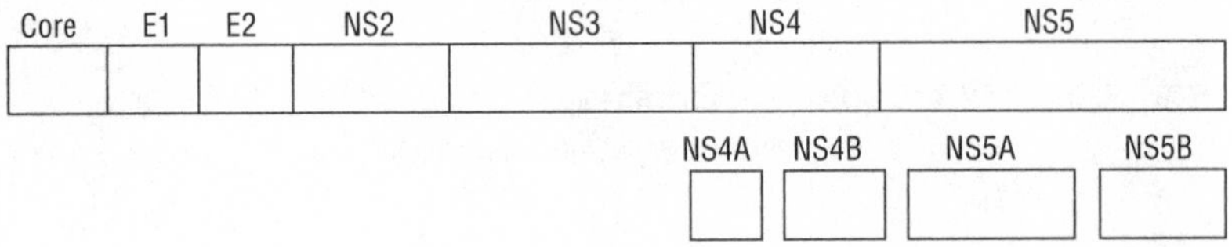

Core, E1, and E2 are structural proteins of the viral particle. The proteins NS2, NS3, NS4A, NS4B, NS5A, and NS5B are not present in the mature virus but are expressed in infected cells. A small protein known as P7, which derives from cleavage between E2 and NS2, is not shown. The functions of these proteins are listed in Table 4.4.

teins. Viral isolates that have significant degrees of dissimilarity belong to different genotypes. There are six major hepatitis C virus genotypes. In the most commonly used current nomenclature, they are referred to as *genotypes 1 through 6*. There are some sub-genotypes within the six major genotypes identified using letters, for example, 1a and 1b.

Table 4.4 Proteins of Hepatitis C Virus

Protein	Function
Structural Proteins	
Core	Forms the viral particle nucleocapsid, or core; may have other effects when expressed in host cells
E1	Protein of the envelope
E2	Protein of the envelope
P7	Ion channel
Nonstructural Proteins	
NS2	A protease that cleaves the viral polyprotein at a specific site
NS3	A protease that cleaves the viral polyprotein at specific sites and an RNA-helicase that can unwind the viral RNA in cells
NS4A	A cofactor necessary for the NS3 protease activity
NS4B	Possibly involved in altering cell membranes necessary for or advantageous to viral replication
NS5A	Phosphoprotein; function not entirely clear but plays some role in determining sensitivity of viral infection to interferon
NS5B	RNA-polymerase necessary to replicate the viral RNA

Figure 4.5 Hepatitis C Virus

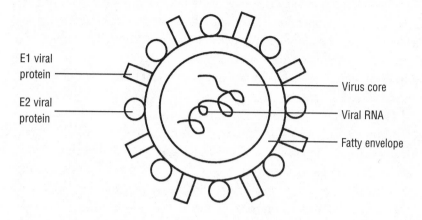

Hepatitis C virus contains a single RNA molecule associated with a nucleocapsid in its center. This is surrounded by a fatty envelope that contains two viral proteins—E1 and E2.

Several studies have shown that patients chronically infected with genotypes 1a and 1b and genotype 4 are less likely to respond to treatment with currently available drugs.

Strains of the hepatitis C virus with more subtle differences that may result from either one or several spontaneous mutations are known as *quasispecies*. The concept of quasispecies may seem like molecular esoterica to the average patient; however, it may be of clinical relevance. Quasispecies represent a way in which the virus changes to avoid being eliminated by the immune system. The emergence of hepatitis C virus quasispecies in an individual with hepatitis C may be associated with more aggressive disease and poor response to treatment. At the present time, quasispecies cannot be determined in commercial laboratories. Their detection requires specialized research procedures.

The hepatitis C virus causes both acute and chronic hepatitis. By far the major concern about being infected with the hepatitis C virus is the development of chronic hepatitis. Acute infection with the hepatitis C virus usually is not associated with symptoms and often goes undiagnosed. Acute infection with the hepatitis C virus usually does not cause clinically apparent disease. Most people who are chronically infected cannot recall an acute episode of jaundice or liver disease. Some may have nonspecific symptoms at the time of infection but never associate them with liver disease. In some cases, however, infection with the hepatitis C virus does cause acute disease. Rare cases of fulminant hepatic failure caused by acute hepatitis C virus infection have been reported and convincingly demonstrated. Although acute hepatitis caused by the hepatitis C virus should always be suspected in an individual with new, sudden-onset liver disease, it usually does not turn out to be the cause.

The major concern about hepatitis C virus is that infection becomes chronic in the large majority of cases. It is estimated that, of all people infected with the hepatitis C virus, 50 to 85 percent become chronically infected. This appears to be the case in adults and probably in children, too. Although acute infection is usually not accompanied by apparent disease, once the virus enters an individual's body, it has a very high chance of staying there and replicating in the liver during the person's lifetime.

Chronic hepatitis C has been referred to by some as a *silent killer*. Perhaps this term is a bit alarmist as only a minority of patients chronically infected with the hepatitis C virus die as a result. There is some accuracy to this term, however. Acute infection with hepatitis C virus is almost always silent and patients almost never remember how they caught the disease. Once a person is chronically infected with the hepatitis C virus, the symptoms of chronic hepatitis are often not present or are so nonspecific that the diagnosis is not readily made.

Most patients with chronic hepatitis C have no symptoms or only nonthreatening symptoms such as tiredness, lack of energy, mild depression, and mild loss of appetite. In a sense, the disease is silent. Unless a history of risk factor is elucidated—for example, past intravenous drug use or blood transfusion prior to 1992—the doctor usually does not suspect hepatitis C upon first seeing a patient. The disease is often first suspected when routine blood tests are performed. Abnormal elevations in blood ALT and AST activities are frequently detected that suggest chronic hepatitis. If alcohol abuse is not in the differential diagnosis, hepatitis C is a likely cause. Even if the patient is a moderate to heavy alcohol drinker, he or she may still have chronic hepatitis C. This may be due to the combination of viral hepatitis and even moderate alcohol use, which is more likely to cause liver disease than either condition alone. Hence, patients with both diseases may be more likely to seek medical attention for liver problems.

What is the course of disease in a chronic hepatitis C patient? The big problem for physicians and patients is that its course is extremely variable and usually cannot be predicted in a specific case. Some patients will have mild, low-grade hepatitis for life and never develop cirrhosis or complications of liver disease. Some patients may develop cirrhosis several years after infection while others will never exhibit symptoms during decades of infection and see a doctor later in life with clinical evidence of cirrhosis. A few hypothetical case histories are illustrative.

- **Case 1.** A forty-year-old woman who is very healthy donates blood. She is told that she has antibodies against the hepatitis C virus. She sees a doctor who conducts a normal physical examination with completely normal blood tests, including normal ALT and AST activities. Upon questioning her mother, the patient discovers that she received a blood transfusion as a baby. A reverse transcription-polymerase chain reaction test detects low levels of hepatitis C virus RNA in her blood. A liver biopsy shows an essentially normal liver.

- **Case 2.** A thirty-nine-year-old man who works as an investment banker is refused life insurance because of "abnormal liver function tests." He routinely works twelve- to fifteen-hour days in a stressful job and jogs and plays tennis regularly. He says that he has never felt better in his life. In college, he experimented only a few times with intravenous drugs but has not used any in twenty years. His doctor finds that a test for antibodies against the hepatitis C virus is positive, and a liver biopsy shows moderate liver inflammation with fibrosis (scarring) progressing to cirrhosis.

- **Case 3.** A fifty-five-year-old woman who works as a nurse remembers sticking herself with a needle about five years ago. She paid little attention to this accident at the time. She feels chronically tired and has mild swelling in her abdomen and ankles and yellowing in the whites of her eyes. She sends off some of her blood to the laboratory and finds elevated ALT and AST activities, a low albumin concentration, and slightly prolonged PT. She sees a doctor who performs a liver biopsy that indicates cirrhosis.

- **Case 4.** A seventy-four-year-old woman sees her doctor, complaining of swelling of the abdomen, swollen ankles, and some pain in her abdomen. She has never consumed alcohol. When she was thirty-four years old, she had a hysterectomy and needed a blood transfusion because of extensive bleeding during surgery. She was an active, healthy woman for the next forty years with few visits to doctors. Physical examination now reveals ascites, edema, and jaundice. Blood tests show normal ALT and AST activities, low albumin concentration, elevated bilirubin concentration, and prolonged prothrombin time. An ultrasound shows ascites and a shrunken, nodular liver consistent with cirrhosis with a mass very typical for hepatocellular carcinoma. A blood test for antibodies against the hepatitis C virus is positive.

These four cases demonstrate the wide variety of presentations of chronic hepatitis C. In some cases, it is a relatively benign disease, in others a "silent killer," and in still others something in between. The patient in Case 1 has been infected with the hepatitis C virus for forty years but is completely healthy and has a liver biopsy with no evidence of chronic hepatitis. She will probably not suffer any consequences of liver disease in her lifetime and would never have known that she had a chronic hepatitis C virus infection if she had not donated blood. There are millions of people like this around the world. They are chronically infected with hepatitis C, will probably never know it, and will probably never get sick from it. In such cases, the disease is clearly "silent" but not a "killer."

The patient described in Case 2 is typical. He was infected with the hepatitis C virus twenty years earlier by experimenting with intravenous drugs. He has never used drugs since and is now a wealthy and successful man. He finds out about possible liver disease through a life insurance examination and is diagnosed with hepatitis C by his doctor. However, he is less fortunate than the patient in Case 1 because, after twenty years of hepatitis C virus infection, this patient already has evidence on liver biopsy that he is developing cirrhosis. In his case, the hepatitis C virus may indeed be behaving like a "silent killer." However, the infection may have been detected early enough so that treatment can prove beneficial. He may or may not develop cirrhosis and complications in later years.

The woman in Case 3 represents a less common but possible course of hepatitis C infection. She was infected only five years earlier and already has cirrhosis and clinical complications. The hepatitis C virus usually does not cause such rapid progression of liver disease, but it is certainly capable of doing so. Here, the virus is also acting as a "killer," but it is less silent. It may be too late for treatment to prevent progression of this woman's liver disease. Fortunately, liver transplantation may stop the virus from acting as a "killer" in her case.

The patient described in Case 4 manifests the real "silent killer" aspect of the hepatitis C virus. She was infected for forty years with the virus and never knew it. The diagnosis of chronic hepatitis C was not made until she had advanced cirrhosis and primary liver cancer. This otherwise healthy woman will probably die of liver disease relatively soon after diagnosis.

How many patients infected with hepatitis C virus will be like the patient in Case 1? How many will be like the less fortunate patients in Cases 2–4? The available data do not permit these questions to be answered precisely, but some estimates can be provided.

Of all the patients who are diagnosed by doctors, most are probably similar to the patient in Case 2. Chronic hepatitis C is usually diagnosed in a patient who was infected several years in the past. Patients usually are asymptomatic and see a doctor because somewhere along the line elevated ALT or AST activity was detected on blood tests taken for another reason. Often, blood tests are performed as part of a life insurance examination or to evaluate nonspecific symptoms such as fatigue, irritability, depression, or loss of appetite that is observed in individuals with chronic viral hepatitis. Some patients diagnosed by doctors will be similar to those in Cases 3 and 4 that already have clinical signs and symptoms of chronic liver disease.

There are probably many more patients like the one in Case 1; however, they are usually not diagnosed. If all patients who have a risk factor for hepatitis C virus infection—for example, anyone who ever received a blood transfusion prior to 1992 or anyone who ever used intravenous drugs—were tested for the virus, many more cases of chronic infection would be diagnosed. Many would probably be similar to the patient described in Case 1, others like the patient described in Case 2. Some authorities have, in fact, recommended that all individuals with risk factors for hepatitis C infection, for example, all recipients of blood transfusions prior to 1992, be tested.

Studies, and the experiences of doctors over the past several years, suggest that there are probably three "worlds" of individuals with chronic hepatitis C. One contains patients similar to the one described in Case 1. The second world contains patients like the man in Case 2. The third contains those similar to the patients in Cases 3 and 4.

In one published study, sixty healthy blood donors infected with the hepatitis C virus were identified by blood screening. Liver biopsies were performed on all of them, and only one had evidence of significant liver disease. These patients—most of whom will probably do well and never suffer from complications of liver disease—comprise the first "world."

On the other hand, a published study of more than one hundred patients referred to a center that specializes in liver disease indicated that greater than 50 percent of patients already had cirrhosis and that many had hepatocellular carcinoma. These patients comprise the third "world" and are similar to those in Cases 3 and 4. These are patients who are already very sick from chronic hepatitis C, most of whom will ultimately need liver transplantation to survive.

The second "world" of patients with chronic hepatitis C consists of people similar to the patient described in Case 2. These are individuals with chronic infection, diagnosed by doctors, who do not yet have evidence of serious liver disease. This "world" contains most of the patients who know that they have chronic hepatitis C and are being monitored for it by doctors. Most of these patients have liver biopsies that indicate ongoing inflammation of the liver with either mild to moderate fibrosis, developing cirrhosis, or, sometimes, established cirrhosis without clinical symptoms or complications. Although there are no definitive numbers, most medical researchers estimate that about 25 percent of patients with chronic hepatitis C who are diagnosed by doctors will develop cirrhosis over two or more decades of infection. Of this 25 percent who develop cirrhosis, some will develop liver failure and require liver transplantation and some will develop hepatocellular carcinoma. It is this second "world" of patients that treatment with interferon and other drugs will probably help the most.

A major challenge for doctors who treat patients with chronic hepatitis C is to determine which of the second "world" patients, such as the patient described in Case 2, will enter the third "world" of patients with cirrhosis, advanced liver disease, or cancer. It is also not entirely clear if some of the first "world" patients, such as the patient described in Case 1, will someday develop cirrhosis and complications after many years. Unfortunately, there are no absolute predictors of which patients will do relatively well and which will go on to develop cirrhosis and complications over time. However, a comprehensive evaluation can provide some useful predictive information.

Liver biopsy is the best test to obtain predictive data about a specific patient with chronic hepatitis C infection who does not already have clinically apparent complications of cirrhosis. Liver biopsy will establish the degree of inflammation, the degree of fibrosis, and the presence or absence of cirrhosis. Patients with significant inflammation or significant fibrosis are more likely to develop cirrhosis over time than those who do not have fibrosis or only minimal fibrosis. Patients who already have cirrhosis are at much greater risk for developing complications, liver failure, and hepatocellular carcinoma.

Viral genotype and concentration of hepatitis C virus RNA in the blood ("viral load") have been studied as possible predictors of disease progression in chronic hepatitis C. Some researchers have shown that infection with hepatitis C virus genotype 1a or 1b is correlated with a poorer prognosis than infection with non-type 1 genotypes. However, conflicting reports have also been reported and there are methodological and design limitations to all published studies that have addressed the issues of genotype and prognosis. The only fact most liver specialists agree upon is that type 1 and type 4 genotypes are less likely to respond to available treatments based on interferon alpha. The same holds true for viral loads. Blood viral RNA concentrations can show considerable fluctuation in a given individual, and viral load is not a reliable predictor of who will or who will not develop cirrhosis.

It is important to emphasize the effects of excessive alcohol consumption as a cofactor for liver damage in patients with chronic hepatitis C. Several studies and clinical observations suggest that alcohol is an independent risk factor for progression of liver disease and development of cirrhosis. Other studies have suggested that alcohol consumption accelerates the progression to cirrhosis in patients with chronic hepatitis C. In fact, the diagnosis of "cirrhosis caused by alcohol and hepatitis C" is heard more and more in medical wards these days. Perhaps the most famous person who suffered from this unfortunate combination was the late baseball player Mickey Mantle, a magnificent New York Yankee.

What is not clear about alcohol as a risk factor for the progression of liver disease in patients with hepatitis C is the amount of alcohol consumption that increases risk. Certainly, alcohol consumption of six or more drinks a day will increase the risk of liver disease, probably at an even faster rate than in individuals who do not have chronic hepatitis C virus infection. The data, however, are less clear for lower amounts of alcohol consumption. Virtually all liver specialists will agree that no patient with chronic hepatitis C should have more than two alcoholic drinks a day. Many experts in this field would even argue that patients with chronic hepatitis C should consume no alcohol. My personal feeling at this time, given the lack of data from well-controlled, forward-looking studies, is that patients with chronic hepatitis C should limit their alcohol intake to no more than a few drinks a few times per week. A couple of glasses of wine with an occasional nice dinner, a beer at a ball game, or an occasional cocktail at a party will probably not be detrimental to the person with chronic hepatitis C. However, this level of drinking may become problematic if it occurs on a daily basis. Patients with chronic hepatitis C certainly should not exceed two drinks per day and should probably keep their alcohol intake well below this amount.

Other organ systems besides the liver can be affected by chronic hepatitis C. The kidneys can be damaged in some cases of hepatitis C because of a condition known as *cryoglobulinemia*. Abnormal kidney function is detected by elevations in the blood creatinine concentration and the blood urea nitrogen (BUN) concentration. These laboratory tests are abnormal in any cause of kidney disease. The precise cause of kidney dysfunction in a person with hepatitis C requires additional testing. A urinalysis is usually the first test in helping to establish the possible cause of a kidney disease. The take-home message for patients with hepatitis C is that abnormalities in the blood creatinine or BUN indicate kidney problems that may or may not be caused by hepatitis C. Further evaluation is required to determine the cause.

Cryoglobulinemia is the presence of cryoglobulins in the blood. *Cryoglobulins* is a term for proteins in the blood that precipitate out at cold temperatures. The test for cryoglobulins involves placing a tube of blood (actually serum, which is blood minus the blood cells) in the cold and seeing if proteins that are soluble at room temperature come out of the solution. In chronic hepatitis C virus infection, cryoglobulins are a combination of viral components and antibodies against the virus. The cryoglobulins can deposit in the kidney and cause them to malfunction.

Cryoglobulins can also deposit in the joints and cause pain (arthragias) and swelling (arthritis) as well as skin rashes and other symptoms.

The most important points to remember about the course of chronic hepatitis C virus infection are:

1. Chronic hepatitis C virus infection is frequently "silent" as the patient has no or only nonspecific symptoms.
2. The course of chronic hepatitis C virus infection can vary significantly. Some individuals may develop cirrhosis after several years of infection. Other infected individuals will never develop significant liver disease or complications.
3. It is extremely difficult to predict the rate or progression of liver disease in an individual with chronic hepatitis C. Liver biopsy is the best source of predictive information.
4. Liver disease progresses more rapidly in patients with chronic hepatitis C who consume too much alcohol, but what constitutes a "safe" lower limit is not known at present.
5. Organs other than the liver can be affected in rare cases of hepatitis C.

Transmission

Hepatitis C virus is transmitted primarily by blood and blood products. Only since 1990, after the virus was discovered, could epidemiological studies of transmission be carried out in which it could be detected in subjects. Since then, we have learned a lot about transmission. The major risk factors for infection are listed in Table 4.5.

Transfusion of Blood and Blood Products

Since 1990 the blood supplies in the United States and most other industrialized countries have been screened for antibodies against the hepatitis C virus. A more sensitive antibody detection test was introduced in 1992, making the risk of getting hepatitis C by a transfusion extraordinarily low. Patients who received blood transfusions before 1990 (and to some extent before 1992), however, are at risk for having hepatitis C. The more units of blood transfused, the higher the risk.

Table 4.5 Risk Factors for Hepatitis C Virus

Transfusion of blood and blood products before 1990 or 1992 in developed countries[1]

Organ or tissue transplant before 1990 or 1992

Injection of illicit drugs (even in remote past)

Hemodialysis

Tattooing and body piercing

Sex with infected partner (higher risk in sexually promiscuous individuals; lower risk in monogamous individuals with infected partner)

Household contacts of infected individuals

Transmission from infected mother to newborn baby

Health care and laboratory workers exposed to blood

Infected health care workers (to patients)

Intranasal cocaine use[2]

Ear piercing in men[2]

---

1 Blood supply screening began in developed countries in 1990 and was improved by the introduction of better tests in 1992; those receiving blood transfusions between 1990 and 1992 are still at some risk.

2 It is unclear if these are actually the modes of transmission or factors associated with other lifestyle activities that may increase transmission (e.g., intranasal cocaine abusers may also be more likely to have used injection drugs at some time).

The risk is extremely high for individuals who received transfusions of blood products derived from multiple donors. Hemophiliacs, who received frequent injections of clotting factors purified from human blood before 1987 when they were treated in a special way to inactivate viruses, have a very high chance of having hepatitis C.

Since the improved 1992 test for detecting antibodies against the hepatitis C virus, the risk of contracting hepatitis C by blood transfusion has been vanishing in the developed world. It has been estimated that since 1992, the chance of receiving a unit of blood contaminated with the hepatitis C virus is less than one in one hundred thousand. One very important thing to remember is that hepatitis C is a chronic disease that can last a lifetime. Therefore, individuals who are now elderly and received transfusions of blood or blood products long before 1990—even when they were babies—can still be infected with the hepatitis C virus.

In underdeveloped countries, where the entire blood supply is not screened, the hepatitis C virus may still be transmitted by blood transfusion. This is especially true where individuals may sell their blood, such as poor areas of rural China. In underdeveloped countries, contaminated blood may also be transmitted by the use of unsterile medical equipment in hospitals and doctor's offices.

Organ or Tissue Transplantation

Transplantation of organs from infectious donors to a recipient carried a high risk for transmitting the hepatitis C virus infection before donor screening was available in 1990 and improved in 1992. This includes recipients of heart, kidney, and liver transplants. Currently, this risk is extremely low in developed parts of the world where organ donors are tested for infection with the hepatitis C virus.

Injection of Illicit Drugs

Illicit injection drug use remains a significant mode of transmission of the hepatitis C virus. Virtually all injection drug users share needles and syringes, making direct exposure to other people's blood common. Very active intravenous drug users are at an extremely high risk for contracting hepatitis C. Infection rates may be near 90 percent in recurrent urban users.

Even *one-time* injection drug use in the *remote past* is a risk for having hepatitis C virus infection. Many individuals are middle-aged when they are first diagnosed with chronic hepatitis C. Many are now "upstanding" members of the community with important jobs, nice families, and a high standard of living. Many used intravenous drugs once or a few times "back in the sixties when everyone was using them." For thirty or more years these patients have lived clean and healthy lives. Little did they know that, for all that time, the hepatitis C virus was lurking in their bodies.

Other viruses, in particular the hepatitis B virus and HIV, also are transmitted by contaminated blood. Therefore, recurrent injectors of illicit drugs have an increased risk of infection with these viruses as well. It is not uncommon for frequent injection drug users to have hepatitis B and C, hepatitis C and AIDS, or all three diseases at the same time.

Hemodialysis

Patients with kidney failure may undergo hemodialysis, a means of purifying the blood. In hemodialysis the patient's blood circulates through a machine that removes metabolic waste products and toxins. Although these machines are disinfected each time they are used, residual blood may be present in these heavily used machines. Patients with kidney failure are also frequently anemic and may receive blood transfusions while getting hemodialysis. Therefore hemodialysis, especially before 1990, is a risk factor for hepatitis C. It is also a well-known risk factor for hepatitis B virus infection.

Tattooing and Body Piercing

Tattooing and body piercing are sometimes done with unsterile equipment. Contaminated blood can potentially be transmitted during these procedures. Individuals with tattoos or pierced body parts, therefore, may be at a slightly increased risk for hepatitis C. This is especially true for people who had these procedures done in underdeveloped countries. One study from the United States has suggested that ear piercing in men, but not in women, is a risk factor for hepatitis C. It is not clear if ear piercing is an actual transmission mode in the United States or if men with pierced ears are more likely to have other risk factors for infection than women with pierced ears. Men may also be more likely than women to have ear piercing performed using unsterile conditions.

Sexual Contact

Perhaps the most common questions about the transmission of hepatitis C involve sex. Most studies suggest that individuals with multiple sex partners are at increased risk for infection with the hepatitis C virus. The prevalence of chronic hepatitis C virus infection is significantly higher in promiscuous homosexual men, patients in sexually transmitted disease clinics, and female prostitutes than in the general population. This suggests that sexual transmission of the virus is a probable route, although it is not entirely clear if the risk is higher in these groups because of other concurrent lifestyle factors such as past or current injection drug use. Based on these findings, the U.S. Centers for Disease Control and Prevention currently recommends that sexually promiscuous individuals should use latex condoms to prevent contracting the hepatitis C virus. This will also prevent transmission of HIV, hepatitis B virus, chlamydia, gonorrhea, syphilis, herpes simplex, and other sexually transmitted pathogens.

Individuals in long-term, monogamous sexual relationships with a partner infected with the hepatitis C virus are at a relatively low risk of becoming infected. Some studies suggest that the sexual partner is at no greater risk for infection than other household contacts. For example, the young son of an infected father has roughly the same low risk of getting infected as his wife. Condoms, therefore, are not considered essential to prevent the spread of the hepatitis C virus for individuals in monogamous sexual relationships with infected partners. Condoms should be considered an option, however, as the risk of sexual transmission, although very low in monogamous relationships, is still real. Each individual will have to determine their own tolerance regarding even this small risk.

Household Contacts of Infected Individuals

Several studies have reported an association between nonsexual household contact and acquiring hepatitis C. This likely occurs as a result of unknown exposure to infectious blood. In the United States, transmission to household contacts is extremely low. In some other countries rates as high as 4 percent have been reported. Hepatitis C is not transmitted by casual contact such as kissing, hugging, holding hands, sharing a bathroom, sharing utensils, or similar situations.

Transmission from Infected Mother to Newborn Baby

The results of several studies suggest that the rate of transmission of the hepatitis C virus from infected mothers to their newborn babies is about 5 percent. In mothers also infected with the HIV virus, the rate of hepatitis C virus transmission appears significantly higher, at around 15 percent. Available data suggest that the hepatitis C virus is not transmitted by breast-feeding.

Health Care and Public Safety Workers Exposed to Blood

Health care personnel, laboratory workers, emergency medical technicians, and public safety workers exposed to blood in the workplace are at risk for being infected with the hepatitis C virus. However, the prevalence of hepatitis C virus infection among health care workers in the United States appears to be about the same as for the general population. Nonetheless, there are several documented cases of the hepatitis C virus being transmitted by needle sticks or other accidents involving exposure to contaminated blood.

Infected Health Care Workers

The risk for hepatitis C virus transmission from infected health care workers to patients appears to be very low. One report from Spain demonstrated transmission from a heart surgeon to five patients. In these cases, transmission occurred during highly invasive open-heart surgery. There have also been rare reports of transmission by contaminated medical equipment; in one case a colonoscope was implicated. The risk of transmission of the hepatitis C virus from doctors and other health care workers to patients is probably real but extremely low.

Intranasal Cocaine

Some data have demonstrated that intranasal cocaine use (snorting) is a risk factor for infection with the hepatitis C virus. Some investigators have hypothesized that the sharing of straws can transmit the virus as a small amount of bleeding can occur inside the nose while snorting cocaine. This mode of transmission has not been clearly proven, however, and it is possible that intranasal cocaine use may only be a "surrogate" risk factor for hepatitis C virus infection because such individuals are more likely to use, or to have used, injection drugs. Nonetheless, intranasal cocaine use should be considered as a possible mode of transmission of the hepatitis C virus.

Unknown Risk Factors

Of all patients in whom chronic hepatitis C infection is diagnosed, as many as one-third report no known risk factor. Studies in the United States have shown that, upon detailed questioning, some individuals will ultimately admit to past intravenous drug use. However, some have not used drugs. A possible mode of transmission is having been treated with unsterile medical equipment in the past. This is probably a mode of transmission in underdeveloped countries where needles for vaccination and drawing blood are frequently reused. Other hidden past exposures to blood and blood products are also possible in virtually anyone.

Diagnosis

The diagnosis of chronic hepatitis C is suspected in several types of patients:

- Individuals with risk factors
- Individuals with elevated ALT and/or AST activities on blood tests
- Individuals with signs and symptoms of liver disease
- Individuals with unexplained nonspecific symptoms
- Individuals with a diagnosis of alcoholic liver disease

Even in the absence of evidence of illness, chronic hepatitis C infection should be suspected in individuals who have used illicit injection drugs, have had blood transfusions prior to 1992 (before a very good screening test was used on the blood supply), or have the other risks outlined in Table 4.5. Chronic hepatitis C virus infection should even be suspected in individuals with risk factors who are asymptomatic and/or have normal ALT and AST activities on blood testing. In addition, chronic hepatitis C should be considered a possible diagnosis in any individual who has elevated ALT and/or AST activities, even if the elevations are only minimal and the patient has no obvious risk factors. Finally, chronic hepatitis C virus infection should be suspected in all individuals with signs and symptoms of liver disease, again, even if there are no identifiable risk factors and if the ALT and/or AST activities are normal. Some may have unexplained nonspecific complaints such as fatigue or mild depression. As hepatitis C virus infection is often found concurrently in individuals with alcoholic liver disease, patients with a diagnosis of alcoholic liver disease should also be tested for antibodies against the hepatitis C virus.

Several blood tests are now available for the diagnosis of infection with the hepatitis C virus, as listed in Table 4.6. The first test that was available in the diagnosis of hepatitis C virus infection was the enzyme-linked immunosorbent assay, or ELISA. Since it first became available in 1990, the ELISA has been repeatedly improved. ELISA detects the presence of antibodies against proteins of the hepatitis C virus. The actual test now contains parts of several viral proteins coated on a plastic dish. The patient's blood is incubated in the dish, the dish is then washed, and a second antibody that recognizes human antibodies is added. The second antibody is attached to an enzyme that will change the color of an indicator that is added next. If the patient has antibodies against hepatitis C virus proteins, they will stick to the viral proteins coated on the dish. The stuck antibodies will then be recognized by the second antibodies, which will change the color of the added indicator. If the color changes, the patient has antibodies against the hepatitis C virus. The ELISA will be negative in acute hepatitis C as it usually takes at least a few weeks or longer for an infected person to develop antibodies.

Currently available ELISAs are about 99 percent sensitive for the diagnosis of chronic hepatitis C. This means that of all patients with chronic hepatitis C, 99 percent will have positive ELISA tests. ELISA is the first test that most doctors will use in the diagnosis of chronic hepatitis C. ELISA is also the test used currently to screen the blood supply, and donated blood that tests positive in this assay is discarded. It should be assumed that an individual with a positive ELISA test has chronic hepatitis C until proven otherwise.

In rare cases, the ELISA test for antibodies against the hepatitis C virus will be "false positive," which means the test will be positive even

Table 4.6 Blood Tests for Hepatitis C Virus

Component Detected in Blood	Test Name
Antibody	Enzyme-linked immunosorbent assay (ELISA)
	Recombinant immunoblot (RIBA)
RNA	Branched chain DNA (bDNA)
	Reverse transcription-polymerase chain reaction (RT-PCR)

though the patient does not have hepatitis C. This occurs if antibodies indiscriminately stick to the plastic dish or any protein. This is a rare occurrence and should be suspected in individuals who have normal ALT on blood testing and no risk factors. In these individuals with a positive hepatitis C ELISA test, a confirmatory test should be performed. A false positive test should also be suspected in individuals with rare diseases that cause elevations in immunoglobulins in the blood. One disease in which immunoglobulins may be elevated, and which is sometimes confused clinically with the diagnosis of hepatitis C, is autoimmune hepatitis. In individuals with a positive hepatitis C ELISA and elevated blood immunoglobulins, a confirmatory test should also be performed.

A test that adds specificity to the detection of antibodies against the hepatitis C virus is the recombinant immunoblot assay, or RIBA. In this test, several proteins of the hepatitis C virus are coated onto a plastic strip. A control or irrelevant protein is added to the same strip. The strip is then incubated with the patient's blood and processed similar to the ELISA. However, with the RIBA it is possible to determine the exact proteins recognized by the antibodies. If the patient has antibodies that react with two or more viral proteins and not the control protein, it is positive. If the patient's blood contains antibodies that react with the control protein only, it is negative. If it contains antibodies that react with only one viral protein, or more than one viral protein and the control protein, it is indeterminate. RIBA is not used often anymore given the advent of RNA tests, which can test directly for the presence of the virus. Like the ELISA, the RIBA will also be negative in acute hepatitis C infection.

The commercial availability of tests to detect hepatitis C virus RNA in blood has improved the diagnosis of hepatitis C virus infection. These tests are for a viral component itself and not for antibodies. The most sensitive test for viral RNA is reverse transcription-polymerase chain reaction, or RT-PCR (commonly called *PCR*). In this test, RNA is extracted from the blood and copied to DNA by an enzyme known as *reverse transcriptase*. A biochemical reaction known as the *polymerase chain reaction* (PCR) is then used to amplify the viral DNA copy so that it can be detected by routine chemical methods. Another test for hepatitis C viral RNA in the blood is branched chain DNA, commonly called *bDNA*. In this test, a fraction of the blood is incubated with a synthetic

DNA molecule that binds to hepatitis C viral RNA. If viral RNA is present, it is captured in a tiny dish and then detected by a chemical reaction involving a second synthetic DNA molecule.

The main advantage of PCR is that it is more sensitive than bDNA. Another advantage is that it can be modified to determine the genotype of the infecting hepatitis C virus. The major disadvantages of PCR are that it is more expensive and requires greater expertise to perform. Both PCR and bDNA can be modified to estimate viral load, which is the concentration of viral RNA in the blood. The trend today is to use PCR to detect hepatitis C viral RNA in blood.

RNA tests are not screening tests. One role of RNA tests is to confirm or refute the results of an antibody test. They also can be used in suspected acute hepatitis C infection and in chronic cases where the doctor suspects the antibody test result may be a false positive or false negative. In these instances, the PCR test is probably a better choice than the bDNA assay because it is more sensitive. If an antibody test is negative and the clinical suspicion of chronic hepatitis C is low (no risk factor and normal ALT and AST; elevated ALT and AST but obvious other diagnosis), the patient probably does not have chronic hepatitis C. If the doctor has a strong clinical suspicion of hepatitis C despite a negative antibody test, however, then a PCR test should be performed because about 1 percent of patients infected with hepatitis C virus will have negative antibody tests.

PCR testing is also a good idea to confirm the diagnosis of chronic hepatitis C in patients in whom an antibody test may be false positive, such as those with high concentrations of blood immunoglobulins. An RNA test should probably be performed also in a patient with a positive antibody test but who has no risk factor for hepatitis C virus infection and normal serum ALT activity. An RNA test must also be performed to diagnose acute hepatitis C as the antibody tests will be negative in acute cases.

The other major role of hepatitis C virus RNA tests is for tracking response to treatment in patients with chronic hepatitis C. PCR should probably be performed prior to treatment and at certain intervals during treatment. (See Chapter 5.) RNA tests, preferably PCR because of its increased sensitivity, should also be performed immediately after treatment is finished, six months after treatment is discontinued, and periodically thereafter to determine if the patient has "cleared" the virus and if this response persists. Patients who have successfully cleared the virus after treatment will have negative RNA tests but usually still have antibodies.

After infection with the hepatitis C virus has been established by antibody or RNA testing, a liver biopsy is usually indicated in the diagnosis of a patient with chronic hepatitis C. The major reasons for performing a liver biopsy have already been outlined here and in Chapter 2. A liver biopsy may also prove useful in the evaluation of patients with two concurrent diseases, for example, someone who abuses alcohol and is infected with hepatitis C virus. Findings on liver biopsy may also help guide decisions regarding if and when treatment should be started. (See Chapter 5.)

Prevention

There is no vaccine yet for the prevention of hepatitis C. Prevention of transmission depends upon protection of exposure to infected blood and blood products. While the rate of sexual transmission is low, sexually promiscuous individuals should use condoms. In long-term monogamous relationships, the transmission rate is very low and the U.S. Centers for Disease Control and Prevention currently recommends that condoms are not necessary if both partners agree. Those living in a household with a hepatitis C virus-infected individual should exhibit caution by avoiding contact with blood. For example, they should not share razors, toothbrushes, or similar items. Caution should be used in tending to injured individuals who are bleeding. In hospitals and doctor's offices, caution should be used in drawing blood and in properly disposing of needles and surgical instruments.

Treatment

The demonstration that alpha-interferons are effective in the treatment of patients with chronic hepatitis C has radically changed the practice of hepatology. It is probably for this reason alone that more gastroenterologists today also consider themselves "hepatologists" compared to over a decade ago. In rare cases when acute hepatitis C virus infection is detected, the available treatment based on an alpha-interferon is even more effective than in chronically infected patients. As the use of the drugs is basically the same in acute infection and chronic infection, and as the vast majority (probably more than 99.99 percent) of treated patients have chronic disease, the treatment of hepatitis C and long-term follow-up of patients with the disease is discussed in detail in Chapter 5, which deals with chronic infection.

Hepatitis D

The hepatitis D virus is a small, circular RNA virus also referred to as *hepatitis delta virus* and classified in the family *Deltaviridae*. The hepatitis D virus is replication defective and cannot propagate in the absence of another virus. In humans, hepatitis D virus infection occurs only in the presence of hepatitis B virus infection; in other words, it cannot infect individuals unless they also have hepatitis B.

The hepatitis D virus causes acute and chronic hepatitis in individuals infected with the hepatitis B virus. It should be suspected either in individuals who have chronic hepatitis B and a sudden worsening in condition or in those who present with very severe acute hepatitis B. In co-infection, a person is infected with both the hepatitis B virus and hepatitis D virus at the same time. Persons with co-infection may present with a more severe acute disease and higher risk of fulminant hepatic failure compared to those infected with hepatitis B virus alone. Co-infection usually results in acute hepatitis. Adults who are co-infected with both the hepatitis D virus and hepatitis B virus are less likely to develop chronic hepatitis B than those infected with hepatitis B virus alone.

In superinfection, an individual already infected with the hepatitis B virus becomes infected with hepatitis D virus. This might occur in a drug user who already has chronic hepatitis B and continues to inject drugs. Superinfection with the hepatitis D virus may be associated with a sudden worsening of liver disease and symptoms such as jaundice. The blood ALT and AST activities may become more elevated. Individuals with chronic hepatitis B who are superinfected with hepatitis D virus usually become chronically infected with hepatitis D virus, too. The risk of developing cirrhosis is greater in individuals chronically infected with both the hepatitis B and hepatitis D viruses compared to those infected with hepatitis B virus alone. As many as 80 percent of individuals chronically infected with both of these viruses may ultimately develop cirrhosis.

Transmission

The hepatitis D virus is transmitted in ways similar to the hepatitis B virus. One mode of transmission is intravenous drug use. Transmission from multiple blood transfusions is also possible, but screening of the blood supply for hepatitis B virus eliminates the hepatitis D virus. Sexual transmission of the hepatitis D virus is less efficient than for the hepatitis B virus. Although hepatitis D virus can be transmitted from mothers to their newborn babies, transmission by this route is rare.

The global distribution of hepatitis D virus infection is similar to that for hepatitis B virus. In some parts of the world, such as southern Italy and Russia, hepatitis D virus infection is fairly common among individuals chronically infected with hepatitis B. It is found in about 20 percent of so-called chronic carriers and in as many as 60 percent of individuals with clinical hepatitis caused by hepatitis B virus. In northern Italy, Spain, and Egypt, about 10 percent of asymptomatic chronic carriers infected with hepatitis B and about 30 to 50 percent of symptomatic patients with hepatitis B are infected with the hepatitis D virus. In most of China and other parts of Southeast Asia where the prevalence of chronic hepatitis B virus infection approaches 10 percent of the entire population, hepatitis D virus infection is rare.

Diagnosis

Diagnosis of hepatitis D virus infection is determined by blood testing. In acute co-infection, IgM and IgG antibodies to hepatitis D virus are detectable during the course of infection. IgM antibodies will be detected earlier after acute infection and IgG later or while the patient is recovering. IgG antibody concentrations in blood generally fall to levels that cannot be detected after the acute infection resolves. There is no reliable marker that persists to indicate past infection with hepatitis D virus. In hepatitis D virus superinfection, high levels of both IgM and IgG antibodies against the hepatitis D virus become detectable after infection. Both IgM and IgG antibodies persist in serum as long as the patient remains infected.

Hepatitis D virus co-infection often is not diagnosed. In cases in which acute hepatitis B is not too severe, the doctor will not search for hepatitis D co-infection. If liver disease is unusually severe in a high-risk individual, testing for antibodies against hepatitis D virus may be performed and the diagnosis of acute co-infection made. In chronic hepatitis D, which occurs usually as superinfection, the presence of IgG antibodies in blood against hepatitis D virus, in a patient with detectable blood HBsAg, establishes the diagnosis. Testing will usually be performed in a patient with known chronic hepatitis B whose condition deteriorates.

While tests for IgG against hepatitis D virus are commercially available in the United States, tests for IgM antibodies are available only in research laboratories. Tests for a hepatitis D virus protein known as *hepatitis D antigen* and PCR tests for hepatitis D virus RNA are also available in research laboratories. They are not part of routine diagnostic testing, however. Tests for hepatitis D antigen and viral RNA directly detect the presence of virus in the patient's blood.

Prevention

Because the hepatitis D virus needs hepatitis B virus to replicate, co-infection can be prevented if hepatitis B virus infection is prevented. Patients immune to hepatitis B infection cannot get infected with the hepatitis D virus. Therefore, vaccination against hepatitis B virus will eliminate the chance of contracting hepatitis D. As a result, universal vaccination for hepatitis B should theoretically eliminate hepatitis D as a human disease.

Individuals not immune to hepatitis B infection, who have knowingly been exposed to the hepatitis B and hepatitis D viruses, can receive passive immunization with hepatitis B immune globulin (HBIG). Prevention of hepatitis B virus infection by HBIG will not permit hepatitis D virus infection. No vaccine exists to prevent hepatitis D virus superinfection of persons with chronic hepatitis B virus infection. In these cases, prevention rests entirely upon avoiding high-risk behaviors. High-risk sexual activities should be avoided and latex condoms used. Intravenous drugs should not be used.

Treatment

Treatment of acute hepatitis D virus co-infection is supportive. Either the patient gets better spontaneously or develops fulminant hepatic failure. Emergency liver transplantation is an option for fulminant hepatic failure. In chronic hepatitis D infection, treatment with interferon alpha is a consideration. Although not much data are available at present, some studies suggest that higher doses of interferon alpha, such as 10 million units every day, are necessary in hepatitis D co-infection compared to the 5 million units used every day for chronic hepatitis B.

Hepatitis E

The hepatitis E virus is a small, spherical virus that has been provisionally classified as a member of the *Caliciviridae* family. It is possible that this family assignment will change because the hepatitis E viral genome is different than that of most other caliciviruses. Its genome is composed of RNA.

The hepatitis E virus causes only acute liver disease. The disease caused by hepatitis E virus infection is known as *hepatitis E,* which is very similar to hepatitis A in its symptoms and clinical course. The disease can range from extremely mild to fulminant hepatic failure. Some cases of acute infection with hepatitis E virus may not produce any symptoms at all and go undiagnosed. In most hepatitis E outbreaks, the highest rates of clinically evident hepatitis have occurred in young to middle-age adults. It is possible that infected children, as is the case with hepatitis A, are more likely to have no obvious disease after infection. The time from infection to symptoms varies from fifteen to sixty days, with forty days being the average. It is not yet clear when the greatest danger of infecting others occurs, but virus excretion in feces has been demonstrated up to fourteen days after acute illness.

Patients with relatively mild disease may suffer from nausea, vomiting, fever, fatigue, and loss of appetite. Blood tests may reveal elevations in ALT and AST activities and possibly elevations in bilirubin concentration. Patients with more severe disease may develop jaundice, and blood tests will reveal an elevation in bilirubin concentration, a prolongation of prothrombin time, and sometimes markedly elevated

ALT and AST activities. Most patients with mild or moderate hepatitis E recover without complications. Some patients become so sick that they cannot eat or drink. Some patients with hepatitis E infection develop fulminant hepatic failure.

Transmission

Hepatitis E virus infection does not occur in the United States. Virtually all cases reported in the United States involve travelers returning from parts of the world where hepatitis E is common. Outbreaks have occurred in many geographic locations around the world, mostly in underdeveloped countries. Hepatitis E virus is primarily spread by the fecal-oral route, that is, from feces of infected individuals to food or water that is then ingested by others. Drinking contaminated water is probably the most common mode of infection. Person-to-person transmission appears to be rare. Similar to hepatitis A, hepatitis E is more common in parts of the world having poor sanitary conditions. Travelers from developed countries to such regions are at increased risk for infection from hepatitis E.

Diagnosis

The clinical diagnosis of hepatitis E infection is suggested by the sudden onset of liver disease fifteen to sixty days after suspected exposure to the hepatitis E virus. Sometimes, patients will present with new-onset jaundice immediately suggesting acute liver disease. Such patients should be questioned about a risk factor for hepatitis E, which in North America and most European countries is recent travel to an area where the disease is endemic. Southern and central Asia, northern Africa, and Central America are regions of the world where hepatitis E outbreaks are the most common.

The diagnosis of hepatitis E infection is made through blood testing. Tests for antibodies against the hepatitis E virus are not commercially available in the United States but are available at research laboratories or specialized centers, such as the U.S. Centers for Disease Control and Prevention. Both IgM and IgG antibodies against the hepatitis E virus are elicited following acute viral infection. Detection of IgM antibodies is the best test to diagnose acute disease, as they are present during the illness and disappear as the patient recovers. IgG antibodies persist for some period of time after infection and may provide protection against recurrent infection. In addition to testing for antibodies in the blood, other tests for hepatitis E infection are available on a research basis in the United States. PCR tests can detect hepatitis E virus RNA in blood or stool during infection. Tests to detect viral proteins in blood and liver are also available in some research laboratories.

Prevention

The most important issue regarding hepatitis E is prevention, which depends primarily upon avoiding contaminated water. Travelers to developing countries should avoid drinking from local water supplies and consuming beverages with ice of unknown purity. Uncooked shellfish, uncooked fruits, and vegetables that are not peeled or prepared by the traveler should not be consumed. At the present time, there are no postexposure prophylactic measures nor vaccines for hepatitis E.

Treatment

There is no specific treatment for hepatitis E. In many cases, the disease is mild and self-limiting. If the patient is so sick that he or she cannot eat or drink, hospitalization may be necessary for the administration of intravenous fluids. The patient can be discharged once there is adequate oral intake. In serious cases, generally those causing fulminant hepatic failure, hospitalization and intensive care are required. Preferably, these patients should be hospitalized in a medical center where liver transplantation can be performed if necessary.

Hepatitis G: Probably Not Liver Disease

In 1995 and 1996, three novel RNA viruses were identified as members of the *Flaviviridae* family and shown to be somewhat similar to the hepatitis C virus. These three viruses were termed GB-A, GB-B, and GB-C by workers who discovered them at Abbott Laboratories. The genetic material of the GB-A and GB-B viruses was isolated from the blood of a tamarin (a species of monkey) infected with the blood of a surgeon with initials GB who died from what appeared to be, at the time, non-A, non-B hepatitis. Subsequent work determined that these two viruses are likely tamarin viruses that do not infect humans. Based on genetic information about GB-A and GB-B viruses, the scientists who discovered them isolated the genetic material of a related virus they called *GB-C* from the blood of a human with chronic hepatitis.

Concurrent with the discovery of the GB-C virus, another group at Genelabs Technologies discovered a virus they called *hepatitis G virus*. They identified the virus in blood from a patient with chronic hepatitis C. They ultimately discovered that the genetic material of this virus was different than that of the hepatitis C virus. It was the same as that of the GB-C discovered by workers at Abbott Laboratories.

The hepatitis G/GB-C virus appears to infect humans and is present in the blood supply. It seems to be transmitted by blood and blood products. However, most doctors and scientists now think that the hepatitis G/GB-C virus does not cause liver disease. The general belief is that the hepatitis G/GB-C virus is an "innocent bystander" that can infect humans but not cause disease.

Due to their similar modes of transmission, the hepatitis G/GB-C virus is often found in patients who are already infected with hepatitis C virus. These individuals do not appear to do any worse than those infected with only hepatitis C. At the present time, there is probably no reason to test patients for infection with the hepatitis G/GB-C virus.

Other Viruses That Cause Hepatitis

Hepatitis A, B, C, D, and E viruses are the major hepatotropic viruses that cause liver disease in humans (there is no hepatitis F). Some other viruses can also cause acute liver disease in otherwise healthy individuals. In most cases, these viruses cause systemic diseases that concurrently affect the liver. These viruses include dengue virus, yellow fever virus, and Epstein-Barr virus (EBV), which causes mononucleosis. Individuals with mononucleosis can suffer from a mild form of acute hepatitis that always resolves. Available data suggest that poxvirus and measles virus cause hepatitis in children.

Some viruses that are generally harmless in healthy individuals may cause liver disease in patients with compromised immune systems. These viruses may infect patients with AIDS or cancer. They may also infect patients who have received organ transplants and are taking medications that suppress their immune systems. The most important of these viruses is cytomegalovirus, or CMV. CMV can cause hepatitis in recipients of organ transplants, including transplanted livers. CMV can also cause hepatitis and serious bile duct abnormalities in patients with AIDS.

Some doctors will test patients with chronic hepatitis for antibodies against CMV and EBV. These viruses are endemic in the human population, and the detection of IgG antibodies means virtually nothing. Furthermore, these two viruses do not cause any significant chronic liver disease in people with normal immune systems. If someone tells you that you have chronic hepatitis caused by EBV or CMV, you should be suspicious and see another doctor.

5

Chronic Hepatitis B and C: Treatment and Long-Term Care

THE DIFFERENT TYPES of viral hepatitis were explained in Chapter 4. You now know that infections with the hepatitis C and hepatitis B virus can be chronic and can cause chronic liver disease. Until relatively recently, there were no treatments for individuals with chronic hepatitis B and chronic hepatitis C (known as *non-A, non-B hepatitis* prior to 1990). Now, there are a variety of drugs for these two diseases. However, the available treatments may not be appropriate for all individuals and still are not effective in many cases. This chapter discusses the available treatments and long-term care for patients with chronic hepatitis B and chronic hepatitis C. Potentially promising future treatments, currently in the research and development stage, are discussed in Chapter 14.

Treatment of Chronic Hepatitis B

There are basically two classes of drugs currently available for the treatment of chronic hepatitis B: alpha-interferons and nucleoside analogues that inhibit the viral DNA polymerase. Interferons are naturally occurring proteins made by the body that stimulate the immune system and activate innate antiviral responses. Alpha-interferons have activity against several viruses, including hepatitis B and hepatitis C. Interferons cannot be taken orally (at least at this time); they must be injected.

There are two main types of therapeutically available alpha-interferons for patients with hepatitis B and hepatitis C: unmodified and pegylated. Unmodified interferons are the proteins themselves, and two extremely similar ones (essentially identical from a clinical perspective) are most often used in the United States for patients with hepatitis B: interferon alpha-2a (Roferon) and interferon alpha-2b (Intron A). Different sized and shaped polyethylene glycol (antifreeze) molecules have been covalently (a type of chemical bond) added to these interferons to prolong their half-lives in the body. This pegylation process has allowed for decreased frequency of injections with better steady-state blood levels. The two pegylated alpha-interferons available in the United States are peginterferon alpha-2a (Pegasys) and peginterferon alpha-2b (Peg-Intron). Because the different manufacturers have sponsored different studies with different doses of these various interferon alpha preparations for hepatitis B, it is complicated to discuss precise dosing and protocols "formally" recommended for each one. I believe that interferon alpha-2a and interferon alpha-2b are clinically equivalent. I also believe that peginterferon alpha-2a and peginterferon alpha-2b are clinically equivalent in terms of safety and efficacy. Therefore, I will use the terms *interferon alpha* and *peginterferon alpha* and not specify between them as to the 2a and 2b forms.

The U.S. Food and Drug Administration has currently approved three nucleoside analogues that inhibit the hepatitis B virus polymerase: lamivudine (Epivir-HBV), adefovir (Hepsera), and entecavir (Baraclude). Over the next several years, there likely will be additional similar drugs of this type approved for chronic hepatitis B. While the basic mechanism of action of all of these drugs is the same, there are some differences, primarily in dosing and potential for the virus to become resistant.

Given that several drugs have been recently approved for certain patients with chronic hepatitis B, we still do not know the best option for each patient. Provided here is some general information about which patients with chronic hepatitis B should be considered for treatment and what can be expected from treatment with these drugs. It is likely that over the next few years, the results of clinical trials and various recommendations from professional societies will modify the way doctors use these available drugs and any similar new drugs. Different doctors are also likely to have their own preferences using these approved drugs.

Who Should Be Treated for Chronic Hepatitis B?

It is important to emphasize that all of the available drugs really only work when there is evidence of active viral replication. If there is no evidence of active viral replication, these drugs are not effective. The following criteria should be met before starting treatment for chronic hepatitis B:

- Chronic hepatitis B (infection lasting longer than six months) with detectable serum hepatitis B virus surface antigen (HBsAg)
- Replicative infection with detectable serum hepatitis Be antigen (HBeAg) and/or viral DNA
- No ascites, encephalopathy, and/or bleeding esophageal varices
- Normal, stable serum albumin concentration
- Normal or almost normal serum bilirubin concentration
- Prothrombin that is not significantly prolonged
- Evidence of active inflammation

Patients should have chronic hepatitis B (longer than six months with infection) documented by the presence of HBsAg in their blood. To be eligible for treatment, patients should have replicative hepatitis B infection, that is, they should have detectable HBeAg and/or viral DNA in their blood. Prior to commencing treatment, patients should have a liver biopsy to confirm the diagnosis and demonstrate inflammation. Patients who have clinical complications of cirrhosis, such as ascites, encephalopathy, and/or bleeding esophageal varices, should probably not be treated, except in research studies or as part of a pretransplant protocol. Patients with biochemical evidence of compromised liver function, including low blood albumin concentration, elevated bilirubin concentration, or significantly prolonged prothrombin time, should probably not be treated. Patients with significantly low platelet counts, low white blood counts, or significant anemia should probably not receive an alpha-interferon; however, the exact cutoff values for exclusion are not agreed upon by all doctors. Patients with hypothyroidism, hyperthyroidism, or diabetes mellitus and poorly controlled blood sugars should not be treated with an alpha-interferon until these conditions are medically controlled.

As with any treatment for any disease, there should be some expectation that the patient will benefit. For example, it may be unreasonable to treat a patient with chronic hepatitis B who also has multiple other medical problems that are more immediately life-threatening. It may also be of little value to treat elderly patients who have had hepatitis B for many decades; however, there is no clear age cutoff. It is here that a doctor's judgment comes into play, and trust between the patient and the doctor is very critical.

Treatment Goals

What are the goals of therapy for chronic hepatitis B? The primary goal is to change the infection from replicative (blood HBeAg-positive or detectable DNA) to nonreplicative (blood HBeAg and DNA negative). Studies have shown that conversion from HBeAg-positive to HBeAg-negative after treatment for chronic hepatitis B is associated with a better patient outcome. Another goal is to decrease inflammation, as can be assessed by decreased blood alanine aminotransferase (ALT) and aspartate aminotransferase (AST) activities and, if performed, follow-up liver biopsy. A third goal is to slow progression of fibrosis, which can be assessed only by repeat liver biopsy. An elusive goal, achieved by very few patients, is loss of HBsAg from blood, which likely demonstrates a cure. Another goal is to decrease the chance of developing hepatocellular carcinoma, which may make reasonable the treatment of select patients with cirrhosis who can tolerate the drugs.

A major difficulty with these goals is that it is hard to determine if some of them are achieved. Loss of HBeAg, viral DNA, or HBsAg from blood is relatively easy to measure. Blood AST and ALT activities are also easy to measure as approximations of liver inflammation. However, assessment of fibrosis and accurate assessment of inflammation require repeat liver biopsies. Furthermore, progression of fibrosis, and the development of hepatocellular carcinoma, may only occur after years or even decades—longer than these drugs have been given to patients.

Which Drug Should You Use?

Given that multiple drugs are not available and approved, this is a difficult question to easily answer. First, the patient should understand the treatment and the chances of obtaining the desired results. Second, the patient should understand the goals of treatment. Third, the adverse event profiles of the different drugs should be considered. Treatment with an alpha-interferon is associated with more side effects and is more difficult to tolerate than treatment with the oral nucleoside analogues.

As studies have shown that conversion from HBeAg-positive to HBeAg-negative after treatment for chronic hepatitis B is associated with a better outcome, this is the main goal of treatment in patients who are HBeAg-positive. Ideally, loss of HBeAg should be associated with the emergence of antibodies against HBeAg, but this does not always occur. For patients without cirrhosis, this is probably more often achieved after treatment with an alpha-interferon (15 to 40 percent) than with nucleoside analogues (10 to 20 percent). Therefore, in patients who have HBeAg in blood and can tolerate treatment with an alpha-interferon, I recommend trying it first. I may also try it in patients who are HBeAg-negative but have high blood concentrations of viral DNA. My preference would be to use a peginterferon, which gives better effective steady-state blood levels with less frequent injections. Although a peginterferon alpha is taken for a longer time period (forty-eight weeks compared to sixteen weeks), it is injected only once a week as opposed to every day or three times a week at fairly high doses. This likely makes taking peginterferon for a year much more tolerable than taking an unmodified interferon at high doses more frequently for a few months.

For patients who cannot tolerate an alpha-interferon, or for patients who have tried one and either stopped because of adverse events or because they did not respond after a full course of treatment, I recommend trying a nucleoside analogue. While lamivudine is the oldest and the most inexpensive, about 20 percent of patients treated with lamivudine develop resistance in which a mutant virus arises and starts to replicate. Resistance is much less frequent with adefovir or entecavir. Emergence of resistance is detected by recurrence of replication during treatment after initial suppression. Viral replication during treatment is assessed by blood viral DNA concentrations. One possibility is to start a patient on lamivudine and periodically check blood hepatitis B virus DNA. If it remains detectable or becomes detectable after an initial decrease, the patient can be switched to adefovir or entecavir. Another possibility, which more and more doctors are choosing, is to use adefovir or entecavir as the first-line nucleoside analogue. In some studies, entecavir has been shown to achieve better responses than lamivudine in terms of reducing blood viral DNA levels and possibly in improving inflammation on liver biopsy after forty-eight weeks of treatment.

An obvious question is: What about giving combinations of these drugs? That is an excellent question, but, unfortunately, there is not much data available yet about these drugs' efficacy or toxicity when used together. A few studies have looked at peginterferon alpha combined with lamivudine and have shown that adding lamivudine to peginterferon alpha does not improve the chance of losing HBeAg from blood, suppressing blood viral DNA, or losing HBsAg from blood. Hence, this combination is not recommended. Other combinations will likely be studied over the next few years. Until more data are available, these combinations probably should not be used outside of approved clinical trials.

Course of Treatment

Unmodified interferon alpha is given at a fairly high daily dose every day or at a higher dose three days a week for sixteen weeks. Peginterferon alpha is given once a week for forty-eight weeks (some studies have given it for fifty-two weeks). At the end of treatment and several months afterward, patients are checked for blood HBeAg, antibodies against HBeAg, HBsAg, and viral DNA. As loss of HBeAg, ideally with the emergence of antibodies against it, and rarely loss of HBsAg can occur a few months after treatment is stopped, patients are checked again sometime after completing treatment. If several months after treatment the patient has lost blood HBeAg (or in rare cases HBsAg, too) and/or has undetectable blood DNA, treatment is considered a "success." If blood HBeAg and viral DNA are detectable, treatment is considered to have "failed."

The optimal duration of treatment with the oral nucleoside analogues is not known. Most doctors will probably anticipate giving these for at least one year. If at the end of a year of treatment there is loss of blood HBeAg (and rarely also HBsAg), treatment is considered a success and the drug may be stopped. However, this is achieved in only a minority of patients. Many more patients will have suppression of viral replication as assessed by undetectable blood viral DNA while taking the drug. But when the drug is stopped in most of these patients, viral replication will begin again and blood DNA will again be detectable. It is not clear if treatment in such patients should be maintained for another year, for several years, or for life, or if a different nucleoside analogue should be tried. It is also not known if prolonged treatment with nucleoside analogues will slow the progression of fibrosis, prevent hepatocellular carcinoma, or prolong life. Many doctors feel that at least patients with significant inflammation and/or fibrosis on liver biopsy, and possibly those with higher blood viral DNA levels, should be treated for the long term. However, the safety and efficacy of treatment with lamivudine, entecavir, or adefovir for hepatitis B for more than one year has not been firmly established. An informed patient and a hepatologist should together make a decision about long-term duration of treatment with nucleoside analogues, with an understanding that all of the answers regarding efficacy and safety are not yet in.

Some patients with chronic hepatitis B will have a flare in liver inflammation as indicated by an elevation in blood ALT activity during treatment. This flare may paradoxically be associated with loss of HBeAg, resulting from the immune system being stimulated to destroy the virus-infected liver cells. Therefore, if a sudden rise in ALT activity occurs during treatment in an individual with chronic hepatitis B, therapy may be cautiously continued unless evidence of worsening liver function or failure is detected. A flare in inflammatory activity could also represent development of resistance to the drug, in which case the blood viral DNA will usually increase. And a flare in inflammatory activity could always indicate another problem or perhaps even a rare adverse event to the drug. It is therefore critical that a physician experienced in the medical treatment of chronic hepatitis B assess the patient very carefully to determine if the drug should be continued or stopped.

Who is more likely to respond to treatment for chronic hepatitis B? A shorter duration of infection correlates to a better chance of response. Therefore, individuals from countries where hepatitis B virus infection is endemic and who were likely infected at birth or in early childhood are less likely to respond. People infected as adults and who have been infected for less than three years usually have the best response. Younger patients are more likely to respond than older patients. Patients without cirrhosis will respond more often than those with cirrhosis; however, patients with greater inflammation on biopsy may surprisingly respond better than those with minimal inflammation.

Drugs to Treat Chronic Hepatitis B

Let's examine more specific information on the currently approved drugs for treating chronic hepatitis B.

Interferon Alpha and Peginterferon Alpha

Patients with chronic hepatitis B should be treated with a dose of 5 million units of interferon alpha every day. An alternative regimen is 10 million units three times a week. For peginterferon alpha, the dosing is 180 micrograms once a week. Interferon alpha and peginterferon alpha are generally provided as premixed solutions in ready-to-use syringes. The premixed solutions are stable if stored in the refrigerator.

Interferon alpha and peginterferon alpha are administered by subcutaneous (under the skin) or intramuscular (into the muscle) injections. Most patients self-administer injections with small syringes similar to those used by diabetics to inject insulin. Most people choose to inject the interferon into the thigh; however, other areas such as the abdomen can also be injected. Patients should obtain brief training from a doctor or nurse before beginning self-injections.

Interferon alpha treatment for chronic hepatitis B is for sixteen weeks, with injections every day or three days a week depending on the dose. Peginterferon alpha treatment generally is for forty-eight weeks with injections once a week. Because low blood counts are a side effect of interferon alpha, patients should have their blood drawn and complete blood counts and platelet counts checked as their doctor instructs them after treatment has begun. ALT activity, bilirubin concentration, and albumin concentration should also be checked periodically during therapy. Patients should probably be seen by their doctors, or a nurse, at least once a month during treatment and instructed to contact their doctor if they experience side effects.

The most common and potentially serious side effects of interferon alpha and peginterferon alpha are low neutrophil counts and low platelet counts. Neutrophils, also called *granulocytes*, are a particular type of white blood cell important in fighting bacterial infections. Platelets are blood cells involved in clotting that may also be low in individuals with cirrhosis. As mentioned, patients should have their blood counts monitored during treatment with interferon alpha. If the neutrophil or the platelet count falls below certain levels, the dose of interferon alpha may have to be temporally reduced or the drug may even have to be discontinued.

There are many other side effects of interferon alpha and peginterferon alpha therapy beside low blood counts. The most common is development of flu-like symptoms. These can be quite disabling and include fever, cold sweats, shaking chills, muscle aches and pains, and joint aches and pains. Flu-like symptoms are usually worse near the start of treatment and less common later in the course of therapy. To help tolerate mild to moderate flu-like symptoms, I generally recommend that patients inject the interferon about an hour before going to sleep and take acetaminophen just before injecting the interferon. The acetaminophen will provide some relief from symptoms and, if taken at bedtime, possibly help the patient to sleep through the side effects. Flu-like symptoms rarely require stopping treatment, but on occasion they are so intolerable that there is no other option.

Interferon alpha and peginterferon alpha can aggravate diabetes mellitus and thyroid disorders. Patients with diabetes mellitus who are treated with interferon alpha should carefully monitor their blood sugars. Patients with thyroid disease—and possibly all treated patients—should have blood tests for thyroid function checked periodically during treatment. Significant abnormalities in blood sugar or thyroid tests may necessitate stopping treatment.

Nervous system and psychiatric problems can occur in individuals receiving interferon alpha and peginterferon alpha. Tingling in the hands, feet, arms, and legs is the most common nervous system side effect. Depression, irritability, confusion, nervousness, impaired concentration, anxiety, and insomnia have all occurred in individuals taking interferon alpha. Sometimes these psychiatric problems are so severe that treatment must be stopped. Severe depression has occurred in individuals taking interferon, and suicides have been reported. Patients with serious preexisting depression or other psychiatric disorders probably should not be treated with interferon alpha. If severe depression develops, the drug should be discontinued immediately and the patient closely followed and referred to a psychiatrist as necessary.

Patients receiving interferon alpha and peginterferon alpha have reported virtually every imaginable complaint. Other, more frequent side effects, which are usually not severe, include fever, rash, headache, muscle aches, fatigue, back pain, dry mouth, nausea, diarrhea, and inflammation at the injection site. Rarely patients have what appear to be allergic reactions to interferon alpha, and the drug must be discontinued if these occur. Despite numerous side effects, interferon alpha therapy is rather safe if patients are monitored closely. Most patients complete the recommended course of therapy.

Lamivudine

Lamivudine is a molecule that looks like a building block of DNA. Its mechanism of action is to inhibit the DNA polymerase of the hepatitis B virus. The activity of this enzyme is essential for replication of the virus. Lamivudine belongs to the class of drugs known as *nucleoside analogues*. Lamivudine (also known as 3TC) is also approved for another indication: the treatment of human immunodeficiency virus (HIV) infection. HIV has a DNA polymerase called *reverse transcriptase* that is inhibited by lamivudine (as well as other drugs). Similarly, lamivudine inhibits the hepatitis B virus DNA polymerase. For the treatment of chronic hepatitis B, the dose is 100 milligrams of lamivudine a day. The daily dose for HIV infection is higher. The dose may have to be adjusted in patients with abnormal kidney function.

Lamivudine is approved for subjects who have chronic hepatitis B and evidence of viral replication. Large clinical studies indicate that lamivudine works better than a placebo (dummy drug) in reducing liver inflammation measured on biopsy and in causing a loss of serum HBeAg from blood. Most studies have examined treatment for one year, but the most effective duration of treatment has not been firmly established. The efficacy and safety of treatment beyond one year in patients with chronic hepatitis B has not been well established.

Lamivudine is generally well tolerated in patients with chronic hepatitis B. In clinical trials, the most common adverse events were ear, nose, and throat infections, plus fatigue and headache. These were reported by approximately one-fifth to one-quarter of patients. More serious adverse events were rare.

A major advantage of lamivudine (and the other nucleoside analogues) compared to interferon is that it is administered orally. One possible drawback is that liver inflammation may recur after the drug is discontinued. Another drawback is that the hepatitis B virus can mutate and become resistant to lamivudine during treatment. It is associated with a specific type of mutation in the viral gene (pol) that encodes the DNA polymerase. Resistance is seen in about 20 percent of treated patients. If the virus becomes resistant to lamivudine, blood ALT and AST activities may rise and the concentration of hepatitis B virus DNA in the blood becomes elevated. When the lamivudine is stopped, the mutant virus appears to die out and a nonmutant virus replaces it in the blood. Fortunately, the onset of resistance does not appear to be associated with severe liver disease.

Adefovir

Adefovir is another nucleoside analogue that inhibits the hepatitis B virus DNA polymerase. It is indicated for patients with chronic hepatitis B who have evidence of viral replication. Adefovir is taken orally. The recommended dose is 10 milligrams a day. The dose may have to be reduced in patients with abnormal kidney function.

Studies have demonstrated that, compared to placebo, adefovir reduces hepatitis B viral DNA and improves findings on liver biopsy compared to placebo. Resistance to adefovir is rare. In studies, viral isolates from patients that show resistance to adefovir in the laboratory occur in only about 4 percent of subjects who have taken the drug for three years. The optimal duration of treatment has not been established.

Entecavir

Similar to lamivudine and adefovir, entecavir is an oral nucleoside analogue with activity against the hepatitis B virus DNA polymerase. It is indicated for the treatment of chronic hepatitis B in adults with evidence of viral replication. The recommended dose is 0.5 milligram a day for patients who have never been treated with a nucleoside analogue and 1.0 milligram a day for patients who have received lamivudine and had evidence of viral replication during treatment or who have known resistance to lamivudine. The dose may have to be adjusted in patients with abnormal kidney function.

In some studies, treatment with entecavir has led to loss of viral DNA from blood in more subjects than in similar subjects treated with lamivudine. These studies also suggested slightly greater improvement in inflammation on liver biopsy after forty-eight weeks. While resistance to entecavir has been demonstrated in the laboratory, it is rarely observed in patients. As with the other nucleoside analogues, not known are the optimal duration of treatment nor the efficacy and safety of treatment longer than one year.

Medical Follow-Up and Cancer Screening

Patients with chronic hepatitis B infection should have regular medical checkups whether or not they are candidates for treatment. Even chronic carriers should see their doctors periodically. If a patient has clinically apparent chronic hepatitis B for many years without significant clinical changes, that patient should probably see a doctor at least once every twelve months. The same should probably hold true for chronic carriers. A physical examination should be performed to ensure there are no signs of cirrhosis. Blood tests should also be taken periodically. Individuals with cirrhosis caused by chronic hepatitis B may have to be seen more frequently for changes in their condition and referral to a liver transplantation center if complications become difficult to control, or if blood tests indicate progressive liver dysfunction.

An important aspect of follow-up care for patients chronically infected with hepatitis B virus is screening for hepatocellular carcinoma. Individuals with chronic hepatitis B infection, especially those with cirrhosis, are at a significantly increased risk of developing hepatocellular carcinoma. Screening protocols to measure blood alpha-fetoprotein concentrations and image the liver using real-time ultrasound have mostly been developed in Japan, where chronic hepatitis B infection is more prevalent than in Western countries. Although formal guidelines have not been established regarding testing frequency, and little to no data exist on overall efficacy and cost-effectiveness, in the United States, it is generally agreed that patients with chronic hepatitis B virus infection should have periodic screening for liver cancer. These patients should have periodic ultrasound studies to check for small liver masses. In addition, blood periodically should be tested for alpha-fetoprotein, which is a marker for hepatocellular carcinoma. Most liver specialists would probably perform such screenings once a year or twice a year in individuals with known cirrhosis. Even individuals without known cirrhosis should probably be periodically screened, including chronic carriers. Again, good data on the efficacy and cost-effectiveness of this type of screening in Western countries do not exist; it is up to the individual doctor's judgment to determine how frequently "periodic" cancer screening should be performed.

Special Situations

The hepatitis B virus often infects patients with other chronic viral diseases or problems. Two relatively common special situations are concurrent infection with HIV and/or hepatitis C virus and concurrent substance abuse.

Infections with Hepatitis B Virus and HIV and/or Hepatitis C Virus

The modes of transmission of hepatitis B virus are quite similar to those for hepatitis C virus and HIV. As a result, it is not unusual for individuals to be infected with any two, or even all three, of these viruses at the same time. A detailed discussion of all the possible diagnostic and treatment options for co-infected patients is beyond the scope of this book, and a lot depends upon the particular case and the doctor's judgment. In general, patients with HIV infection but a "healthy" immune system (normal CD4 or "T-cell" counts) and no complications of AIDS, who have hepatitis B infection, should probably be treated just like patients without HIV infection. Equally aggressive diagnostic procedures and treatments should probably be used if there are no contraindications. In individuals with low CD4 counts or with AIDS, a less aggressive approach to hepatitis B may be taken as other problems may be more immediate. Notably, lamivudine, which is used to treat hepatitis B, is also active against HIV and taken by many patients with this disease. Tenofovir (Viread), which is used to treat HIV, is also active against the hepatitis B virus (and may someday be approved for this indication). Again, the approach to patients with HIV and hepatitis B infection depends upon the individual case and the judgment of an experienced doctor.

For patients with chronic hepatitis B virus and hepatitis C virus infection, both diseases should be approached together. Many of the diagnostic and treatment considerations are similar to both. If there are not contraindications, patients with chronic hepatitis B, who also have chronic hepatitis C, should probably first be treated with a peginterferon alpha for forty-eight weeks. The treatment protocols using this drug are very similar for both diseases.

Alcohol and Drug Abusers with Chronic Hepatitis B

Hepatitis B virus infection is common in people with active drug and alcohol use problems. Treatment with interferon alpha or peginterferon alpha requires frequent medical monitoring and the injection of medications. It is almost impossible to treat an active alcohol or drug abuser with injection interferons. Successful control of the substance use disorder must be accomplished in virtually all cases before using interferon alpha. Treatment with oral nucleoside analogues may be a better option in patients with active drug and alcohol use problems, and the substance abuse disorder should be treated simultaneously.

Treatment of Chronic Hepatitis C

Current treatment of chronic hepatitis C is based on interferon alpha. Interferon alpha is a reasonably good treatment for hepatitis C, but it is *far from perfect*. Under the best circumstances, only about half of patients have the most desired outcome: not having detectable hepatitis C virus in the blood several months and longer after stopping treatment. Interferon alpha causes myriad side effects, including draining the pocketbook (usually of the government or insurance company).

Interferon alpha is not absorbed orally and must be administered by injection. Interferon alpha-based treatment of chronic hepatitis C, while not perfect, is currently the only option available.

Interferon alpha-based treatment for chronic hepatitis C has become more and more complicated as several pharmaceutical companies have similar competing products. Various doctors may also use slightly different treatment protocols. The best results are obtained when interferon alpha is combined with ribavirin, an oral antiviral agent. *At the time of writing this book, the gold standard treatment for most individuals with chronic hepatitis C is a peginterferon alpha plus ribavirin.* The usual duration of treatment is twenty-four or forty-eight weeks, depending on the genotype of the infecting virus.

It would be incredibly boring to provide every detail on all the dosages and possible treatment protocols involving interferon alpha to treat chronic hepatitis C. I will instead review in this section the drugs that are currently approved in the United States (and many other countries) and the most common protocols for using peginterferon plus ribavirin. The major side effects of treatment and the retreatment options will be summarized for those who have had an unsuccessful first, second, or third course. I will also provide some thoughts on who should and should not be treated, realizing that the decision in a specific case must be left up to the individual patient and his or her doctor. (See Chapter 14 for potentially better treatments for chronic hepatitis C that may be available someday.)

No particular treatment is suitable to all patients. This section is meant as a general overview of the options and not as a formal treatment guide. *A patient must always see a doctor about appropriate medical treatment for his or her case.*

Who Should be Treated for Chronic Hepatitis C?

Not all people with hepatitis C are good candidates for the currently available treatments. The decision to treat or not must be made by an experienced doctor in conjunction with an informed patient. The doctor should be a specialist familiar with the treatment of chronic hepatitis C.

Almost all patients with chronic hepatitis C should be *considered* for treatment. If a primary doctor who is not familiar with treatment makes the diagnosis of chronic hepatitis C, the patient should be referred to a specialist. Although all patients are not necessarily candidates for treatment, most deserve evaluation by a specialist experienced with treating hepatitis C. Exceptions to this rule include patients with more pressing concurrent illnesses, such as serious heart disease or cancer; elderly patients; and patients with advanced cirrhosis, who should generally be referred for evaluation for liver transplantation. Many patients with significant depression or mental illness are also poor candidates for treatment, as life-threatening mood alterations and even suicide can occur while receiving currently available treatments. Similarly, people who are actively abusing illegal drugs or alcohol are not good candidates for treatment.

Which patients would liver specialists treat? At present there is no complete consensus. Some liver specialists are aggressive and will treat virtually all patients with chronic hepatitis C, even those for whom it may be potentially dangerous. Others will only aggressively treat certain groups of patients. Some liver specialists will not recommend treatment for individuals who have had hepatitis C virus infection for many years and have only minimal inflammation and fibrosis on liver biopsy. Some think that treatment is not indicated for patients over age sixty-five, and there are some published studies that suggest this may be a valid opinion.

The decision about who should be treated depends upon the judgment of an experienced physician and the individual patient's overall physical and mental health. I cannot provide highly specific recommendations. I can, however, stress a few general points that should be considered, based on what is known about chronic hepatitis C and the currently available drugs.

1. Hepatitis C is generally a very slowly progressive disease. Those without significant inflammation or fibrosis on their liver biopsies have the option of thinking about treatment, starting at their convenience, and even waiting until newer and more effective drugs are available. *The treatment of hepatitis C is never an emergency.* (There are, however, two rare instances in which the treatment of hepatitis C is relatively urgent. One is the patient with hepatitis C-related cryoglobulinemia [see Chapter 4] who is developing kidney failure, in which treatment may

prevent kidney damage. The other is the rare patient in which acute infection is detected, as very early treatment of acutely infected individuals has been associated with better responses.)

2. Individuals with significant inflammation and fibrosis on liver biopsy are probably at an increased risk of developing cirrhosis and should probably be treated sooner rather than waiting too long. However, waiting several months will probably not be detrimental to anyone (except, perhaps, for the two rare instances mentioned in the first item).

3. Individuals with cirrhosis on biopsy but no complications should probably consider earlier treatment to prevent progression of complications. However, these patients are also less likely to successfully respond to currently available treatments or to tolerate them.

4. Because hepatitis C is a slowly progressive disease, elderly patients should probably not be treated with currently available medications. However, *elderly* is tough to define, and there is no exact age cutoff. The decision should depend on the person's overall state of health and possibly liver biopsy findings.

5. People with more pressing physical diseases, mental illness, or social problems that prevent them from complying with a complex treatment regimen should not be treated. Some patients with uncontrolled diabetes mellitus, thyroid disease, kidney disease, blood disorders, and other conditions also may not be able to take interferon alpha and/or ribavirin.

6. Patients with complications of cirrhosis should not be treated except perhaps in an approved clinical trial or in conjunction with doctors at a transplant center.

7. A patient who has received the currently available gold standard of peginterferon alpha plus ribavirin, without a successful response, should, in most cases, probably not be treated again with these drugs and should wait until new drugs are available.

Treatment Goals

Before explaining the goals of treatment, some of the jargon regarding the therapy of chronic hepatitis C must be defined. These terms are not all scientifically accurate or precise, and they are sometimes confusing. Nonetheless, most doctors and many patients use them.

The first concept that needs to be clarified is the parameter that is measured to gauge a "response" to treatment. The most commonly used parameter of response to treatment today is loss of hepatitis C virus RNA from the blood when measured by PCR testing. This is termed a *virological response*. In older studies, before routine RNA testing was readily available, response to treatment was defined as normalization of blood ALT activities. This was called a *biochemical response*. Measuring blood ALT activity is not an ideal way to determine response to treatment because in some patients it may be elevated for reasons other than hepatitis C, such as excessive alcohol or fatty liver. Patients who have normal blood ALT activities may also still have inflammation detectable on liver biopsy. Another type of response that is sometimes measured in studies but rarely in the routine care of patients is called a *histological response*. This is determined by decreased inflammation and possibly fibrosis on liver biopsy after treatment, compared to before treatment. *In routine clinical practice today, a virological response is generally regarded as the desired goal of treatment.*

Additional terminology is commonly used to define the nature of the measured response. The goal of treatment is to become a "sustained responder." So-called sustained responders have undetectable hepatitis C virus RNA in the blood six months and longer after stopping treatment. It is presumed, although not yet strictly proven, that many such individuals will have cleared the virus from their bodies and that the liver inflammation from hepatitis C will stop. This may not be strictly true as the hepatitis C virus may be present in the liver at very low levels—just not replicating rapidly enough to produce significant levels in the blood. It is also possible that an apparent sustained response may be transient and that hepatitis C virus RNA will again become detectable in blood more than six months after stopping treatment. For this reason, it may be reasonable for sustained responders to have PCR testing for virus in their blood performed every year or every few years after treatment is stopped.

Many patients with chronic hepatitis C treated with an interferon-based therapy have a virological response during treatment and then "relapse" after treatment is stopped. "Relapsers" are patients who have undetectable hepatitis C virus RNA in their blood during treatment that becomes detectable after stopping the drugs. The long-term benefit of having a response during treatment and then relapsing is not clear. Some studies suggest that these patients may have a histological response if liver biopsy is obtained after treatment. The significance of this in terms of long-term prognosis is not clear.

Roughly a quarter to a third of patients treated with interferon-based therapy will be "nonresponders." In nonresponders, hepatitis C viral RNA will persist in the blood during treatment. Some of the initial responders will experience a "breakthrough" during treatment, and viral RNA will be detected in the blood later during the course of therapy. Some will be considered "partial responders" because their blood hepatitis C viral RNA concentrations will decrease but not become undetectable by PCR testing. Most liver specialists generally group partial responders and individuals who break through with nonresponders because they never had persistently undetectable hepatitis C viral RNA in the blood during treatment.

Although a sustained response with undetectable viral RNA in blood six months and longer after stopping treatment is the goal of most doctors and patients, it is possible that treatment with interferon alpha, with or without ribavirin, may be somewhat beneficial even if this goal is not attained. Some studies suggest that treatment slows the development of fibrosis. Others suggest that interferon alpha may prevent the development of hepatocellular carcinoma in patients with hepatitis C and cirrhosis. However, longer-term studies are necessary to confirm the benefits of treatment in those who are not sustained responders.

Although it seems obvious that achieving a sustained virological response is of benefit to a patient, rigorous, long-term studies still must be completed to definitively prove this. An improvement in survival or decrease in the incidence of liver transplantation in patients with chronic hepatitis C who are sustained responders to interferon alpha-based therapy has not been demonstrated. Preliminary case reports of a few patients with chronic hepatitis C examined ten or more years after achieving a sustained response to interferon alpha have shown that none have developed cirrhosis. However, formal, long-term studies of such patients, with relevant comparison groups, remain to be completed. Despite the fact that the hard scientific data are lacking, I believe that patients can assume that a sustained response to treatment will lead to long-term benefits.

Course of Treatment

Alpha-interferons and peginterferons are generally supplied as pre-mixed solutions in ready-to-use syringes ("injection pens"). They are stable if stored in the refrigerator. Interferon alpha, unmodified or pegylated, is administered by subcutaneous or intramuscular injections. Most patients administer the injections themselves and choose to inject the interferon into their thighs; however, other areas such as the abdomen can work. Patients should obtain brief training from a doctor or nurse before starting self-injections.

Peginterferon alpha is generally injected once a week. Unmodified interferons are generally injected every other day, three times a week, for chronic hepatitis C. The doses of the different unmodified and peginterferon alphas vary depending upon the different manufacturers' preparations, and a patient must follow his or her doctor's instructions carefully. For unmodified interferon alpha-2a and interferon alpha-2b, the single dose is 3 million units. For interferon alfacon-1, the dose is in micrograms. Peginterferons are dosed in micrograms, and the amounts vary for the different preparations. Weight-based dosing is recommended for peginterferon alpha-2b (Peg-Intron), in which the amount injected each week depends upon the patient's weight. A single dose (180 micrograms) is recommend for peginterferon alpha-2a (Pegasys). Again, patients injecting interferon, unmodified or pegylated, should pay careful attention to their doctors' instructions regarding appropriate doses.

Ribavirin for chronic hepatitis C comes as 200 milligrams (0.2 gram) capsules or tablets. The capsules are stable at room temperature. Ribavirin is taken two times every day, in the morning and at night. The recommended dose depends upon the patient's weight (usually from 800 milligrams to 1,200 milligrams daily divided between the morning and evening doses).

Interferon alpha-based treatments for chronic hepatitis C are generally given for twenty-four or forty-eight weeks. In general, individuals infected with genotype 1 or genotype 4 are treated for forty-eight weeks and those infected with genotype 2 and genotype 3 for twenty-four weeks. Studies suggest that having detectable viral RNA in the blood after twelve weeks of treatment with peginterferon alpha and ribavirin is a predictor of nonresponsiveness. Many doctors will stop the drug if this is the case.

Before treatment with peginterferon or interferon, with or without ribavirin, patients should have a battery of blood tests to make sure that there are no contraindications to receiving the drugs. If thyroid disease, diabetes mellitus, or kidney disease are suspected based on blood testing, treatment should be deferred until these conditions are investigated further. Anemia, low white blood cell counts, and low platelet count may also make a patient ineligible for treatment with interferon alpha or ribavirin.

First-Time Treatment

Patients with chronic hepatitis C who have never been previously treated are referred to by the silly term *naive*. Most naive patients who have chronic hepatitis C and are good candidates for treatment should receive a peginterferon and ribavirin. Those patients who for some reason cannot tolerate ribavirin should probably be treated with peginterferon alpha alone.

Overall, approximately 50 percent of naive patients treated with peginterferon alpha plus ribavirin will achieve a sustained response to treatment. There are several predictors for which patients with chronic hepatitis C are more likely to respond. In general, the following are correlated with a lower probability of responding: age greater than forty-five years; duration of infection longer than five years; the presence of fibrosis or cirrhosis on liver biopsy; infection with genotype 1a, 1b, or 4; and possibly higher blood hepatitis C virus RNA concentrations (viral loads) at the start of treatment. Despite these facts, it is not possible to apply these predictors to an individual patient to calculate his or her exact chance of responding to treatment. A doctor may be able to better *guess* ahead of time which patient is more or less likely to respond but cannot make such predictions with certainty in an individual patient. One good predictor of nonresponse after treatment has been started is the presence of hepatitis C viral RNA in blood after twelve weeks of taking peginterferon plus ribavirin.

In summary, individuals with chronic hepatitis C who are good candidates for treatment with a peginterferon plus ribavirin have about a 50 percent overall chance of achieving a sustained response of no detectable viral RNA in the blood after treatment with peginterferon plus ribavirin. For those who cannot take ribavirin, the sustained response rate with a peginterferon alone is approximately 30 percent. The chances are better for those infected with genotypes 2 and 3 and less for those infected with genotypes 1 and 4. A fifty-fifty chance isn't that bad, but better treatments are clearly needed.

Retreatment

One of the growing issues in the treatment of patients with chronic hepatitis C is what to offer patients who are nonresponders or relapsers after a first course of treatment. The current options are basically limited to:

1. Retreatment with peginterferon alpha and ribavirin for patients who received interferon alone for their first course of treatment
2. Retreatment with peginterferon alpha plus ribavirin for those who have received unmodified interferon alpha plus ribavirin for their first course of treatment
3. Retreatment with interferon alpha or peginterferon alpha, at a higher dose and/or for a longer duration, with or without ribavirin
4. Enrollment in approved clinical trials of different interferon-based treatment protocols
5. Enrollment in approved clinical trials of novel drugs

The results of clinical trials clearly show that the combination of interferon alpha plus ribavirin or peginterferon plus ribavirin improves the response rate of relapsers who were previously treated with interferon alpha alone. For patients with chronic hepatitis C who relapse after treatment with interferon alone, retreatment with a peginterferon alpha plus ribavirin is a good option. The treatment of relapsers to interferon alpha alone was, in fact, the first indication for which combination therapy with interferon plus ribavirin was approved.

Retreatment of nonresponders to interferon alpha alone is more difficult. Most liver specialists will offer retreatment with peginterferon alpha plus ribavirin to patients who did not respond to interferon alone. Overall, the retreatment rate of such subjects is probably somewhere between 10 and 20 percent. The results may be significantly better for those infected with non-type 1 genotypes. Therefore, it is probably reasonable for nonresponders to interferon alpha alone to be retreated with peginterferon alpha plus ribavirin, especially if they are infected with hepatitis C viral genotypes other than type 1.

What about treatment for patients with chronic hepatitis C who have failed treatment with interferon alpha (unmodified or pegylated) plus ribavirin? At present, no specific recommendations can be made. Such patients may want to consider participating in clinical trials; however, most trials right now only involve various types of interferon and ribavirin. There are some long-term studies of low-dose "maintenance" interferon alpha, but the results are not yet available. Several studies have looked at higher doses of interferon alphas, most without promising results. Some doctors may offer interferon alfacon-1 to those patients who did not respond to a preparation based on interferon alpha-2a or interferon alpha-2b. Data from some uncontrolled studies suggest that this may work in some patients, but trials comparing interferon alfacon-1 to an equivalent dose of another interferon alpha for retreatment of such patients are not available.

In my opinion, the most reasonable option for patients who have failed treatment with a peginterferon alpha plus ribavirin is observation until new and more promising drugs are available. Another alternative is enrollment in approved clinical trials that are testing new drugs with novel mechanisms of action. (See Chapter 14.) The choice among these options depends upon the wishes of the particular patient, his or her doctor's opinion, and the opportunity to participate in clinical trials. Regardless of the choice, patients should realize two important things:

1. Most people with chronic hepatitis C do well in the long term and never develop cirrhosis and its complications, with or without treatment.
2. Chronic hepatitis C is a slowly progressive disease and treatment is almost never an emergency.

Currently Available Drugs to Treat Chronic Hepatitis C

As of January 2006, the U.S. FDA has approved several different drugs for patients with chronic hepatitis C as shown in Table 5.1. A quick glance at this table shows that things are a little confusing. Much of this is a result of healthy competition between pharmaceutical companies and government regulatory policies, not always scientific reasons. There are three different unmodified interferon alphas, produced by three different manufacturers, approved for chronic hepatitis C. There are two peginterferon alphas, produced by two different manufacturers. Two manufacturers sell ribavirin as a proprietary drug and recently generic ribavirin has been approved. Ignoring business issues and marketing efforts of the companies that make these drugs, I can simplify things as follows:

1. An interferon alpha is an interferon alpha. They all work the same. There are no proven, clinically significant differences at equivalent doses between interferon alpha-2a, interferon alpha-2b (for biochemists reading this, the difference is only one conservative amino acid substitution between 2a and 2b), and interferon alfacon-1.

2. Although there are chemical differences between the polyethylene glycol modifications of peginterferon alpha-2a (Pegasys) and peginterferon alpha-2b (Peg-Intron), there are no available data to suggest that they are different in terms of their safety and efficacy in the treatment of chronic hepatitis C. These two preparations should be considered equivalent.

3. Because of the way clinical trials were done to get the drugs approved, there are slight differences in the recommended doses of peginterferon alpha-2a and peginterferon alpha-2b. For peginterferon alpha-2a, one dose is recommended for all patients. For peginterferon alpha-2b, the recommended dose varies depending upon the patient's weight. The recommended doses of concurrently administered ribavirin also vary slightly.

4. The active ingredient of peginterferon alpha is still interferon alpha. However, because it is administered less frequently and gives

Table 5.1 Drugs Approved for Treating Chronic Hepatitis C (January 2006)

Generic Name	Trade Name	Manufacturer
Interferon alpha-2b	Intron A	Schering
Interferon alpha-2a	Roferon	Roche
Interferon alfacon-1	Infergen	Valeant
Ribavirin (approved for	Rebetol[1]	Schering
use with an interferon alpha)	Copegus	Roche
	None (generic)	Teva
Peginterferon alpha-2b	Peg-Intron	Schering
Peginterferon alpha-2a	Pegasys	Roche

1 Combination of Schering Intron-A and Rebetol is also sold as Rebetron.

better blood concentrations of interferon alpha, peginterferon is easier to take and more effective than the unmodified interferon alphas.

5. All of the available ribavirins are equal (some are tablets and
some are capsules).

Since all approved treatments of chronic hepatitis C depend upon
use of interferon alpha, let's again review what it is. Interferon alphas
are proteins that are naturally produced by the body, especially in
response to viral infections. Those currently approved for hepatitis C
in the United States are recombinant preparations: they are produced
using recombinant DNA methodology. Interferon alphas have a multi-
tude of effects on the body, including the activation of general antiviral responses and stimulation of the immune system to seek out and kill
virus-infected cells. *Interferon alphas were not specifically designed to
attack the hepatitis C virus.* They stimulate a wide range of responses
and, because of this, have a wide range of side effects. Interferon alphas
were available before the hepatitis C virus was discovered and, in fact,
were used in clinical trials to treat patients with non-A, non-B hepatitis. They were selected for use in chronic hepatitis C because of their
general antiviral and immune system effects. Interferon alpha used alone
was the first treatment approved for chronic hepatitis C because well-
designed clinical trials showed that some chronic hepatitis C patients

treated with it had decreased liver inflammation. Subsequently it has been shown that about 10 to 20 percent of patients treated with interferon alpha alone for six to eighteen months have no detectable hepatitis C virus in their blood several months after stopping treatment.

The U.S. FDA later approved the combination of interferon alpha-2b and ribavirin for patients with chronic hepatitis C. Ribavirin is a synthetic compound with activity against several different viruses. *Similar to interferon alpha, ribavirin was not specifically designed to attack the hepatitis C virus.* Ribavirin was around for many years before the discovery of the hepatitis C virus and was shown to have efficacy against several viruses in the laboratory, in humans, and in other animals. In the United States, ribavirin was first approved in aerosol form for the treatment of respiratory syncytial virus that causes respiratory infections in children. In several studies, oral ribavirin was examined as a single agent for the treatment of adults with chronic hepatitis C but shown not to be effective. However, the combination of interferon alpha and ribavirin was subsequently shown in several studies to be more effective than interferon alpha alone in the treatment of chronic hepatitis C. The combination led to undetectable hepatitis C virus in the blood several months after treatment at a rate of more than twice that of interferon alpha alone (greater than 40 percent compared to less than 20 percent). As a result of these studies, the U.S. FDA approved interferon alpha plus ribavirin for the treatment of chronic hepatitis C.

Peginterferon alpha is a newer preparation of interferon alpha. *The active ingredient of peginterferon alpha is interferon alpha.* Administered by an injection, it has the same effects as regular interferon alpha against viruses and on the immune system. The difference between peginterferon alpha and unmodified interferon alpha is in the pharmacokinetics (absorption, elimination from the body) and not the pharmacodynamics (mechanism of action). By attaching a polyethylene glycol molecule to the interferon molecule, it is eliminated more slowly from the body. As a result, the drug can be administered less frequently, generally one injection a week, compared to three injections a week for unmodified interferon alpha. As a result, more constant effective blood concentrations are achieved. Less frequent injections also generally lead to better patient compliance. More constant effective blood concentrations may also lead to greater antiviral efficacy.

Peginterferon alphas have virtually replaced unmodified interferons in the treatment of chronic hepatitis C. A peginterferon alpha and ribavirin is now the first treatment of choice for most patients with chronic hepatitis C. For all patients treated, approximately 50 percent achieve a sustained response. Based on genotype of the infecting virus, the rate is less for type 1a and type 1b (about 40 percent) and greater for those with genotypes 2 and 3 (about 60 percent).

Some individuals cannot take ribavirin. These include patients with anemia, kidney failure, and heart disease. Ribavirin can cause modest to serious anemia. So those already anemic may encounter problems. Patients with significant heart disease could be at risk for a heart attack if they become suddenly anemic as a result of taking ribavirin. For this reason, people with known heart disease or risk factors for it should have a cardiac stress test before taking the drug. Since the kidney clears ribavirin from the body, it should not be used in individuals with significant kidney disease, except perhaps in approved clinical trials. For patients who cannot take ribavirin, treatment with a peginterferon alpha alone is currently the next best choice. The chance of a sustained response with a peginterferon alpha alone is approximately 30 percent.

Side Effects of Currently Available Hepatitis C Treatments

There are numerous side affects associated with all the preparations of interferon alpha. For this reason, careful monitoring is necessary during treatment. Because low blood counts are a potential side effect, patients should have their blood drawn and complete blood counts and platelet counts checked one, two, and four weeks after treatment is started and roughly once a month thereafter. Blood ALT activity, bilirubin concentration, and albumin concentration should also be checked periodically during therapy. Patients should probably be seen by their doctors or a nurse at least once every few months during treatment and be instructed to contact their doctors if they experience side effects.

Common and potentially serious side effects of interferon alpha at the doses generally used to treat patients with chronic hepatitis C are low neutrophil counts and low platelet counts. Neutrophils, also called *granulocytes*, are a particular type of white blood cell important in fighting bacterial infections. Platelets, which are involved in blood clotting, also may be low in individuals with cirrhosis. As mentioned, patients should have their blood counts monitored during treatment with interferon alpha. If the neutrophil count falls below 750 cells per cubic millimeter of blood, or the platelet count falls below 50,000 cells per cubic millimeter of blood, the daily dose can be reduced until these values rise above these levels. If the neutrophil count falls below 500 cells per cubic millimeter of blood or the platelet count below 30,000 cells per cubic millimeter of blood, interferon therapy should probably be discontinued. Resumption of treatment can be considered when the blood counts return to higher, safe levels. Both interferon alpha and ribavirin can cause anemia (low red blood cell count). If anemia occurs, the dose of ribavirin or both of these drugs may have to be reduced or stopped. They may be carefully restarted in some cases when the anemia improves.

Many doctors will use drugs such as epoetin alpha (Procrit, Epogen) in patients with chronic hepatitis C who develop anemia during treatment. This drug stimulates the bone marrow to produce more red blood cells. Others will use drugs such as filgrastim (Neupogen) or pegfilgrastim (Neulasta) to treat low neutrophil counts. These drugs stimulate the bone marrow to produce neutrophils. It must be emphasized that these drugs are *not* approved to treat anemia or low neutrophil counts that may occur during treatment for chronic hepatitis C. Their efficacy and safety has not been established for this purpose. These drugs should be considered experimental for these conditions and, in my opinion, should not be used outside of approved clinical trials.

There are many other side effects of interferon alpha therapy besides low blood counts. The most common is the development of flu-like symptoms. These can be quite severe and include fever, cold sweats, shaking chills, muscle aches and pains, and joint aches and pains. Flu-like symptoms are usually worse near the start of treatment and less common later in the course of therapy. To help tolerate mild to moderate flu-like symptoms, I generally recommend that patients inject the interferon about an hour before going to sleep and take acetaminophen right before injecting the interferon. The acetaminophen will provide some relief of the symptoms and, if taken at bedtime, possibly help the patient to sleep through the night. Flu-like symptoms rarely require stopping treatment, but on occasion they are so intolerable that there is no other option but to stop.

Interferon alpha treatment can aggravate diabetes mellitus and thyroid disorders. Patients with diabetes mellitus who are treated with interferon alpha should carefully monitor their blood sugars. Patients with thyroid disease (and possibly all treated patients) should have blood tests of thyroid function checked periodically during treatment. Significant abnormalities in blood sugar or thyroid tests may necessitate stopping treatment. Patients with preexisting thyroid disease and poorly controlled diabetes may not be able to tolerate interferon alpha.

Psychiatric problems, some severe, have been reported in individuals being treated for hepatitis C. Severe depression, including suicide, has occurred in patients with chronic hepatitis C treated with interferon alpha or peginterferon alpha with or without ribavirin. Patients with serious preexisting depression or other psychiatric disorders probably should not be treated with interferon alpha. Those with a history of depression or other psychiatric illnesses should probably be evaluated by a psychiatrist before treatment is initiated and during treatment, if it is started. If severe depression develops during treatment, the drugs should be immediately discontinued and the patient closely followed and referred to a psychiatrist as necessary. If more mild signs of depression occur, the addition of an antidepressant medication during treatment may be helpful. The main thing to remember is that depression can be very serious, even life-threatening. If depression becomes a problem during treatment, the best response is always to stop the interferon plus ribavirin, as the treatment of chronic hepatitis C is never an emergency.

Irritability, confusion, nervousness, impaired concentration, anxiety, and insomnia also may occur in individuals taking interferon alpha and ribavirin. Sometimes these psychiatric problems are so severe that treatment must be stopped. As with depression, psychiatric consultation should be considered if these symptoms become significant. If in doubt about the severity of the psychiatric symptoms, the drugs should be stopped.

Virtually every other complaint imaginable has been reported by patients being treated for hepatitis C with interferon alpha or peginterferon alpha with or without ribavirin. Some of the more frequent

side effects, which are usually not severe, include fever, rashes, headache, muscle aches, fatigue, back pain, dry mouth, nausea, diarrhea,
tingling in the arms and legs, and inflammation at the injection site.
These usually are mild to moderate and do not require stopping treatment. Rarely, patients have what appear to be allergic reactions to interferon alpha, and the drug must be discontinued if these occur. Despite
the numerous side effects, interferon alpha therapy is rather safe if
patients are followed closely by their doctors. Most patients complete
the prescribed course of therapy.

The major side effect caused by ribavirin is the hemolytic anemia.
This is a sudden drop in the red blood cell count, hemoglobin, and
hematocrit that results from the rupture of red blood cells. For this
reason, the blood count must be monitored after starting therapy. If
the hemoglobin concentration drops to below 10 grams per deciliter
during treatment, the dose of ribavirin should be cut in half until it
returns to normal. If the hemoglobin concentration drops to below 8.5
grams per deciliter, ribavirin treatment should be discontinued.
Depending upon the situation, the interferon dose may also have to be
altered. Because sudden-onset anemia can be very dangerous in individuals with heart disease, patients known to have significant heart disease should not receive ribavirin. Patients at risk for heart disease
should be evaluated with a stress test prior to treatment. As mentioned
previously, some doctors are using epoetin alpha to treat anemia that
occurs during treatment with interferon alpha plus ribavirin, but this
is not an approved indication and has not been shown to be safe or
effective at the time of this writing.

Ribavirin may cause birth defects and should not be given to
women who are pregnant. Women who are taking ribavirin should not
get pregnant, and men who are taking ribavirin should not get their
female sexual partners pregnant. People having sex while taking ribavirin must use contraceptive agents.

Summary of Current Treatment of
Chronic Hepatitis C

When considering treatment of chronic hepatitis C, patients and their
doctors should consider the following:

1. Treatment of chronic hepatitis C is almost never an emergency. Chronic hepatitis C is a slowly progressive disease that does not progress to cirrhosis in most patients. In virtually all cases, there is time to think about treatment, whether and when to start it, and if it is the right choice.

2. Treatment can always be stopped once started if problems or significant side effects occur.

3. Currently available treatments are far from perfect. The current gold standard treatment of a peginterferon alpha plus ribavirin achieves the desired sustained response only about half the time.

4. Better treatments will very likely be available in the future.

Patients and their doctors must realize that the treatment of chronic hepatitis C is rapidly evolving and subject to radical change. Some clinical studies are still in progress to optimize available interferon-based treatments. Also in clinical trials are several ribavirin-like drugs, which may cause anemia less frequently. Most important, as discussed in Chapter 14, many pharmaceutical companies, biotechnology companies, and academic laboratories are working on novel drugs to attack the hepatitis C virus and prevent the complications resulting from infection. When such drugs are developed, they will add greater specificity to the treatment of hepatitis C and will either complement, or hopefully be used instead of, interferon alpha-based therapies. Some of these drugs are already in early-stage clinical trials; however, it is unlikely that any will be approved in the next few years. Like all new drugs, they must first be tested in large-scale, controlled clinical trials to prove their safety and efficacy.

Medical Follow-Up and Cancer Screening

Patients with chronic hepatitis C should have consistent medical follow-up whether or not they are candidates for drug treatment. Even individuals with no symptoms, normal blood ALT and AST activities, and minimal inflammation on liver biopsies should see their doctors periodically. On the whole, such individuals will probably do extremely well in the long term; however, it is clear that an individual patient without any apparent liver disease at one point in time may develop a more aggressive disease later. Therefore, periodic physical examinations and laboratory tests are reasonable recommendations. If a patient has chronic hepatitis C over many years without significant clinical change, he or she should probably see a doctor about once a year. A physical examination should be performed to confirm there are no signs of cirrhosis. Blood tests should be checked for evidence of inflammation or change in liver function.

As with chronic hepatitis B virus infection, chronic infection with hepatitis C virus is associated with development of hepatocellular carcinoma. While almost all patients with chronic hepatitis C who develop cancer also have cirrhosis, cancer in noncirrhotic livers has been reported. An important aspect of follow-up care for the chronically infected patient with hepatitis C virus is screening for hepatocellular carcinoma. There are no strict guidelines regarding frequency, and no data exist on overall efficacy and cost-effectiveness of such screening. Patients with chronic hepatitis C should probably have periodic ultrasound tests to check for small liver masses. Blood should also be tested periodically for alpha-fetoprotein, a marker for hepatocellular carcinoma. Patients with cirrhosis should probably have more frequent "cancer screenings" than patients without cirrhosis. Again, good data on the efficacy and cost-effectiveness of cancer screening do not exist, and it is up to the individual doctor to determine how frequently "periodic" screening should be performed.

Vaccination against hepatitis A and hepatitis B are recommended for individuals with chronic hepatitis C. Some studies have suggested that patients with chronic hepatitis C are at increased risk for developing fulminant hepatic failure as a result of hepatitis A virus infection compared to healthy individuals. Acute hepatitis B virus infection may also be more dangerous in someone having another chronic liver disease. For these reasons, vaccination against hepatitis A and B for individuals with chronic hepatitis C who are not immune to these other viral infections is indicated.

Special Situations

Patients with chronic hepatitis C are sometimes also infected with HIV or hepatitis B virus. Chronic hepatitis C is also common in substance abusers. These special situations are briefly discussed here.

Hepatitis C Virus and HIV Infection

Concurrent infection with the hepatitis C virus and HIV is not unusual. Many years ago, chronic hepatitis C was not treated in individuals infected with HIV, as their life expectancy was short. However, since the recent revolution in the treatment of HIV with highly active antiretroviral therapy (HAART), patients have been living long and productive lives. Some have been living long enough to develop complications of cirrhosis from hepatitis C.

In general, patients with HIV infection and a healthy immune system (normal CD4 or "T-cell" counts) and no complications of AIDS, who also have chronic hepatitis C, should probably be approached just like a patient with chronic hepatitis C without HIV infection. Equally aggressive diagnostic procedures and treatments should be considered in patients with hepatitis C virus and HIV co-infection without laboratory evidence of a compromised immune system or AIDS. Keep in mind, however, the numerous different drugs that such patients will take and the potential for drug interactions and compliance problems. Patients on several drugs to treat HIV and two drugs to treat hepatitis C are at an increased risk for developing side effects and should be monitored closely.

In individuals with very low CD4 counts or with AIDS, a less aggressive approach to hepatitis C is usually indicated. In such patients, other problems may be more immediate. The approach to every individual patient depends upon the particular case and the doctor's judgment. Treatment of chronic hepatitis C can also be considered if such patients eventually become stable on anti-HIV medications.

Hepatitis C Virus and Hepatitis B Virus Infection

The hepatitis B virus and hepatitis C virus are transmitted in similar fashions. In Western countries, hepatitis B virus infection is less common than hepatitis C. In Eastern countries and parts of Africa, the opposite is true. In patients with both, the two diseases should be approached together. Patients with chronic hepatitis B infection and evidence of viral replication are potential candidates for drug treatment. Treatment with peginterferon alpha for one year at the same dose is approved for treatment of certain patients with chronic hepatitis B and chronic hepatitis C and is a logical first approach for many patients.

People eligible for treatment for both hepatitis B and hepatitis C should see a specialist who has experience in treating both conditions.

Alcohol and Drug Abusers with Chronic Hepatitis C

Chronic hepatitis C is common in people with active drug and alcohol use problems. Current treatment protocols for chronic hepatitis C require good compliance, frequent medical monitoring, and the injection of medications. It is almost impossible to treat an active alcohol or drug abuser for chronic hepatitis C. In virtually all such cases, the substance abuse should be treated first.

6

Alcoholic Liver Disease

MOST PEOPLE READILY recognize alcohol (specifically ethyl alcohol or ethanol) as a major cause of liver disease. In the United States, it is the number one cause of liver disease. Although it has been estimated that as many as 10 percent of Americans abuse alcohol, most people who drink excessively do not develop liver disease. It is not known why some individuals who regularly have only a few drinks per day will develop liver disease, while others who drink a bottle or more of hard liquor a day will not. What is important to realize is that excessive alcohol consumption can potentially cause liver disease in an individual, and it is not possible to predict in whom this will happen. Anyone who consumes too much alcohol on a regular basis is at risk to develop liver disease.

Alcoholic liver disease presents in many different ways. Some examples may help illustrate the many different signs and symptoms.

• **Case 1.** A thirty-five-year-old homeless man is brought to the emergency room by a city emergency medical services ambulance after being found lying in the street confused and agitated. He is dirty and disheveled and looks much older than his actual age. He has a fever, is deeply jaundiced, and is breathing rapidly. Laboratory examination reveals elevated blood alanine aminotransferase (ALT) and aspartate aminotransferase (AST) activities with the AST activity being almost three times higher. Bilirubin is elevated, albumin is low, and prothrombin time is prolonged. Chest X-ray indicates pneumonia and many old fractured ribs. The medical resident who admits the patient recognizes him as someone who is always seen on the street near her apartment with a bottle of hard liquor or fortified wine. He is hospitalized and treated with antibiotics but becomes tremulous, suffers a seizure, and remains critically ill for about a week. He is treated with benzodiazepines. After several weeks in the hospital, his condition gradually improves. Upon discharge, he is no longer jaundiced and ALT and AST activities are near normal, though blood albumin concentration is still a little low. He refuses referral to an inpatient rehabilitation center, and the medical resident who admitted the patient sees him on the street with a bottle of fortified wine a few days after discharge.

• **Case 2.** A fifty-two-year-old woman is the mother of two grown children and wife of a CEO of a large multinational corporation. Her children no longer live at home, and her husband, who travels frequently, is now seeking a divorce. She has been arrested twice in the past year for driving her luxury car while under the influence of alcohol. After considerable urging by her daughter, she sees her family doctor. She denies having more than a few drinks a week, but blood tests indicate numerous abnormalities, including elevated serum ALT and AST activities, elevated gamma-glutamyltranspeptidase (GGTP) activity, and slightly low albumin concentration. She is referred to a liver specialist who performs a liver biopsy. Cirrhosis is confirmed.

• **Case 3.** A twenty-year-old student at an Ivy League college starts drinking heavily for the first time in his life. After a few months, he is consuming at least twelve beers a night plus hard liquor. He goes to the student emergency health services facility because of nausea and vomiting mixed with red blood. Blood tests show mildly elevated ALT, AST, and GGTP activities; a complete blood count reveals mildly elevated mean corpuscular volume (slightly enlarged red blood cells). He is admitted to the local hospital. An upper endoscopy indicates a tear in his esophagus (Mallory-Weiss tear) that was bleeding, and he is discharged. He attends a campus support group for students with alcohol problems, gives up drinking, and starts exercising regularly. On follow-up examination a few months later, he is in excellent health and a laboratory examination is completely normal.

One theme central to these three hypothetical cases of alcoholic liver disease, and all real cases, is excessive alcohol intake. Alcoholic liver disease is virtually always associated with the psychiatric diagnoses that are known as *alcohol use disorders*. Most people refer to these conditions as "alcoholism" and individuals that suffer from them as "alcoholics." Therefore, before discussing the effects of alcohol on the liver, it is essential to understand something about misuse of alcohol.

Alcoholism

Alcoholism is an ill-defined term for the condition characterized by alcohol consumption that causes psychosocial or medical problems. Everyone would recognize the patient in Case 1 as the typical "skid row alcoholic" but may have a harder time recognizing the patients in Cases 2 and 3 as having disorders caused by alcohol until it is too late. In fact, an alcohol use disorder was recognized too late in Case 2. Fortunately for the patient described in Case 3, he had a problem that brought him to medical attention early in life.

Like *alcoholism*, the adjective *alcoholic* is an imprecise term used to describe an individual who has psychosocial or medical problems resulting from excessive alcohol consumption. The American Psychiatric Association's *The Diagnostic and Statistical Manual of Mental Disorders*, Fourth Edition, provides specific diagnostic criteria for two chronic alcohol use disorders: alcohol dependence and alcohol abuse. The less precise term *alcoholic* would include individuals with either of these conditions, and although it is less precise, *alcoholic* will be used in this book.

The clinical criteria for alcohol abuse are maladaptive patterns of use leading to clinically significant impairment or distress occurring within a twelve-month period. This basically means persistent and serious social and personal problems that result from drinking alcohol. An example would be failure to perform adequately at work, in school, or at home as a result of being drunk or hung over. Another example would be the use of alcohol in physically hazardous situations, such as driving a car or operating machinery while intoxicated. Individuals with alcohol abuse disorders may experience other substance-related social problems, such as arrests for disorderly conduct or fighting while intoxicated. More important, people with alcohol abuse disorders will continue to drink despite having the types of problems that are caused or exacerbated by consuming alcohol. To have a diagnosis of substance abuse, the individual must have never met the criteria for substance dependence, in which case he or she would instead have a dependence disorder.

Two central features of alcohol dependence are tolerance and withdrawal. Tolerance is characterized by a need for increased amounts of alcohol to achieve intoxication or diminished effects with continued use of the same amount of a substance. Withdrawal is a constellation of signs and symptoms that occur if a dependent individual suddenly stops drinking alcohol. Other criteria for alcohol dependence include consumption of large amounts or over longer periods than intended, persistent desire or unsuccessful efforts to reduce consumption, and the spending of a great deal of time in activities necessary to obtain alcohol. Individuals with alcohol dependence may also reduce important social, occupational, or recreational activities because of alcohol use. An important aspect of alcohol dependence, especially concerning the patient with alcoholic liver disease, is continued use of alcohol despite knowledge of having a physical or psychological problem caused or exacerbated by it. In other words, an individual with liver disease related to alcohol who continues to drink, despite knowing that it is harmful, has already met one of the criteria for alcohol dependence.

Alcohol withdrawal is a characteristic syndrome that occurs when a dependent individual stops or reduces alcohol intake that has been heavy and prolonged. The hypothetical patient in Case 1 suffered from alcohol withdrawal after admission to the hospital. The syndrome of alcohol withdrawal includes tremor, insomnia, sweating, rapid pulse rate, nausea, vomiting, psychomotor agitation, and anxiety. Alcohol withdrawal also can cause delusions and hallucinations. One common hallucination is that bugs are crawling over the individual's body (this is known as *formication*). The syndrome of alcohol withdrawal is sometimes called *delirium tremens* (DTs) because delirium and tremulousness are characteristic symptoms. Alcohol withdrawal can also cause seizures. Alcohol withdrawal is a very serious medical condition that can be fatal. Hospitalization and treatment with benzodiazepines such as diazepam (Valium) or chlordiazepoxide (Librium) are usually necessary for alcohol withdrawal and may be lifesaving.

Who Gets Alcoholic Liver Disease?

Most individuals with liver disease caused by alcohol probably suffer from alcohol dependence. However, some individuals who have abused alcohol over many years may also develop liver disease. It is also possible that individuals who do not strictly meet the diagnostic criteria for either of these conditions will develop liver disease after many years of drinking. There are multiple genetic and environmental factors that determine if a person who consumes alcohol is at risk for liver disease, most of which have not been identified.

An alcoholic "drink" generally contains 10 grams of alcohol. This is roughly the amount of alcohol in a 12-ounce bottle of beer, a glass (4 ounces) of wine, or 1.5 ounces of distilled spirits. There is no magic number of drinks a day that cause alcoholic liver disease. Probably two alcoholic drinks a day for many years is a very conservative minimum amount necessary to develop alcohol-related liver disease. Six or more alcoholic drinks every day significantly increase the risk for developing liver disease. Some individuals, however, will never develop liver disease no matter how much alcohol they consume. For reasons that are unclear, women may be more likely to develop liver disease than men at relatively low amounts of daily alcohol consumption. It should also be realized that alcohol consumption can cause serious social and physical problems other than liver disease. Therefore, the risk for developing liver disease from alcohol is not the only reason to limit alcohol consumption. Perhaps the most important aspect of alcoholic liver disease is that once a patient develops liver disease from alcohol consumption, that individual is drinking too much and should never drink again.

Spectrum of Alcoholic Liver Disease

Excessive alcohol consumption causes three different liver disorders: fatty liver, alcoholic hepatitis, and cirrhosis. Fatty liver and alcoholic hepatitis are completely reversible if the patient stops drinking. As explained in Chapter 3, cirrhosis is not reversible, yet cessation of alcohol consumption can prevent further deterioration of liver function in a patient with alcoholic cirrhosis. Any combination of fatty liver, alcoholic hepatitis, and cirrhosis can occur simultaneously in the liver of someone who consumes excessive alcohol. A common example is the occurrence of alcoholic hepatitis in an individual who starts a binge of heavier drinking and already has cirrhosis caused by alcohol. Although cirrhosis is not reversible, this individual's condition may improve dramatically upon cessation of alcohol consumption as the hepatitis resolves itself.

Fatty Liver

Excessive alcohol consumption can lead to the accumulation of fat in liver cells. The individual with fatty liver caused by alcohol usually does not have physical signs or symptoms of liver disease. He or she may suffer from nonspecific symptoms such as fatigue. Fatty liver can cause blood test abnormalities and usually mild elevations in the blood AST and/or ALT activities. A diagnosis of fatty liver can be made with certainty only by liver biopsy. Fatty liver caused by alcohol will resolve itself if the patient stops drinking. The patient described in Case 3 probably had fatty liver from alcohol that later resolved itself.

Alcoholic Hepatitis

Excessive alcohol consumption can cause hepatitis or inflammation of the liver. Clinically, alcoholic hepatitis can range from relatively mild illness with fever, pain in the right upper abdomen, nausea, and vomiting to a severe life-threatening condition. Blood AST and ALT activities are usually elevated. In alcoholic hepatitis, AST activity is frequently two or more times higher than ALT activity. In severe cases, alcoholic hepatitis can cause many of the same complications as cirrhosis, including ascites, hepatic encephalopathy, and bleeding esophageal varices. If these complications are caused by alcoholic hepatitis, they will reverse themselves as the inflammation resolves if the individual stops drinking. In contrast, they will not reverse if caused by cirrhosis. The patient described in Case 1 is an example of someone with both cirrhosis and alcoholic hepatitis.

When examined under the microscope, liver inflammation caused by alcohol appears very different than liver inflammation caused by hepatitis viruses or most other drugs. The inflammation of alcoholic hepatitis can be readily distinguished from these other types by performing a liver biopsy. However, liver biopsy is usually not necessary in patients with alcoholic hepatitis as the diagnosis is readily made based upon typical symptoms in a patient with excessive alcohol consumption. Once the clinical symptoms of alcoholic hepatitis resolve themselves, liver biopsy may be indicated to determine the presence of underlying cirrhosis.

Cirrhosis

Chronic consumption of excessive amounts of alcohol can cause cirrhosis. (See Chapter 3.) In the United States, alcohol is the number one cause of cirrhosis. Very often, cirrhosis will be the initial condition the first time a patient with alcohol liver disease sees a doctor. This is exemplified by the hypothetical patient in Case 2.

Effects of Alcohol on Metabolism by the Liver

Excessive alcohol consumption affects its own metabolism plus that of other drugs by the liver. In most individuals, alcohol is primarily broken down by enzymes known as *alcohol dehydrogenases*. These enzymes speed up the chemical reaction that converts ethyl alcohol to its metabolite acetaldehyde.

Acetaldehyde is an important metabolite of alcohol because it is associated with unpleasant effects such as flushing, nausea, and vomiting. It may also play a role in long-term liver damage caused by alcohol. In the body, acetaldehyde is metabolized to acetic acid (vinegar) by a chemical reaction enhanced by the enzyme known as aldehyde dehydrogenase. An individual with a genetic deficiency of aldehyde dehydrogenase, which is not uncommon in persons of Asian descent, becomes red and warm after just a few sips of alcohol. Pharmacological inhibition of aldehyde dehydrogenase is also accomplished by the drug disulfiram (Antabuse). This drug is sometimes taken by individuals with alcohol use disorders to deter them from drinking as they will feel sick after consuming alcohol due to acetaldehyde buildup.

Chronic excessive alcohol consumption induces synthesis of an enzyme in the liver known as *cytochrome P450* (actually a family of related enzymes in which alcohol affects specific ones). Cytochrome P450 can metabolize alcohol, and it becomes a major pathway for alcohol metabolism in the chronic alcohol drinker. Oxidation of alcohol by cytochrome P450 utilizes certain cofactors in the cell at a high rate. This influences the body's overall metabolism and may play some role in causing liver and other organ dysfunction. Induction of cytochrome P450 also explains, in part, the "tolerance" to alcohol present in some individuals with alcohol dependence. Because alcohol is more readily metabolized in the liver by cytochrome P450, it takes more alcohol to achieve a desired blood concentration.

Cytochrome P450 enzymes metabolize other drugs besides alcohol. For this reason, the doses of some drugs must be adjusted in alcoholics. Some drugs become relatively ineffective in the alcoholic as cytochrome P450 catalyzes their breakdown into harmless metabolites that are excreted. Other drugs may potentially become more toxic in heavy alcohol drinkers if the metabolites that result from the action of cytochrome P450 are toxic. There are hundreds of drugs whose metabolism is influenced by alcohol.

Effects of Alcohol on Other Parts of the Body

Alcohol affects many organs of the body besides the liver, and disorders can occur in individuals without liver disease. Frequently, individuals with alcoholic liver disease also have problems with other organ systems resulting from excessive alcohol consumption. These complicating problems can complicate the clinical picture of the individual with alcoholic liver disease.

Nervous System

Alcohol obviously affects the brain. Virtually every adult has either experienced or has observed in others the intoxicating effects of alcohol consumption. Individuals with alcohol dependence may develop a tolerance to alcohol's intoxicating effects. Some component of tolerance is metabolic in that alcohol is more readily metabolized by induced cytochrome P450 enzymes. However, some component of tolerance to alcohol's intoxicating effects occurs because of nerve cell structure changes. The resulting higher concentrations of blood become necessary to alter brain function. A component of tolerance to alcohol is also behavioral as chronic alcohol drinkers "learn" how to perform certain tasks while intoxicated.

Chronic alcohol consumption also affects the brain in more severe ways. Many alcohol-dependent individuals eventually become deficient in thiamine (vitamin B_1). Thiamine deficiency can lead to a serious neuropsychiatric condition known as *Wernicke-Korsakoff syndrome.* Structural changes are observed in particular parts of the brain in individuals with this condition, and the syndrome has two separate components that often occur together but can be seen separately: Wernicke encephalopathy and Korsakoff psychosis. Wernicke encephalopathy is characterized by profound alterations in brain function. It can be diagnosed on physical examination by abnormal function of one of the nerves that moves the eye in certain directions. Korsakoff psychosis is a dramatic psychiatric condition characterized by confabulation (making up stories) and loss of some memory functions, usually of more recent events. Wernicke-Korsakoff syndrome can complicate the overall clinical picture of a patient with alcoholic liver disease. It can also combine with hepatic encephalopathy and alcohol withdrawal symptoms, resulting in complex neurological problems. Treatment with thiamine usually reverses Wernicke encephalopathy but does not always improve the memory disturbances associated with Korsakoff psychosis.

Alcohol has other effects on the nervous system. It can damage peripheral nerves and cause loss of sensation. Chronic alcohol consumption can cause cerebellar degeneration, or loss of nerve cells in the cerebellum, the portion of the brain that regulates coordination. Finally, years of excessive alcohol consumption can cause diffuse loss of nerve cells in the brain and generalized dementia.

Gastrointestinal System

Alcohol can cause disease in other parts of the gastrointestinal system besides the liver. Alcohol causes pancreatitis, or inflammation of the pancreas. This is characterized by severe abdominal or back pain, fever, and the inability to eat or digest certain foods. Pancreatitis can be life-threatening and require hospitalization and even intensive care. Alcohol also causes gastritis and possibly stomach and duodenal ulcers. Gastritis and ulcers can complicate the diagnosis of gastrointestinal bleeding in an individual with alcoholic liver disease because the chances of bleeding from esophageal varices, gastritis, or stomach ulcers are all increased in the alcoholic. Emergency endoscopic examination of an alcoholic is almost always required to diagnose sources of bleeding in the stomach, esophagus, or intestines. Alcohol can also cause excessive vomiting and retching. The result can be tears in the esophagus that can bleed (Mallory-Weiss tears).

Heart and Skeletal Muscle

Excessive alcohol consumption can affect the heart and skeletal muscles. Cardiomyopathy, a condition characterized by decreased effectiveness of heart pumping and an enlarged heart, may be caused by alcohol. Abnormal heart rhythms can also result from alcohol consumption and withdrawal. Further, alcohol can cause myopathy, or inflammation of the skeletal muscles leading to weakness.

Blood

Alcohol suppresses the bone marrow where blood cells are made. Chronic alcohol drinkers may become anemic from alcohol consumption and also have low white blood counts. Alcohol can directly lower the platelet count and further decrease it in cirrhotic individuals who may also have low platelet counts secondary to trapping of platelets in an enlarged spleen. Low platelets can cause a tendency to bleed.

Other Complications

Excessive alcohol drinkers are also at risk for other complications. They include:

- **Falls and injuries.** An old radiologist's tale says that "the radiological diagnosis of alcoholism is made by finding multiple broken ribs on a chest X-ray." Head injuries from falls can result in skull fractures and cause bleeding in the space around the brain (subdural hematoma).

- **Infections.** Because alcoholics are often in a stupor or near-unconscious state, they are at risk for aspirating vomit into their lungs that can cause serious pneumonia (aspiration pneumonia). Because their immune systems may be compromised, alcoholics are also at increased risk for infections from bacteria that do not usually infect healthy individuals.

- **Predisposition to certain cancers.** Long-term heavy alcohol use increases the chances of developing throat cancer. Because the large majority of individuals who abuse alcohol also abuse tobacco, many are also at increased risk of developing lung cancer. The combination of tobacco and alcohol makes the risk for developing throat cancer even higher.

- **Psychosocial problems.** Individuals with alcohol use disorders have higher rates of psychosocial problems such as unemployment, personal financial difficulties, homelessness, and incarceration for crimes.

Individuals with alcohol use disorders are at risk for many problems in addition to liver disease. Because of alcohol's multiple negative effects on the body, treating individuals with alcoholic liver disease presents one of medicine's greatest challenges. This challenge is complicated even further by the alcoholic's inevitable psychological and social problems.

Diagnosis of Alcoholic Liver Disease

A history of excessive alcohol consumption in a patient with liver abnormalities suggests a diagnosis of alcoholic liver disease. The diagnosis can sometimes be made clinically when a patient with a known alcohol dependence disorder has signs, symptoms, and laboratory abnormalities of liver disease. However, other causes of liver disease, such as chronic viral hepatitis, drugs, and congenital disorders, should not be immediately excluded as possible diagnoses because patients who consume excessive amounts of alcohol may also have these problems. Sometimes, a history of alcohol consumption is difficult to obtain from a patient or family members, and individuals with alcohol use disorders are notorious for lying about the amount of alcohol they consume. A general rule is that the patient usually consumes at least three times more alcohol than he or she tells the doctor. In these cases, various laboratory tests may suggest excessive alcohol consumption. The blood GGTP activity may be elevated from alcohol consumption and the mean corpuscular volume of red blood cells may be decreased. In patients with alcoholic hepatitis, blood AST activity may be two or more times higher than blood ALT activity, whereas in other forms of hepatitis ALT and AST activities are usually roughly equal.

If a diagnosis of alcoholic liver disease cannot be made on clinical grounds, liver biopsy may be necessary, such as with a patient with a questionable history of alcohol abuse who comes to the doctor with elevated blood AST and ALT activities. Liver biopsy may be necessary to diagnose fatty liver, alcoholic hepatitis, or cirrhosis. Liver biopsy also may be necessary to establish the presence of cirrhosis if it is not clinically apparent. Old studies have shown that liver biopsy reveals a liver disease other than alcohol liver disease in about 25 percent of patients who drink and in whom alcoholic liver disease is suspected by clinical criteria. Therefore, liver biopsy is also helpful to exclude another or concurrent liver disorder in a person with an alcohol abuse disorder.

Treatment

The cornerstone of treatment of an individual with alcoholic liver disease is complete and unconditional abstinence from alcohol. This cannot be emphasized enough. Fatty liver and alcoholic hepatitis will resolve if alcohol consumption is stopped. While cirrhosis is not reversible, the patient's condition may improve or not progress if he or she stops drinking alcohol.

Abstinence from alcohol is often easier said than done. Substance abuse and dependence are diseases, and a component of these diseases is an inability to stop using the substance despite knowing it is harmful. Individuals with alcohol dependence may suffer withdrawal upon stopping drinking, and this can prove fatal. Hospital admission for detoxification, therefore, may be required for alcohol-dependent individuals. In many cases, detoxification should ideally be followed up by inpatient rehabilitation for at least one month. Additional outpatient psychotherapy is often necessary, and participation in Alcoholics Anonymous should probably be continued for life. Despite this course of action, the relapse rate is quite high.

Supportive medical care may be necessary for the patient with alcoholic liver disease. Complications of cirrhosis are treated as described in Chapter 3. Acute alcoholic hepatitis may require hospitalization and treatment. Some studies suggest that steroids may be beneficial in severe cases, and other complications caused by alcohol such as gastritis may also respond to treatment. Although medical treatment is often essential to support patients with alcohol-related illnesses, no medication or procedure is a substitute for abstinence when it comes to treating alcoholic liver disease.

7

Drugs and Toxins and the Liver

MANY DRUGS AND CHEMICALS can potentially affect the liver. Some of these drugs and chemicals affect the liver in a predictable manner. For these drugs, the type of liver injury can be expected in most individuals who consume the compound. In these cases, the injury is usually dose-dependent, with the chance of developing an injury and the degree of its severity dependent upon the amount of the substance consumed. A classical example is the necrosis (death) of liver cells caused by carbon tetrachloride, a chemical that used to be included in cleaning fluids.

Many drugs and chemicals cause liver injury in an idiosyncratic manner. In idiosyncratic liver injury, the liver damage cannot be readily predicted. Typically, only one in many, perhaps millions, of individuals who consume the compound will develop an idiosyncratic liver injury. The doctor cannot predict which individual will develop the liver injury, and the chance of developing the injury does not necessarily depend upon the dose. Idiosyncratic liver injury often occurs after a person has been taking a drug without problems for weeks or months. Doctors and scientists do not understand very much about the mechanisms of idiosyncratic liver injury, but undiscovered genetic differences among individuals are likely to be the major factors.

The signs and symptoms associated with liver damage induced by drugs or toxins can vary tremendously. Many patients will have no obvious problems, and liver damage can only be ascertained by blood testing. Some patients will have no symptoms for years and eventually develop cirrhosis from chronic drug use or toxin exposure. Some drug-induced liver diseases will appear as fulminant hepatic failure.

It is extremely important that doctors and patients realize that many different drugs can potentially cause liver damage. A comprehensive history regarding medications—both prescription and over-the-counter—is an essential part of evaluating a patient with liver disease. In older adults, prescription medications are a fairly common cause of liver abnormalities that are picked up on routine blood tests suggesting liver diseases (elevated blood aminotransferase, alkaline phosphatase, and gamma-glutamyltranspeptidase, or GGTP, activities). One intelligent approach with a patient on medications causing liver problems is to suspect that any drug may be causing the liver disease or blood test abnormality. The drug causing the problem can sometimes be established by the known adverse event profile of the drug plus the exclusion of other liver disorders. Another way to determine if a drug is causing a liver problem is for the doctor (not the patient without the doctor's knowledge) to discontinue it. If the abnormality resolves, the drug is then a suspected culprit. Restarting the drug and witnessing return of the abnormality more strongly suggests this.

After a drug is established to be the cause of liver disease, the decision to stop or continue use of the drug requires the judgment of an experienced physician. For example, mild cholestasis indicated by slightly elevated blood alkaline phosphatase and GGTP activities may be less significant than the repercussions of stopping a medication to prevent seizures or psychosis. On the other hand, continued use of a particular agent to lower blood pressure that is causing hepatitis may not be reasonable if equally effective alternative drugs are available. Therefore, the doctor's experience and judgment are critical in deciding if the risk of continuing a drug affecting the liver outweighs the potential danger. It is not possible to provide specific guidelines for these decisions.

Overdoses of certain drugs or exposure to certain toxins can cause acute liver disease and even fulminant hepatic failure. As alluded to, some individuals also may have idiosyncratic reactions that can cause severe liver disease with normal doses of a generally safe drug. In cases of severe or life-threatening liver injury caused by a drug or toxin, the goal is to identify the causative agent and immediately stop the drug or toxin.

It is beyond the scope of this book to provide an exhaustive list of drugs and compounds that affect the liver. There are thousands and they affect the liver in many different ways. This section will discuss liver toxicities associated with some commonly used drugs and classical hepatotoxins, as shown in Table 7.1.

Acetaminophen

Acetaminophen is the active ingredient in many over-the-counter pain relievers, including Tylenol. At recommended doses and durations of treatment, acetaminophen is an extremely safe compound used by millions of people worldwide. Despite a few unconfirmed case reports in the literature, there are no controlled studies showing that acetaminophen is toxic to the liver when taken as recommended on package labels.

Table 7.1 Drugs That Can Affect the Liver and Classical Hepatotoxins

Drugs	Acetaminophen overdose
	Isoniazid (INH)
	Statins
	Halothane
	Methotrexate
	Anticonvulsants
	Psychiatric medications
	Cancer chemotherapy
	Antiretroviral drugs (HAART to treat HIV infection)
	Antihypertensive agents
	Cardiovascular drugs
	Antidiabetic agents
	Estrogens (birth control pills)
	Anabolic steroids
Classical Hepatotoxins	*Amanita phalloides* mushrooms compounds (death caps)
	Carbon tetrachloride
	Pyrrolizidine alkaloids
	Aflatoxins

An overdose of acetaminophen, however, can cause liver damage. Overdosing on acetaminophen, which is also known as *paracetamol* in some parts of the world, was first recognized as a method for committing suicide in Great Britain and later in the United States. Overdoses of acetaminophen, usually more than 15 grams at a time in adults (each "extra-strength" tablet or capsule contains half a gram), can cause fulminant hepatic failure. Some individuals have been reported to have taken overdoses of acetaminophen for various reasons but not as deliberate suicide attempts. Therefore, in patients with acute liver disease of unclear etiology, a very careful history of all over-the-counter drug use (acetaminophen is in many over-the-counter products) and amounts consumed is extremely important.

The diagnosis of acetaminophen overdose is made by history and detection of toxic levels in the blood. The time of ingestion must be known to determine if the blood level is toxic. The clinical picture of acetaminophen overdose can be one of massive liver cell death as manifested by extremely high blood aminotransferase activities within a couple of days after the overdose that rapidly return to normal. Signs and symptoms of liver failure usually first occur about two days later. Some patients, however, will not develop serious liver damage, even with large doses.

N-acetylcysteine (Mucomyst) is the treatment for acetaminophen overdose. It has been hypothesized that N-acetylcysteine's mechanism of action is to neutralize a toxic metabolite of acetaminophen that at normal concentrations is easily detoxified by the liver. N-acetylcysteine is most effective if given within ten hours of an acetaminophen overdose and probably not effective if given more than twenty-four hours later. For patients who develop fulminant hepatic failure from acetaminophen overdose, intensive care is essential and liver transplantation may be necessary.

Isoniazid

Isoniazid, or INH, is widely used in the treatment and prevention of tuberculosis. People with active tuberculosis, and many with only positive skin tests, are treated with isoniazid. Treatment usually lasts for six months. About 10 percent of individuals treated with isoniazid develop transient, mild elevations in blood aminotransferase activities.

These are not serious and treatment can be continued. However, about 1 percent of individuals develop severe hepatitis and some even develop fulminant hepatic failure.

Isoniazid hepatitis is rare in younger individuals but occurs in about 2 percent of treated individuals over age fifty. In active tuberculosis, the risk of no treatment is far greater than the risk of liver disease from isoniazid. A more conservative treatment approach may be used in individuals with positive skin tests in whom isoniazid is prescribed to prevent active tuberculosis, however. The decision depends upon the individual's risk factors for developing active tuberculosis and must be made by the patient's doctor using guidelines recommended by public health agencies or professional organizations.

Statins

The HMG-CoA reductase inhibitors or statin class of drugs are used to lower serum cholesterol concentrations. These are the most widely prescribed drugs in the United States. This class of compounds includes atorvastatin (Lipitor), fluvastatin (Lescol), lovastatin (Mevacor), pravastatin (Pravachol), rosuvastatin (Crestor), and simvastatin (Zocor). Hepatitis, as presumed from increases in blood aminotransferase activities, occurs in about 1 percent of patients receiving starting doses of these drugs and in up to 2 percent of those who receive maximum doses. Patients are usually asymptomatic. Therefore, those who receive statins should have their aminotransferase activities checked by blood testing four to six weeks after first taking the drug or increasing dosage and checked periodically thereafter while on the medication. If blood alanine aminotransferase (ALT) or aspartate aminotransferase (AST) activities persistently increase to more than three times normal, the medications should probably be discontinued. Liver inflammation induced by statins is reversible upon stopping the drugs.

Halothane

Halothane has been widely used through the years as a general anesthetic, although is it less often used today. In about one in ten thousand cases, halothane causes hepatitis. The onset of hepatitis usually begins a few days to within three weeks after receiving anesthesia. Halothane can induce a mild hepatitis that is detectable only by finding elevated blood aminotransferase activities or fulminant hepatic failure. Almost all patients with halothane-induced hepatitis have had prior exposure to the drug, and repeated exposure greatly increases the chance of developing hepatitis. Therefore, halothane should be avoided in individuals for whom repeated surgeries are anticipated or who have been exposed previously to the drug. The anesthetics methoxyflurane and enflurane may also cause hepatitis similar to that caused by halothane.

Methotrexate

Methotrexate is commonly used to treat severe psoriasis and rheumatic diseases. Chronic therapy with methotrexate may cause fibrosis (scarring) and cirrhosis of the liver. These changes are dose-related and most studies show that cirrhosis is rare with total cumulative doses of less than 1.5 grams. Methotrexate can cause liver damage without causing abnormalities in the aminotransferase activities or other blood tests. For this reason, liver biopsy to determine fibrosis is sometimes performed after a cumulative dose of 1 to 1.5 grams of methotrexate.

Anticonvulsants

Two commonly used anticonvulsants (drugs to prevent seizures) can cause liver disease. Phenytoin (Dilantin) causes various types of liver damage. Its continued use, if liver abnormalities occur, depends upon the risk of recurrent seizures and availability of alternative effective drugs compared to continued treatment. Rare cases of acute phenytoin liver injury have been reported that can cause fulminant hepatic failure. Valproic acid (Depekote) and its derivatives also can cause liver disease. Mild elevations in blood aminotransferase activities are not uncommon and should be followed by repeated blood testing. Valproic acid can cause clinically significant liver disease. Valproic acid liver damage is characterized by death of liver cells and accumulation of microscopic fat globules in liver cells.

Psychiatric Medications

Various drugs used in the treatment of psychiatric disorders can affect the liver. Phenothiazines such as chlorpromazine (Thorazine) that are used to treat schizophrenia and other forms of psychosis commonly cause cholestasis, or impaired bile flow within the liver, which can lead to jaundice. Elevations in the blood alkaline phosphatase and GGTP activities are often the first indications of this disorder. Some antidepressant medications can cause hepatitis and are usually inferred from elevations in blood ALT and AST activities. Continued use of drugs for these conditions means weighing the risk that their discontinuation will cause life-threatening mood changes or psychotic behavior versus the slight risk of progressive liver damage. Sometimes one type of drug can be substituted for another. This decision will doubtless depend upon careful collaboration between the psychiatrist and liver specialist.

Cancer Chemotherapy

Many drugs used for cancer chemotherapy can cause different types of liver damage. An interesting condition caused by high-dose chemotherapy with several different agents is known as *veno-occlusive disease*. This disease is characterized by damage that causes obstruction of the smallest hepatic veins that exit the liver. Acute veno-occlusive disease can mimic hepatic vein obstruction and clinically present as the sudden onset of abdominal discomfort, enlarged liver, and ascites. Slowly progressive courses can also occur. There is no specific treatment.

Antiretroviral Agents

Highly active antiretroviral therapy (HAART) has had a tremendous impact in treating patients infected with HIV and preventing the development of AIDS. The classes of drugs used for HAART are nucleoside reverse transcriptase inhibitors, nonnucleoside reverse transcriptase inhibitors, and protease inhibitors. Drugs in each of these classes can potentially cause liver damage. Fortunately, severe hepatitis is rare in patients with HIV who receive HAART. Drug-induced liver injury should be suspected in all patients receiving these drugs who develop symptoms or blood test abnormalities suggestive of liver disease. Some HAART drugs also cause fatty liver as well as a condition known as *partial lipodystrophy*, characterized by loss of fat from the arms and legs and excess fat accumulation in other areas, including the liver. The management of liver toxicity depends upon on its clinical impact. Mild hepatitis or fatty liver often spontaneously resolves or can be followed. In some cases, severe liver injury may require discontinuation of the drugs, for example when there is evidence of liver failure, hypersensitivity reaction, or lactic acidosis (accumulation of lactic acid in the blood).

Antihypertensive Agents

Several drugs used to control blood pressure can cause liver damage. A classic example is alpha-methyldopa (Aldomet), though this drug is hardly used today. Rare cases of liver damage have been associated with a variety of other blood pressure medications.

Cardiovascular Drugs

Various drugs used to treat heart disease have also been associated with liver toxicity. Many heart drugs can potentially cause hepatitis, but occurrence is rare considering how frequently such drugs are prescribed. One culprit that causes a unique form of liver disease is amiodarone, which is used to treat heart rhythm abnormalities. Amiodarone liver toxicity is problematic because it is sometimes associated with no clinical or laboratory evidence of liver disease until significant damage has occurred. On liver biopsy, unusual fatty inclusions are often observed.

Antidiabetic Agents

Various oral medications used to treat diabetes mellitus can cause liver damage. Troglitazone (Rezulin), a very effective drug that had been used by many diabetics, was removed from the market after reports that it caused liver disease, even fulminant hepatic failure, and other drugs in the same class (thiazolidinediones) became available. Fortunately, cases of severe liver disease were rare considering troglitazone's widespread use. As other oral antidiabetic agents can potentially cause idiosyncratic liver injury, patients should have their blood aminotransferase activities checked at the start of therapy and periodically thereafter. As many drugs are available to treat diabetes, a specific one should probably be discontinued and can be potentially replaced by another if clinical or laboratory evidence of liver disease develops during treatment. The doctor's judgment and experience are very critical in determining if a suspected drug is causing the problem, if it should be stopped, and how another drug should be substituted.

Birth Control Pills and Other Estrogen Preparations

Estrogens, most commonly present in birth control pills and medications used to treat symptoms of menopause, can cause cholestasis (impaired bile flow within the liver). This is characterized by itching all over the body, possibly jaundice, and elevations in blood alkaline phosphatase and GGTP activities. Cholestasis typically occurs within the first two months of taking birth control pills. Birth control pill use has also been associated with various liver tumors, including benign adenomas and another benign condition known as *focal nodular hyperplasia*. These conditions are rare.

Anabolic Steroids and Androgens

Anabolic steroids are sometimes used by bodybuilders and athletes to enhance performance results. Anabolic steroid use has been associated with a condition known as *peliosis hepatitis*, in which blood-filled spaces in the liver are devoid of cells. Increased incidence of a rare form of liver cancer due to anabolic steroid use may also occur.

Classical Hepatotoxins

Various toxins are known to cause liver disease in a predictable manner. Toxins that damage the liver are referred to as *hepatotoxins* or *hepatotoxic substances*. The most dramatic hepatotoxins are those that cause severe acute disease or fulminant hepatic failure. A classic example is *Amanita phalloides* mushrooms, also known as *death caps*, which can cause fulminant hepatic failure. Another classic example is ingestion of carbon tetrachloride, which used to be present in cleaning fluids and can cause sudden hepatic necrosis and fulminant hepatic failure.

Pyrrolizidine causes liver veno-occlusive disease similar to that caused by various cancer chemotherapeutic agents. Pyrrolizidine toxicity is perhaps most commonly caused by traditional medicines or bush teas prepared in the West Indies. Pyrrolizidine poisoning is not uncommon in Jamaica, where medicinal bush teas prepared from poisonous plants are sometimes given to children.

Although virtually nonexistent in the U.S. food supply, aflatoxins are a common cause of chronic liver disease in other parts of the world, especially tropical regions. Aflatoxins are produced by a mold that is a contaminant of a variety of nuts (most commonly peanuts), beans, and grains. Chronic aflatoxin ingestion can cause cirrhosis. Of most concern throughout the world is the role that chronic ingestion of aflatoxins and their metabolites have in the development of hepatocellular carcinoma (primary liver cancer).

8

Fatty Liver

THE TERMS *fatty liver* and *steatosis* have traditionally been used to describe a pathological observation and not a disease per se. In response to various insults, fat accumulates in the hepatocytes in either large droplets (macrovesicular) or tiny droplets (microvesicular). This can readily be seen on liver biopsy. Some of the causes of fat accumulation in hepatocytes are listed in Table 8.1.

In recent years, nonalcoholic fatty liver disease, or NAFLD, has been used to describe the condition in which fat accumulates in the liver from causes other than alcohol (or other drugs). In the United States, this occurs most frequently in adults who are obese, diabetic, or both. It also can occur sometimes in children. For adults, overweight and obesity ranges are most often determined by using weight and height to calculate a number called the *body mass index*, or BMI, (BMI = [weight in kilograms] ÷ [height in meters squared]). For most people, BMI correlates with their amount of body fat. An adult who has a BMI between 25 and 29.9 is considered overweight; an adult who has a BMI of 30 or higher is considered obese. Given the high prevalence of obesity, nonalcoholic fatty liver disease is an increasingly recognized condition among Americans.

Nonalcoholic fatty liver disease is actually a spectrum of pathological conditions. At one end of the spectrum is the simple accumulation

Table 8.1 Causes of Steatosis or Fatty Liver

Macrovesicular Steatosis	Excessive alcohol consumption
	Obesity
	Diabetes mellitus
	Malnutrition
	After intestinal bypass surgery
	Total parenteral nutrition
	Idiopathic (cause not known)
Microvesicular Steatosis	Reye syndrome
	Fatty liver of pregnancy
	Sometimes with excessive alcohol consumption
	Drugs (common ones include tetracycline and valproic acid)
	Rare inherited metabolic diseases
	Jamaican vomiting sickness (caused by a toxin from the unripened fruit of the ackee tree)

of fat in hepatocytes (steatosis). At the other end of the spectrum is cirrhosis, which can occur after years of fatty accumulation plus inflammation. The condition in which fat accumulation is associated with varying degrees of inflammation (hepatitis) and fibrosis (scarring) is known as *nonalcoholic steatohepatitis* (NASH). While steatosis, or simple accumulation of fat in the liver, generally does not progress to cirrhosis, NASH can. An individual who at one point in time has steatosis can potentially have NASH at another time. Having NASH for many years is likely the major cause of so-called "cryptogenic" cirrhosis, or cirrhosis in which the diagnosis cannot readily be established. This is because once a patient develops cirrhosis from NASH, fat may disappear from the liver cells.

Patients with nonalcoholic fatty liver disease usually do not have symptoms or physical signs of liver disease. Abnormalities usually detected by routine blood tests, or tests performed to evaluate other conditions, are often the first indications of fatty liver. Patients with fatty liver almost always have some degree of insulin resistance and, as a result, are usually obese and/or have type II diabetes mellitus. (Type II diabetes generally begins in adulthood and is associated with insulin resistance and often obesity.)

Diagnosis

When a patient is found to have elevated alanine aminotransferase (ALT) and aspartate aminotransferase (AST) activities in blood tests, the first questions a doctor asks usually concern alcohol use. The initial appropriate blood tests are for hepatitis B surface antigen and antibodies against the hepatitis C virus in order to exclude chronic viral hepatitis. If investigation reveals no history of excessive alcohol consumption and no evidence of hepatitis B or hepatitis C virus infection, fatty liver is often suspected. Drugs, metabolic disorders, and autoimmune hepatitis should also be excluded as possibilities when appropriate. The diagnosis of nonalcoholic fatty liver disease is more strongly suspected in individuals who are obese or have diabetes mellitus.

Many doctors will perform an ultrasound examination on patients with elevated blood ALT and AST activities even though there are few, if any, conditions that cause asymptomatic elevations in these lab tests that can be diagnosed by this procedure. However, as fat has a different ultrasound density than normal liver tissue, the presence of fat in the liver can be suggested by ultrasound examination. But the detection of fat density on ultrasound examination cannot clearly establish the presence of fat in hepatocytes. In addition, ultrasound cannot distinguish between simple steatosis and NASH. Furthermore, in some patients with steatosis or NASH, the ultrasound examination will frequently be normal. Ultrasound and other radiological tests such as a CAT scan are not reliable or precise tests for the diagnosis of fatty liver. While they may suggest the presence of fatty liver, definitive diagnosis and a distinction of steatosis versus NASH can only be made by liver biopsy.

A doctor usually suspects nonalcoholic fatty liver when:

1. The patient has elevated ALT and/or AST activities on blood tests.
2. The patient does not drink significant amounts of alcohol and does not take medications that can affect the liver.
3. The patient is usually (not always) overweight or obese and/or suffers from type II diabetes mellitus.
4. Hepatitis B and hepatitis C virus infections are reliably excluded by history and laboratory testing.

5. Metabolic and autoimmune liver diseases are unlikely based upon history and, if necessary, the results of laboratory testing.
6. An ultrasound examination is done and may or may not be consistent with fatty infiltration of the liver.

At this point, what will most doctors do? And what should be done? As in many other areas of medicine, there are no absolute right or wrong answers.

One important consideration is whether elevations in the blood ALT and/or AST activities have persisted for more than six months. In patients who come to the doctor for the first time with only modest elevations in the aminotransferase activities, when other causes of liver disease have already been reliably excluded, it is reasonable to perform repeat blood testing six months later. If physical examination and/or laboratory tests such as bilirubin, albumin, and prothrombin time suggest abnormal liver function, however, liver biopsy should probably be performed sooner.

What if the patient has had elevations in blood ALT and AST activities for six months or longer? If the diagnosis of fatty liver is strongly suspected on clinical grounds, for example, if the patient is obese and/or suffers from diabetes, many doctors will defer liver biopsy and say that the patient has fatty liver. But the diagnosis can be suspected but not diagnosed conclusively without performing a liver biopsy. For these reasons, most liver specialists would probably perform liver biopsies in a patient suspected of having fatty liver to definitely establish the diagnosis.

There are three reasons why liver biopsy is critical in the evaluation of patients with suspected fatty liver. First, it is the only way to definitively establish the diagnosis. Second, it is necessary to exclude other possible conditions that were deemed to be unlikely based on history, physical examination, and laboratory testing. Even in patients in whom fatty liver is strongly suspected, another diagnosis will sometimes be discovered by liver biopsy. Third, liver biopsy is the only way to distinguish between steatosis and NASH (and sometimes cirrhosis caused by having NASH). This is a critical distinction. NASH carries a worse prognosis than steatosis. Patients with steatosis probably do not have progressive liver disease. However, NASH can progress to cirrhosis and can be diagnosed only by liver biopsy. It is important to note that a doctor cannot state that you have NASH without doing a biopsy.

To summarize some of the major points about fatty liver and its diagnosis:

1. The most common causes of fatty liver (excluding excessive alcohol consumption) are obesity and type II diabetes mellitus. It can occur in individuals without these conditions, however.
2. Fatty liver can be suspected but not definitively diagnosed without performing a liver biopsy.
3. Fatty liver can be definitively diagnosed only by liver biopsy.
4. The distinction between steatosis and NASH can be made only by liver biopsy.

Treatment

Unfortunately, no prospective randomized studies exist that prove any potential treatment to be effective for nonalcoholic fatty liver disease. Based on clinical experience and common sense, however, it is likely that several reasonable interventions will cure or improve steatosis and NASH. The basic logical treatment is to remove the underlying cause of fatty infiltration and lessen exposure to things that can worsen it. This includes:

- Weight loss if obese or even if slightly overweight
- Better control of blood sugar if diabetic
- Low-fat diet
- Aerobic exercise
- Limitations on or avoidance of alcohol

Obese patients, or even only slightly overweight ones, should lose weight. In the experience of many liver specialists and in the results of small observation studies, weight loss has been shown to improve fatty liver based upon return of blood ALT and AST activities to normal. Weight loss is best achieved by a combination of diet and exercise; either one alone will not be as efficient.

Even in patients who are not overweight, or once a patient reaches ideal body weight, a low-fat diet and exercise should be continued. People who have, or have had, fatty liver are likely predisposed to it. Therefore, such individuals should pay careful attention to maintaining a low-fat intake and to burning off fats by aerobic exercise.

Alcohol is the major cause of fatty infiltration of the liver, and NASH appears identical to alcoholic hepatitis on liver biopsy. Patients with steatosis or NASH should limit alcohol intake, although there is no strict lower limit. Besides its direct effects on the liver, alcohol also contains needless calories that are best avoided. Patients with NASH should probably limit alcohol consumption to a very infrequent single drink (perhaps New Year's Eve or a major celebration). The fact that NASH and alcoholic hepatitis look so similar suggests that alcohol could worsen the condition.

Steatosis and NASH are often present in patients with diabetes mellitus, and diabetics whose blood sugars are less well controlled may be more likely to develop them. Therefore, tight control of blood sugars should be attempted in diabetics with fatty liver.

Overall, the prognosis for most patients with nonalcoholic fatty liver disease who have simple steatosis is quite good—from a strictly "liver point of view." However, steatosis may potentially turn into NASH if the patient accumulates more fat. And NASH can lead to cirrhosis. Therefore, patients with steatosis should make the necessary lifestyle changes to prevent this from occurring.

Nonalcoholic fatty liver disease is "treated" by maintaining an overall healthy lifestyle. Eating well, exercising, maintaining ideal body weight, and limiting alcohol intake will improve not only fatty liver but also, perhaps even more significantly, overall health. I often tell an obese patient with fatty liver that although the fat in the liver will probably not lead to significant liver disease, "you should think about what excessive fat in your body will do to your heart." Patients with fatty liver caused by obesity and poorly controlled diabetes are at increased risk for serious diseases such as heart attack, stroke, and, possibly, cancer. Obese patients with fatty liver who lead unhealthy lifestyles should consider fatty liver a warning sign for development of other serious diseases. They should heed this warning and start living healthier lives.

9

Autoimmune Liver Diseases

AUTOIMMUNE DISEASES are those in which tissue injury is caused by the person's own immune system attacking the body. Some autoimmune diseases, such as systemic lupus erythematosus, are systemic in that many different organs are attacked. Others are relatively organ-specific, including the liver diseases discussed in this chapter.

The causes of most autoimmune diseases, including those that affect the liver, are not known. It is not entirely clear why an individual's immune system will, all of a sudden, attack constituents of his or, more often, her own body. There are very likely genetic factors that predispose people to develop autoimmune diseases. Mutations in certain genes in mice are associated with autoimmune diseases, and autoimmune diseases tend to run in families. However, autoimmune diseases are not strictly inherited and a relative of someone with an autoimmune disease still will most likely not get the disease. It is also likely that environmental factors trigger autoimmune diseases in individuals who are genetically predisposed, but these factors have not been clearly identified.

Patients with autoimmune diseases may have specific antibodies in their blood against proteins, fats, or DNA inside their own cells. Antibodies that recognize constituents of a person's own body are known as *autoantibodies*. The recognized constituents are sometimes called *autoantigens*. Autoantibodies are often classified based on the part of the cell in which their autoantigens are localized, for example, as antinuclear antibodies (ANA) or antimitochondrial antibodies (AMA). In most cases, it is not clear how, or if, autoantibodies and the autoantigens they recognize contribute to the disease process. Nonetheless, disease-specific autoantibodies have tremendous utility as diagnostic markers, even if they do not cause the disease being diagnosed. Blood testing for autoantibodies, therefore, often plays a critical role in the diagnosis of autoimmune diseases.

Three major liver diseases are considered to be autoimmune: autoimmune hepatitis, primary biliary cirrhosis (PBC), and primary sclerosing cholangitis (PSC). In autoimmune hepatitis, the immune response is directed against the hepatocytes and the clinical picture is that of hepatitis. In PBC, the immune response is directed against the smallest bile ducts within the liver and the clinical picture is related to their inflammation and obstruction. In PSC, the immune response is against the bile ducts inside and outside the liver and the illness manifests with symptoms attributable to bile duct obstruction.

Autoimmune Hepatitis

Autoimmune hepatitis was first described as "lupoid hepatitis." This term should no longer be used. The term *lupoid* is especially confusing because there is no relationship between autoimmune hepatitis and systemic lupus erythematosus. Autoimmune hepatitis affects primarily women. About 80 percent of affected individuals are women, usually between the ages of fifteen and forty. More rarely, autoimmune hepatitis affects both much older and much younger individuals.

Although it is a chronic disease, when many patients first seek medical attention they are acutely ill with jaundice, fever, symptoms of severe liver dysfunction, and a picture that sometimes can even resemble fulminant hepatic failure. Other patients may first come to medical attention because of nonspecific symptoms or blood test abnormalities suggestive of chronic hepatitis. In addition to liver disease, some patients with autoimmune hepatitis also suffer from fever, joint aches, muscle pains, fluid accumulation in various parts of the body, and low platelet counts. Other patients already have cirrhosis when they are first diagnosed with autoimmune hepatitis. If left untreated (or if it does not respond to therapy), autoimmune hepatitis can lead to severe liver failure before cirrhosis develops. Such patients may suffer from hepatitis for several months, or even weeks, and then develop liver failure and need liver transplantation to survive.

Diagnosis

Diagnosis of autoimmune hepatitis is made based upon a combination of clinical, laboratory, immunological, and pathological criteria. Autoimmune hepatitis should be suspected in any young patient—especially a woman—with clinical evidence of hepatitis. It should be suspected especially in individuals not abusing alcohol, not taking drugs, with no family history of metabolic liver disease, and with no evidence of viral hepatitis. Patients usually present with moderate to severe hepatitis; their alanine aminotransferase (ALT) and aspartate aminotransferase (AST) activities are elevated on blood tests. Some patients with relatively mild liver inflammation may have only laboratory abnormalities when first examined. In some instances, patients with autoimmune hepatitis first come to doctors or emergency rooms with severe liver failure and hepatic encephalopathy that closely resembles fulminant hepatic failure. The blood ALT and AST activities will usually be markedly elevated, the bilirubin concentration high in these patients, and the prothrombin time prolonged.

Serum protein electrophoresis, which measures blood globulin concentrations, or other tests for blood immunoglobulin concentrations, plus testing for autoantibodies, are of central importance in diagnosing autoimmune hepatitis. Patients with one type of autoimmune hepatitis (type 1) have gamma-globulin concentrations more than twice normal and sometimes antinuclear antibodies and/or antismooth muscle antibodies in their blood. Patients with another type of autoimmune hepatitis (type 2) may have normal or only slightly elevated gamma-globulin concentrations but have antibodies against a particular cytochrome P450 protein that are called *anti-LKM antibodies* (liver kidney microsome). Patients with yet another type (type 3) have autoantibodies called *anti-SLA antibodies* (soluble liver antigen). This classification of autoimmune hepatitis into types 1, 2, and 3 is not really that important to patients; what is important is knowing that special blood tests for autoantibodies and gamma-globulin concentration are often very helpful in making the diagnosis.

Patients in whom a diagnosis of autoimmune hepatitis is suspected should have a liver biopsy. If immediate liver biopsy is contraindicated because of a prolonged prothrombin time or low platelet count, treatment should be started prior to biopsy if the diagnosis is likely based on clinical and laboratory criteria (e.g., a young woman with severe hepatitis, an elevated blood gamma-globulin concentration, and negative risk factors and blood tests for viral hepatitis). The patient will often improve rapidly with treatment, and biopsy should be performed to confirm the diagnosis when the prothrombin time and platelet count return to safe ranges. Certain features on liver biopsy strongly support the diagnosis of autoimmune hepatitis, including the presence of plasma cells, a type of white blood cell that secretes antibodies. In addition, liver biopsy is usually the only way to know with certainty if a patient with autoimmune hepatitis has cirrhosis.

A scoring system for diagnosis of autoimmune hepatitis has been devised in which certain diagnostic features are given points depending upon how suggestive they are for autoimmune hepatitis. Features with positive points include female sex, the presence of certain autoantibodies, a high concentration of gamma-globulin, negative tests for viral hepatitis, no excessive alcohol consumption, and certain findings on biopsy. Examples of diagnostic features given negative points are laboratory evidence of hepatitis C virus or hepatitis B virus infection. When these diagnostic features are scored and totaled, the diagnosis of autoimmune hepatitis is classified as unlikely, probable, or likely. It is not important for patients to know the details of the scoring system but to realize that the history and several different investigative measures are considered together in making the diagnosis. There is no one test for the diagnosis of autoimmune hepatitis.

Treatment

Steroids, usually prednisone or prednisolone, and azathioprine (Imuran) form the cornerstones of treatment for autoimmune hepatitis. These drugs suppress the immune system. Once the doctor is confident about the diagnosis, treatment should be started immediately. Some doctors start prednisone or prednisolone alone and others start aza-thioprine along with one of these. Usually, the steroid dose is higher if used alone.

About three-quarters of patients with autoimmune hepatitis respond rapidly to treatment based on improvement in symptoms and laboratory test results. Repeat liver biopsy, if performed, usually indi-cates tremendous resolution of inflammation. Once a patient responds, the steroid and/or azathioprine should be gradually tapered to the low-est possible dose that keeps ALT and AST activities normal or very near normal. Unfortunately, some patients will not have a good response to treatment no matter how much medication is used. Experimental ther-apies in the setting of approved clinical trials may be appropriate for these individuals.

Maintaining a patient on the lowest doses of prednisone and/or azathioprine to keep the disease under control is usually more trial and error than precise science. In some patients, all medications can be stopped after several months of treatment and the patient will not need any to keep ALT and AST normal. However, such patients can relapse and again have clinical or laboratory evidence of liver inflammation in the future. In other patients, a low dose of steroid, azathioprine, or both is necessary to keep disease activity under control. Some patients have a fluctuating course in which blood ALT activities increase and decrease over time. These patients may need slightly more medication at certain times to keep liver inflammation minimal and slightly less medication at other times. For these reasons, all patients with autoim-mune hepatitis should have follow-up visits regularly with a doctor experienced in treating this disease.

Over the long term, many patients with autoimmune hepatitis will develop cirrhosis despite having a response to treatment. Nonetheless, treatment is essential as the progression of disease can be rapid and dramatic without it, sometimes leading to liver failure. Treatment also will very likely significantly slow the progression of cirrhosis. Even patients who already have cirrhosis when first seeking medical care should be treated because stopping the inflammation will halt ongoing liver damage and the rapid development of complications or liver fail-ure. For patients with chronic autoimmune hepatitis who develop com-plications of cirrhosis or liver failure, liver transplantation is an effective procedure. The disease almost never recurs in the transplanted liver, possibly due in part to powerful drugs used to suppress the immune system to prevent transplant rejection.

Primary Biliary Cirrhosis

Generally referred to by doctors and patients as PBC, primary biliary cirrhosis was first described in the 1950s. Primary biliary cirrhosis is actually a misnomer for this disease. The defining abnormality in PBC is not biliary cirrhosis, which is a general term meaning cirrhosis resulting from bile duct disorders. However, after many years of having the disease, patients almost invariably end up with biliary cirrhosis. The defining pathological abnormality in PBC is inflammation of the smallest bile ducts in the liver. Dr. Hans Popper and Dr. Fenton Schaffner, who performed one of the first detailed pathological characterizations of PBC in the 1960s, proposed the name *nonsuppurative cholangitis* for this disease. This is a much better description of the characteristic pathological lesion of PBC that means inflammation of the bile duct (cholangitis) without pus (nonsuppurative). Unfortunately, this term never caught on, and *primary biliary cirrhosis*, or PBC, is the term now used by everyone.

PBC occurs worldwide, but its exact prevalence is not clear. Estimates are that about 150 to 400 of every million people have PBC. One thing is certain about who gets PBC: mostly women. Ninety percent of people with PBC are female.

PBC is diagnosed usually in middle-aged women. The examining doctors do not always immediately suspect PBC as a diagnosis. The presentation can vary. Very often, individuals with early PBC have few or no symptoms and the diagnosis is first suspected based on routine blood testing. Sometimes, patients will not see doctors until they have complications of cirrhosis. The following three hypothetical cases are typical of PBC.

• **Case 1.** A forty-year-old woman has been suffering from itching all over her body for the past several weeks. There is no rash. Various creams and over-the-counter remedies have not helped. She sees her doctor, who also cannot readily explain the itching. The doctor prescribes an antihistamine that still does not help. The patient returns a couple of weeks later with self-inflicted scratch marks all over her body. Before referring the patient to a dermatologist, her doctor performs several blood tests and finds the alkaline phosphatase activity to be markedly elevated. An ultrasound examination of the liver is performed that is normal. The patient is referred to a gastroenterologist who does a blood test for antimitochondrial antibodies, which comes back positive. A liver biopsy is performed that is consistent with PBC.

• **Case 2.** A forty-five-year-old woman who appears completely healthy is found to have elevated alkaline phosphatase and gamma-glutamyltranspeptidase (GGTP) activities on routine blood tests by her gynecologist. The gynecologist refers the patient to an internist who makes a provisional diagnosis of PBC based on clinical history and laboratory testing. She is then referred to a liver specialist who performs a liver biopsy that confirms the diagnosis.

• **Case 3.** A fifty-seven-year-old woman who has seen a doctor regularly for many years due to high blood pressure arrives at an emergency room complaining of increasing abdominal girth and yellow eyes. The emergency room doctor discovers ascites and finds blood bilirubin concentration and alkaline phosphatase activity to be elevated. The patient is admitted to the hospital for further evaluation. A keen young medical student assigned to her case orders all the right tests to make a provisional diagnosis of PBC (and the medical student later graduates with honors). A liver biopsy shows biliary cirrhosis.

The most common presentations of patients with PBC are similar to those described in Cases 1 and 2. A very typical example is that of a woman between the ages of forty and sixty who sees a doctor because of excessive itching (the medical term is *pruritus*). Cholestasis, or stagnation of bile in the bile ducts in the liver, is associated with retention in the body of unknown factors that can cause itching. The retained factor in the blood responsible for the itching is not bilirubin as itching can occur with normal blood bilirubin concentration.

Another very typical presentation of PBC is a woman who has no medical complaints but in whom elevated alkaline phosphatase activity is discovered on blood tests taken for other reasons. There are also less common examples of PBC. Sometimes, the patient does not see a doctor until the disease is fairly advanced. When the disease is more advanced, patients may see a doctor because of jaundice or complications of cirrhosis such as ascites (as described in Case 3). "Extrahepatic," or symptoms not related to the liver, are also sometimes experienced by individuals with PBC. Dry eyes and dry mouth, known in medical jargon as *sicca syndrome* or *Sjögren syndrome*, is a frequent complaint. Various rashes and other skin abnormalities sometimes occur. Bone loss or osteoporosis is also frequently experienced by women with PBC.

PBC is an invariably progressive disease that leads to cirrhosis and ultimately end-stage liver disease. All patients diagnosed with this disease will either develop cirrhosis or die of something else first. What is difficult to predict is the rate of progression to cirrhosis or liver failure in a given patient. Some patients will progress to end-stage cirrhosis just a few years after diagnosis, while others will not develop cirrhosis for twenty years or more. This variability may be due in part to the fact that patients may have the disease without symptoms for a number of years before being diagnosed. Predicting the progression of disease in a patient with PBC is critically important because it allows the doctor to know when referral for liver transplantation is necessary.

Several complex mathematical equations have been devised to predict the progression of patients with PBC. Perhaps the most famous is the so-called Mayo equation. These equations consider a wide range of laboratory parameters, symptoms, physical signs, and biopsy findings. Of all the parameters in these equations, the blood bilirubin concentration is probably the best predictor of disease progression if complications of cirrhosis that predict a rapidly deteriorating course are not yet present. Once the blood bilirubin concentration exceeds 6 milligrams per deciliter, the patient's life expectancy is about two years. Patients with rising bilirubin concentrations should be referred for liver transplant evaluation.

Diagnosis

Diagnosis of PBC depends upon a combination of historical, laboratory, immunological, and liver biopsy data. There is usually no one test that will definitively diagnose PBC, but the presence of antimitochondrial antibodies is extremely suggestive. In rare cases, a unique lesion of lymphocytic cells attacking a small bile duct ("florid duct lesion") can be seen on liver biopsy that is diagnostic. In general, the liver biopsy is consistent with PBC but not conclusively diagnostic.

Clinical criteria are important in diagnosing PBC. If clinical signs and symptoms are not compatible, the diagnosis should be suspect. A diagnosis of PBC in a man also deserves careful scrutiny, but it can occur. Other conditions that can cause biliary disease, including drugs, should be excluded by history.

Blood tests virtually always indicate elevations in alkaline phosphatase and GGTP activities. The AST and ALT activities are usually normal or slightly above normal. The bilirubin and albumin concentrations and prothrombin time are normal early in the course and become abnormal as the disease progresses.

Immunological tests are of central importance to the diagnosis of PBC. More than 90 percent of patients will have antimitochondrial antibodies (AMA) in their blood. These antibodies recognize proteins in mitochondria, which are tiny membrane-bound organelles found in all cells. In the clinical laboratory, these autoantibodies are detected by a type of microscopy in which the part of the cell that contains the recognized autoantigen can be identified. This test is fairly effective for detection of antimitochondrial antibodies, but, in rare cases, it is falsely positive in patients who actually do not have them. Some laboratories may use a more specific test that directly determines if the patient's antibodies react with specific proteins present in mitochondria.

About 10 percent or less of patients with PBC do not have detectable antimitochondrial antibodies on blood testing. These patients are sometimes said to have "AMA-negative PBC" or "autoimmune cholangitis." If all other aspects of the history, laboratory test results, and liver biopsy findings point to the diagnosis, patients who are "AMA-negative" probably have PBC. I do not believe that patients with all other features of PBC but without detectable antimitochondrial antibodies should be considered as having some sort of special or distinct variant. It has not been demonstrated that so-called autoimmune cholangitis is a different disease than PBC. In fact, some studies have reported that when tests that are more sensitive than those used in most routine clinical laboratories are used to look for antimito-chondrial antibodies, about 99 percent of subjects with the diagnosis of PBC have them.

In addition to antimitochondrial antibodies, about 50 percent of patients with PBC will have autoantibodies against nuclei (antinuclear antibodies, or ANA). Except for certain antinuclear antibodies detected only in research laboratories, the presence of ANA is not specific for the diagnosis of PBC. ANA are found in a variety of autoimmune diseases, sometimes even in normal individuals. Their presence in the blood supports but does not make definitive the diagnosis of PBC.

More than 90 percent of patients with PBC have an elevation in the total IgM antibody concentration in their blood. This is not specific for PBC, but if present in someone with other criteria suggestive of the disease, an elevated blood IgM concentration supports the diagnosis. Conversely, the absence of an elevated IgM concentration should make any doctor question the diagnosis of PBC but not exclude it.

An important aspect of the diagnostic evaluation of PBC is liver biopsy. As mentioned previously, the liver biopsy is rarely definitively diagnostic for PBC. However, a diagnosis based on clinical, laboratory, and immunological parameters is strongly supported by a consistent biopsy. Pathologists will usually "stage" the liver biopsy in PBC. A stage 1 biopsy is the "florid bile duct lesion" of lymphocytic white blood cells attacking a small bile duct that is diagnostic for PBC. This lesion is usually not seen. A stage 2 biopsy in PBC shows ductular proliferation or many abnormal small bile ducts. A stage 3 biopsy in PBC shows fibrosis, and a stage 4 biopsy shows biliary cirrhosis. In general, the stages of the biopsy show a continuum of disease, from the least advanced (stage 1) to the most advanced (stage 4). As PBC can affect the liver in a nonuniform fashion, sometimes you will see two or more stages on the same biopsy, for example, ductular proliferation, or stage 2, and fibrosis, or stage 3. The stage of the biopsy in PBC correlates roughly to the rate of disease progression. It is not a precise predictor, however, and there are other criteria that better predict a patient's rate of progression to end-stage liver disease.

In summary, the diagnosis of PBC is made by a combination of clinical, laboratory, immunological, and biopsy criteria. There is rarely one diagnostic test result. Supreme Court Associate Justice Potter Stewart once said in an opinion on a case involving pornography: "I know it when I see it." The same can be said by an experienced liver specialist about PBC.

Treatment

Ursodiol (Actigall or Urso), a bile acid, has been shown to improve the blood test results and clinical symptoms in patients with PBC. The results of some studies also indicate that ursodiol slows progression of the disease. Ursodiol is not a "cure" for PBC, but it may significantly slow disease progression. It is a very safe drug with few side effects. For these reasons, all patients with PBC should probably receive ursodiol as there are benefits and the attendant risks are low. The recommended dose for patients with PBC is 13 to 15 milligrams per kilogram of body weight a day. Despite extensive study, no other medical therapies have been shown to conclusively slow progression of PBC. Notably, steroids may be detrimental. Other drugs are being investigated in clinical trials.

Osteoporosis (loss of bone) is a common complication of PBC. This results, in part, from bile duct damage that causes decreased absorption of fat-soluble vitamins including vitamin D, which is necessary for adequate calcium absorption and bone formation. Patients with PBC, most of whom are women and at a generally increased risk for development of osteoporosis, should probably take supplemental calcium and multivitamins that include vitamin D to prevent bone loss. There are no serious risks to this treatment, and it may reduce osteoporosis, which in later life can be devastating.

Itching can be incapacitating in some patients with PBC. This condition often responds to treatment with a bile acid-binding resin such as cholestyramine. This is a powder mixed with water and consumed as a suspension. If itching does not respond to treatment with cholestyramine, some studies suggest that opioid antagonists (drugs that counter the affects of opiates) such as naltrexone may help. Sometimes, a drug called *rifampin* may help.

Patients with PBC must realize that the disease invariably progresses, sometimes over a time period of many years. Many younger individuals will probably require liver transplants at some time in their lives barring better treatments being developed. Older patients may die with, but not from, PBC. Liver transplantation is remarkably effective for patients with PBC. The key is for the doctor to refer the patient for transplantation at the correct time. Anyone with complications of cirrhosis such as ascites or bleeding esophageal varices should be referred to a transplantation center for evaluation. Most patients, however, do not develop these complications until late in the course of disease. As mentioned, one of the best predictors of progression is blood bilirubin concentration. Once total bilirubin concentration in the blood begins to rise, certainly by the time it reaches 4 milligrams per deciliter, the patient should be referred for liver transplant evaluation. As in all chronic liver disease, no single parameter substitutes for follow-up by an experienced specialist.

Primary Sclerosing Cholangitis

Primary sclerosing cholangitis is often referred to as PSC. It is a chronic liver disease characterized by inflammation, destruction, and fibrosis of the large bile ducts within the liver, as well as the bile ducts outside the liver. The cause of PSC is unknown, but most investigators agree that it is an autoimmune disease. Other causes, such as infectious agents, toxins, or recurrent infections of the bile ducts, have not been absolutely excluded. The worldwide prevalence of PSC is approximately three in one hundred thousand individuals. In contrast to PBC and autoimmune hepatitis and most other autoimmune diseases that primarily affect women, about 70 percent of patients with PSC are men. The strong association of PSC with inflammatory bowel disease also suggests it is an autoimmune disorder. About 75 percent of patients with PSC have inflammatory bowel disease, mainly ulcerative colitis.

Inflammation of the larger bile ducts in PSC can lead to strictures, or narrowing. Sometimes, bile can get plugged in these strictures, resulting in acute and almost complete blockage of bile flow. In such instances, patients will develop jaundice. These recurrent bouts of bile duct obstruction, along with destruction of bile ducts within the liver, eventually lead to biliary cirrhosis in most patients. Patients with PSC also often have recurrent episodes of bacterial cholangitis, which is an infection of the bile ducts with bacteria. Patients with bacterial cholangitis usually experience jaundice, fever, and right upper quadrant abdominal pain. In some patients, recurrent episodes of bacterial cholangitis, which can be fatal, are a very significant problem before cirrhosis develops. In other patients, bacterial cholangitis is not a frequent problem. Patients with PSC also bear an increased risk of cholangiocarcinoma, or primary bile duct cancer. The average survival, or time until liver transplantation, in patients with PSC is around ten years from time of diagnosis.

Diagnosis

Many patients with PSC are identified by discovering elevated alkaline phosphatase and GGTP activities in blood tests taken for other reasons. This testing may be part of an evaluation for inflammatory bowel disease, from which most patients with PSC also suffer. Some patients first see doctors because of itching, jaundice, fatigue, fever, weight loss, or signs of complications from cirrhosis. Others go to their doctors for the first time with signs and symptoms of bacterial cholangitis such as fever, chills, and right upper quadrant abdominal pain.

Blood tests for PSC virtually always indicate elevated alkaline phosphatase and GGTP activities, with lesser or no elevations in the aminotransferase activities. Early in the course of disease, the bilirubin concentration is usually normal or slightly elevated, but it becomes markedly elevated late in the course of disease. Large fluctuations in blood bilirubin concentrations can also occur, even early in the disease, as a result of intermittent bile duct obstructions or bacterial cholangitis. Both albumin concentration and prothrombin time are normal in the disease's early stage. Later, when cirrhosis develops, albumin concentration falls and prothrombin time can be prolonged. The prothrombin time can also be prolonged prior to the development of cirrhosis secondary to decreased vitamin K absorption, in which case it will correct with the injection of vitamin K.

Immunological abnormalities are often, but not invariably, detectable in patients with PSC. None of them is specific to the diagnosis. About 30 percent of affected individuals have elevated blood gamma-globulin concentrations and about half have elevated total blood IgM concentrations. A majority of patients have a particular type of autoantibody known (probably incorrectly) as *antineutrophil cytoplasmic antibodies*, or ANCA. These autoantibodies should really be called "atypical ANCA," as they are really very different than the ANCA that are specific for certain vasculitic diseases. Atypical ANCA can also be detected in patients with inflammatory bowel disease without PSC. Some patients with PSC also may have antismooth muscle or antinuclear antibodies.

The gold standard diagnostic test for PSC is endoscopic retrograde cholangiopancreatography (ERCP). The findings include strictures and dilatations of the medium-sized and large bile ducts inside and outside the liver. The characteristic pattern is often described as "beads on a string" caused by the alternating widening and narrowing of the bile ducts. The diagnosis may also be suggested on magnetic resonance cholangiopancreatography (MRCP). Liver biopsy in PSC is usually confirmatory but rarely diagnostic. Sometimes, a very characteristic finding known as an "onion skin" lesion (layers of fibrosis tissue surrounding a bile duct) is seen on liver biopsy. Liver biopsy in PSC is also important in determining if the patient has cirrhosis.

Secondary causes of sclerosing cholangitis must be ruled out when making the diagnosis of PSC. These secondary causes include some drugs, bile duct cancers, and past biliary tree surgery. Infections of the bile ducts with cytomegalovirus (CMV) and *Crytosporidia* in patients with AIDS can also result in a picture similar to PSC. The causes of secondary sclerosing cholangitis usually can be eliminated based on patient history, physical examination, and appropriate laboratory tests.

Treatment

Current medical therapy does not have a significant impact on PSC. Ursodiol (Actigall or Urso) may improve laboratory test results, but studies have demonstrated that it does not prolong survival until liver transplantation is necessary. Treatment in patients with PSC is directed at complications. Itching can be treated with bile acid-binding resins such as cholestyramine and, possibly, the opioid antagonist naltrexone. Deficiencies in fat-soluble vitamins, such as vitamin K and vitamin D, are treated by supplementation.

Episodes of bacterial cholangitis can be life-threatening, and immediate antibiotic therapy in the hospital is necessary. There may be some role for dilatation of dominant bile duct strictures by ERCP in some cases of PSC, but there have been no controlled trials proving that this is effective. If such a procedure is recommended, a physician with considerable experience in treating patients with PSC should be consulted.

Inappropriate or improperly performed procedures to dilate the bile ducts can be dangerous and lead to additional damage, worsening the patient's prognosis. As there is an increased incidence of cholangio-carcinoma in patients with PSC, this should always be suspected, especially in patients with long-standing disease whose condition worsens. Therefore, ERCP, MRCP, or CAT scan to look for bile duct cancer may be necessary in a patient whose condition deteriorates.

Liver transplantation is highly effective in the treatment of patients with advanced liver disease caused by PSC. Indications for liver transplantation are complications of cirrhosis. In some cases, patients with PSC and recurrent, life-threatening episodes of bacterial cholangitis, even without cirrhosis, warrant consideration for liver transplantation.

10

Inherited Liver Diseases

SOME DISEASES RESULT from alterations in a single gene and are generally referred to as "inherited" or "genetic." They are also said to demonstrate Mendelian inheritance. The term *Mendelian* derives from the monk Gregor Mendel, who was the first person to describe single gene inheritance based on his work breeding pea plants (an excellent online database of human genetic disease is Dr. Victor McKusick's "Online Mendelian Inheritance in Man," which can be found at ncbi.nlm.nih.gov/entrez/query.fcgi?db=OMIM).

In genetic disorders, the normal gene is referred to as wild-type and the gene that causes the disease as mutant. In autosomal dominant disorders, affected individuals need possess only one mutant copy of the responsible gene to cause disease. In autosomal recessive disorders, an individual with the disease must have two copies of the mutant gene. Individuals with two copies of a mutant gene are said to be homozygotes. Individuals with one copy are heterozygotes, or "carriers." Some genetic diseases are passed on by mutant genes on the X chromosome. In mammals, females have two X chromosomes and males only one. Therefore, in X-linked recessive disorders, men need have only one copy of a mutant gene to have a disease while women need to have two.

The most important inherited liver diseases are autosomal recessive. Therefore, a brief discussion on their pattern of inheritance is warranted. If a heterozygote, or carrier, breeds with an individual with two wild-type genes, none of the offspring will have the disease but 50 percent of the offspring will be carriers of the mutant gene. If two carriers breed, 50 percent of the offspring will be carriers, with 25 percent having the disease and 25 percent having two copies of the wild-type gene. If an individual with the disease breeds with a carrier, 50 percent of the offspring will be carriers and 50 percent will have the disease. If breeding takes place between two individuals with the disease, 100 percent of the offspring will have the disease. If someone with the disease breeds with a normal individual, all the offspring will be carriers. These situations are outlined schematically in Figure 10.1.

A detailed discussion of all inherited diseases that affect the liver is beyond the scope of this book. This chapter will address the "big three": hereditary hemochromatosis, alpha-1-antitrypsin deficiency, and Wilson disease. A brief discussion of congenital disorders of biliary metabolism and inherited cholestatic disorders is also included as is a discussion of Gilbert syndrome, which is not really a disease but a very common inherited condition that causes elevated unconjugated bilirubin concentrations in the blood and sometimes jaundice. For additional details on these conditions, and for information on the more esoteric genetic liver diseases not discussed in this book, refer to "Online Mendelian Inheritance in Man."

Figure 10.1 Inheritance Patterns in Autosomal Recessive Genetic Disease

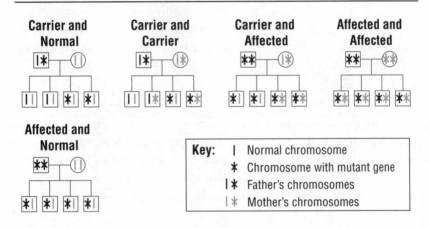

Hemochromatosis

Hereditary hemochromatosis, or primary hemochromatosis, is the most common inherited disease in persons of European descent. It occurs in three to five people in every one thousand. About one in ten individuals are carriers who possess one copy of the mutant gene. People with hereditary hemochromatosis have increased absorption of iron, resulting in excess iron deposition in the liver, heart, joints, and other organs. This abnormal accumulation of iron can cause cirrhosis, heart disease, arthritis, diabetes mellitus, pituitary gland abnormalities, and a bronze coloring of the skin.

The problem with hemochromatosis is that in most cases, the disease is not diagnosed until complications develop. Most individuals will have high body iron for many years without symptoms. Men usually seek medical attention with symptoms earlier in life than women because younger women constantly lose iron during menstruation. Many patients have cirrhosis of unclear cause until a liver biopsy indicates increased iron content. Sometimes, patients will present with complications from iron deposition in other organs. These complications, such as arthritis, diabetes, or heart disease, may occur along with, or independently from, liver disease.

The diagnosis of hereditary hemochromatosis is suspected from the results of blood tests suggesting elevated body iron concentrations. There are three simple blood tests related to iron metabolism: iron, transferrin saturation, and ferritin. Elevations in these, especially elevations in both transferrin saturation and ferritin together, suggest, but are not specific for, hemochromatosis. A diagnosis of hereditary hemochromatosis is usually made by liver biopsy and determination of liver iron content. The doctor should send a sample of liver tissue obtained from the biopsy for measurement of iron content. In hereditary hemochromatosis, the liver iron content is significantly elevated.

For many years, it was known that the gene responsible for hereditary hemochromatosis was on chromosome 6. In 1996, scientists at the biotechnology company Mercator Genetics identified a candidate gene for hemochromatosis on this chromosome. They initially called this gene *HLA-H*, but *HFE* is now the official name for this gene. It appears that about 90 percent of individuals with hereditary hemochromatosis have the same mutation in the *HFE* gene, which can be detected in the clinical laboratory.

The genetic test for mutations in the *HFE* gene now plays an important role in diagnosing carriers and patients with hereditary hemochromatosis. It is especially important in screening the children, brothers, and sisters of patients with the disease, as they are also at risk. Some doctors may argue that liver biopsy is not essential if hereditary hemochromatosis is diagnosed by genetic testing. Others will state that biopsy is still necessary to establish the extent of liver disease and the presence or absence of cirrhosis. No conclusive studies have been completed assessing the need for liver biopsies in patients in whom hereditary hemochromatosis is diagnosed using the genetic test.

There is an effective treatment for hereditary hemochromatosis if the disease is diagnosed early. As the damage to organs in hemochromatosis results from excessive iron deposition, lowering the body's total iron load will prevent it. The treatment, therefore, is blood letting or, in medical terminology, phlebotomy. Repeated phlebotomy is performed to reduce the red blood cell count to a level slightly below normal. The level is then maintained there by periodic repeat phlebotomies. If hereditary hemochromatosis is diagnosed early, phlebotomy is extremely effective in preventing ensuing complications. Unfortunately, hereditary hemochromatosis is frequently not diagnosed until it is rather late and organ damage, such as cirrhosis, has already occurred.

Secondary hemochromatosis is a condition that mimics hereditary hemochromatosis. Secondary hemochromatosis results from iron deposition in the body, including the liver, secondary to nongenetic causes. A common cause is repeated blood transfusions over many years, as may be necessary in individuals with blood diseases such as thalassemias. Some individuals with alcoholic liver disease also develop secondary hemochromatosis for unclear reasons.

Alpha-1-Antitrypsin Deficiency

Inherited deficiency of the protein alpha-1-antitrypsin, which is synthesized in the liver and secreted into the blood, can cause lung and liver disease. The major function of alpha-1-antitrypsin in the body is to inhibit the function of an enzyme known as *elastase*. Elastase breaks down a structural component of the lungs known as *elastin*. If its activity is not partially inhibited by alpha-1-antitrypsin in the body, excessive lung damage and emphysema may occur.

Certain mutations in the gene for alpha-1-antitrypsin lead to production of an abnormal form that is not properly secreted from liver cells. The mutant form of alpha-1-antitrypsin that causes this abnormality is known as the Z *mutation*. In individuals who have inherited two abnormal Z genes, about 85 percent of synthesized alpha-1-antitrypsin accumulates in hepatocytes and forms aggregates. Retained aggregates of the Z form of alpha-1-antitrypsin in the liver can cause hepatitis and eventually cirrhosis.

Between 12 and 15 percent of individuals who have inherited two abnormal alpha-1-antitrypsin Z genes develop liver disease. About 10 percent develop cirrhosis in early infancy or early childhood. The remainder are first diagnosed with chronic liver disease as adults. Patients with the Z form mutation are generally not at increased risk for lung disease because the little bit of alpha-1-antitrypsin that makes it into their blood inhibits elastase. On the other hand, people with other mutant forms of alpha-1-antitrypsin get lung disease because either an inactive form is secreted from the liver or none is made at all. These people, however, do not get liver disease because these other mutant forms do not accumulate in the liver.

The diagnosis of alpha-1-antitrypsin deficiency is made by measuring the amount of alpha-1-antitrypsin in the blood. Patients with two abnormal Z genes have blood concentrations about 15 percent normal. To distinguish the Z mutation from other mutations with decreased amounts of blood alpha-1-antitrypsin, a genetic test is available to directly detect the mutation in the alpha-1-antitrypsin gene. This test can be used to diagnose the condition prenatally if a mother is at risk for passing on the disease to her baby. Abnormal accumulation of alpha-1-antitrypsin can also be observed on liver biopsy in patients with two abnormal Z genes.

Liver transplantation is the only means of treatment for liver disease caused by alpha-1-antitrypsin deficiency. Transplantation is performed when complications of cirrhosis develop.

Wilson Disease

Wilson disease is an inherited disorder that primarily affects the brain and liver. Patients suffer from neurological, psychiatric, blood, and/or liver problems. The Wilson disease gene encodes a protein that transports copper in or out of cells. In individuals with two mutant forms of this gene, copper accumulates in the liver, brain, and other organs. There is decreased secretion of copper into the bile and increased excretion of copper in the urine. About 85 percent of patients with Wilson disease also have low levels of ceruloplasmin, a copper-binding protein that circulates in the blood.

The age of onset of symptoms in patients with Wilson disease varies considerably. About 50 percent of patients develop symptoms by age fifteen. Almost all have symptoms by the time they are age forty. Very rarely, patients with Wilson disease may not have symptoms until they are in their fifties. About half of patients first seek medical attention because of liver disease, about one-quarter with neurological symptoms, about 15 percent with blood problems, and 10 percent with psychiatric abnormalities.

Neurological symptoms usually appear in adolescents and young adults. At first, they are very subtle. A common initial presentation is deteriorating performance in school not related to an intellectual deficiency. More obvious symptoms include lack of coordination, tremors, clumsiness, and difficulty walking. Wilson disease can also lead to the development of debilitating nerve and muscle abnormalities and seizures. Psychiatric abnormalities predominate in some patients and include psychosis, manic-depression, aggressive behaviors, and dementia. These are usually diagnosed in teenagers who may be hospitalized in psychiatric institutions before the diagnosis of Wilson disease is made.

About 15 percent of patients with Wilson disease present with blood abnormalities. The blood disorder in Wilson disease is intravascular hemolysis, which is destruction of red blood cells within the bloodstream. Hemolysis is usually of sudden onset and can be very serious and even life-threatening. More often, it is transient and resolves spontaneously.

Liver involvement in Wilson disease can mimic many other disorders. Patients can display signs and symptoms of chronic or acute hepatitis. Some have clinical symptoms resembling fulminant hepatic failure. Others first seek medical care with cirrhosis. Most common are patients with Wilson disease whose illness resembles chronic hepatitis that progresses to cirrhosis over several years.

Wilson disease should be suspected in all young individuals who present with liver disease, especially if there is a family history of liver disease, neurological, or psychiatric disorders. Several tests are used to establish the diagnosis. Most patients have a characteristic physical sign known as a *Kayser-Fleischer ring*. These are brownish discolorations of the part of the cornea (surface of the eye) surrounding the iris (the part of the eye that is colored). They result from abnormal copper deposition. An ophthalmologist or optometrist can see them using a slit-lamp. Kayser-Fleischer rings are almost always present in patients with both Wilson disease and neurological symptoms but may not be present in patients suffering from liver disease only.

In blood tests, the diagnosis of Wilson disease is suspected due to low ceruloplasmin concentration, which is found in about 85 percent of individuals with the disease. A low blood ceruloplasmin concentration in a person with Kayser-Fleischer rings essentially confirms the diagnosis of Wilson disease. The amount of copper in a twenty-four-hour urine sample also is elevated in patients with Wilson disease. It also may be elevated in individuals with cirrhosis from other causes. All untreated patients having Wilson disease exhibit significantly elevated concentrations of liver copper; however, this also may be observed in patients with other forms of liver disease. Nonetheless, measurement of liver copper content in tissue obtained at liver biopsy is an important test to establish the diagnosis. Liver biopsy, of course, will also establish the extent of liver damage.

Genetic tests for Wilson disease are available in research laboratories only. Because many different mutations in the Wilson disease gene can cause the condition, the entire gene may have to be sequenced (unless the specific mutation in a family member is known). This makes genetic testing laborious at the present time. If the particular mutation in an individual is known, genetic testing of family members becomes somewhat easier.

Drugs that prevent the accumulation of copper in the body are effective treatments for Wilson disease. D-penicillamine and trientine bind to copper and help remove it from the body by enhancing urinary excretion. Zinc acetate blocks the absorption of copper and increases copper excretion in the stool. As it causes no serious side affects, it is often the preferred treatment. Tetrathiomolybdate is an experimental drug that is also effective in treating Wilson disease.

Treatment of Wilson disease can reverse neurological and psychiatric symptoms and some aspects of liver damage. If the disease is diagnosed in an asymptomatic person, such as a family member of someone with Wilson disease, all complications and symptoms can be prevented if the individual starts and continues on drug therapy. Sometimes, patients with Wilson disease have cirrhosis and end-stage liver disease. In these cases, liver transplantation may be necessary. Liver transplantation may also be effective in sudden-onset liver failure caused by Wilson disease.

Congenital Disorders of Bilirubin Metabolism

Several inherited diseases affect the metabolism of bilirubin in the liver. Most are very rare abnormalities resulting from either the defective conjugation of bilirubin or the abnormal secretion of conjugated bilirubin into the bile. The first type causes elevations in unconjugated bilirubin, and the second type causes elevations in conjugated bilirubin in the blood. These disorders usually appear as jaundice at birth. A detailed discussion of each is beyond the scope of this book, but some of the better known of these "classical" (just about every medical student hears about them at least once) inherited liver diseases are explained in Table 10.1.

Congenital Cholestatic Disorders

Mutations in genes encoding proteins involved in bile formation and transport of bile through the bile ducts can cause cholestasis (stagnation of bile flow). Benign recurrent intrahepatic cholestasis (BRIC), or Summerskill syndrome, is caused by mutations in a gene on chromo-

Table 10.1 Rare Inherited Disorders of Bilirubin Metabolism That Cause Jaundice

Impaired Conjugation of Bilirubin

Crigler-Najjar Syndrome Type 1	Results from absent activity of the enzyme that conjugates bilirubin to its glucuronide form. Inherited in an autosomal recessive manner. May be fatal in childhood without liver transplantation.
Crigler-Najjar Syndrome Type 2	Results from decreased activity of the enzyme that conjugates bilirubin to its glucuronide form. Autosomal recessive inheritance. Serum bilirubin concentrations usually range from 8 to 20 mg/dl. Patients generally do well except for being jaundiced.

Impaired Secretion of Bilirubin

Dubin-Johnson Syndrome	Results from mutations in a protein that transports conjugated bilirubin out of hepatocytes and into the bile. Inherited in an autosomal recessive manner. Very rare except in Persian Jews, where it is seen in 1 in 1,300 individuals. A dark pigment found in hepatocytes. Generally benign course.
Rotor Syndrome	Autosomal recessive inheritance. Very rare. Cause not clear. Benign course.

some 18, known as *ATP8B1*, and can be inherited in an autosomal recessive or autosomal dominant manner. Benign recurrent intrahepatic cholestasis is characterized by intermittent episodes of cholestasis, often starting in childhood, which last for days or months. During these transient episodes, patients may suffer from itching and jaundice, which resolves spontaneously. Benign intrahepatic cholestasis does not cause lasting liver disease or cirrhosis.

Different mutations in ATP8B1 cause progressive familial intrahepatic cholestasis type 1 (PFIC1), also known as *Byler disease*. This autosomal recessive disease often presents as intermittent episodes of cholestasis in infancy but progresses to malnourishment, growth retardation, cirrhosis, and end-stage liver disease by childhood. A similar autosomal recessive disorder known as *progressive familial intrahep-*

atic cholestasis type 2 (PFIC2) is clinically similar to PFIC1 but caused by mutations in a gene on chromosome 2 encoding a protein called *BSEP*. Liver transplantation is usually ultimately necessary for patients with both types of progressive familial intrahepatic cholestasis.

Gilbert Syndrome

One very common inherited condition, usually diagnosed in adults or older children, is Gilbert syndrome. Gilbert syndrome is not a serious condition, but it is often of concern to individuals who have it. In addition, it sometimes leads to extensive and inappropriate testing by doctors.

Gilbert syndrome is not a disease but a normal variant in which patients have mildly elevated unconjugated bilirubin concentrations in their blood. They also may occasionally be jaundiced. These abnormalities are of no real clinical significance. Gilbert syndrome tends to run in families but does not always demonstrate strict Mendelian inheritance patterns.

Gilbert syndrome is probably caused by mildly decreased activity of the enzyme UDP-glucuronosyltransferase that catalyzes the conjugation of bilirubin in the liver. Subtle mutations in the regulatory region of the gene encoding this enzyme have been described. There may be other causes of Gilbert syndrome, such as decreased uptake of unconjugated bilirubin from the blood by hepatocytes. As a result of these abnormalities, the concentration of unconjugated bilirubin in the blood is abnormally elevated.

Gilbert syndrome is most frequently discovered when someone is found to have a slightly elevated total bilirubin concentration on blood tests taken for other reasons. The blood bilirubin concentration is usually less than 2 milligrams per deciliter and the individual is not jaundiced. The indirect (unconjugated) bilirubin concentration in the blood is elevated, but the conjugated (direct) bilirubin concentration is normal. Some people with Gilbert syndrome, however, may actually come to doctors because of jaundice, especially while suffering from an unrelated illness. This is because fasting, stress, and infections exacerbate the condition. In such instances, the blood bilirubin concentration may reach 6 milligrams per deciliter.

Gilbert syndrome is diagnosed by the characteristic elevation of the blood indirect bilirubin concentration with a normal direct bilirubin concentration in blood tests. However, similar laboratory test results can be seen in disorders in which bilirubin production is increased, such as those causing abnormal breakdown of red blood cells. Therefore, these should be excluded as a cause of the laboratory abnormality. Few, if any, acquired liver diseases in adults cause elevations of the indirect bilirubin with a normal direct bilirubin. This means that other blood tests related to the liver, such as the aminotransferase and alkaline phosphatase activities, should be normal. (However, Gilbert syndrome can occur in individuals with other liver diseases.) A diagnosis of Gilbert syndrome is further supported by an elevated blood indirect bilirubin concentration in a relative. If the diagnosis remains in question, phenobarbital, a drug that will decrease bilirubin concentration in an individual with Gilbert syndrome, can be given and the blood bilirubin concentration measured again.

An extensive search for structural liver disease is not necessary in individuals with Gilbert syndrome. Unfortunately, some doctors embark on costly and unnecessary evaluations. They sometimes even order CAT scans and ultrasound scans that are not indicated, as liver diseases detectable on these studies would cause elevations in the direct blood bilirubin concentration.

Individuals with Gilbert syndrome have normal life spans. They do not suffer from a disease, and no treatment is indicated.

11

Other Liver Disorders

THE LIVER can be affected by a wide variety of cancers, infections, and benign tumors or by disorders that affect the hepatic vein and heart. Disorders of the gallbladder and bile ducts can involve the liver. There are also liver diseases unique to pregnant women, infants, and young children. While an extensive review of all these liver disorders is beyond the scope of this book, some of the most important ones are discussed in this chapter.

Mass Lesions of the Liver: Cancers, Tumors, Cysts, and Abscesses

There are many different abnormal masses that can be present in the liver. These are most frequently discovered first as lesions on radiological tests such as ultrasound or CAT scans. Sometimes, these scans are ordered to evaluate patients with clinical signs of liver disease or due to blood test results that suggest liver problems. In other instances, lesions are found in the liver on radiological scans performed for other purposes, for example, an ultrasound examination done during pregnancy or to examine the gallbladder or kidneys.

Many people ask about "lesions on the liver" or "spots on the liver"—as if these are specific diseases. The term *lesion* (or *spot*) is a nonspecific, general term that refers to any abnormality seen on any radiological test. Radiological studies are definitive enough to diagnose only a few lesions seen in the liver. In most cases, radiological scans alone are not sufficient to determine what these lesions are, and tissue sampling, that is, biopsy, is necessary to make a diagnosis. This section includes some important points about cancers, other tumors, cysts, and abscesses that can be found in the liver.

Cancer

The term *liver cancer* really does not refer to a particular diagnosis. The reason is that many different cancers can affect the liver. Most "liver cancers" that people in the Western world refer to are cancers that originate in other organs and spread to the liver via the bloodstream. In the East, most liver cancers are just that, hepatocellular carcinomas that originate in the liver itself. This is a very important distinction.

Metastatic Cancer

Metastatic cancers are tumors that spread from the organ of origin to other nearby or distant sites. Because of its rich blood supply, the liver is a common site where cancer will spread. Malignant tumors arising in virtually any organ can spread to the liver. Some of the most common cancers that metastasize to the liver are those originating in the colon, pancreas, lung, and breast. These cancers are known as *carcinomas* because they arise in epithelial tissues. Lymphomas and leukemias, cancers that originate in the lymph nodes and bone marrow, respectively, can also invade the liver. So can sarcomas, which are cancers that originate in tissues such as muscle or cartilage.

Once a diagnosis of cancer metastatic to the liver is made, and the tissue of origin determined (usually requiring a biopsy at a specific site), treatment of metastatic liver cancer usually falls into the domain of an oncologist—a medical cancer specialist. Several different types of treatment may be offered. In some cases, procedures can be performed that relieve symptoms and, perhaps, prolong life. They are usually not curative. Chemotherapy can be instilled directly into the liver via an implanted pump. Surgeons can resect one or two isolated metastatic tumors. Large metastatic tumors can be treated by embolysis. In this procedure, a catheter is passed through the hepatic artery to vessels feeding the tumor, and drugs or other materials are injected to clot off the tumor's blood supply. Many experimental therapies for metastatic cancers are also under investigation in clinical trials at numerous medical schools and hospitals. Organizations such as the American Cancer Society (cancer.org) and the National Cancer Institute (nci.nih.gov) can provide information for patients and doctors interested in such trials.

Most patients with cancers that have metastasized to the liver have a very poor prognosis. Once a carcinoma has spread to the liver, the patient's life expectancy is usually a couple of years at most. A notable exception is testicular cancer, which is very responsive to chemotherapy and can be cured. Some types of lymphomas and leukemias that involve the liver also may respond very well to chemotherapy and be cured.

Primary Liver Cancer

There are two types of primary liver cancer; both cancers originate in the liver itself. Hepatocellular carcinoma is cancer that arises from hepatocytes. Intrahepatic cholangiocarcinoma is cancer that arises from bile duct cells within the liver. (Technically, these cancers may arise from "liver stem cells" that are normally destined to become either hepatocytes or bile ducts; this point has not been resolved.)

Hepatocellular carcinoma, although relatively rare in the United States, is either the number one or number two cause of cancer death worldwide (along with lung cancer). About 80 percent of people with hepatocellular carcinomas have cirrhosis. This type of cancer is especially common in parts of Asia and Africa where hepatitis B virus infection, which is a major risk factor, is endemic. Chronic hepatitis C virus infection is probably the next leading cause. As discussed in earlier chapters, patients chronically infected with hepatitis B virus and hepatitis C virus should have some type of periodic screening for hepatocellular carcinoma. Hepatocellular carcinoma may also develop in patients with cirrhosis from any cause. Aflatoxins have also been implicated as a major risk factor for causing hepatocellular carcinoma. Although virtually nonexistent in the United States, aflatoxins, which are produced by a mold that is a contaminant of nuts (most commonly peanuts), grains, and beans, are common in other parts of the world. Aflatoxins are commonly present in food in some parts of the world where hepatitis B virus infection is endemic.

Hepatocellular carcinomas are usually discovered as masses on CAT scans or ultrasound scans. The majority of patients with hepatocellular carcinomas have cirrhosis. In patients who have cirrhosis, a sudden deterioration in clinical condition may provide a clue to the presence of a hepatocellular carcinoma. Sometimes they will cause pain. Rising blood alkaline phosphatase activity may also suggest the diagnosis. Alpha-fetoprotein is a useful marker for diagnosis of hepatocellular carcinoma. It is often measured as part of routine screening in patients with chronic hepatitis B and chronic hepatitis C. Rising blood alpha-fetoprotein concentration in someone with chronic liver disease suggests the development of hepatocellular carcinoma. CAT or ultrasound scans should be performed in such instances. About 70 percent of patients with hepatocellular carcinoma have elevated blood alpha-fetoprotein concentrations. It is not specific for hepatocellular carcinoma, as individuals with other types of cancer—especially testicular—may also have elevated blood concentrations.

The definitive diagnosis of hepatocellular carcinoma is made by biopsy. Usually, the liver mass is biopsied by a radiologist under CAT scan or ultrasound guidance. Sometimes, it is biopsied using a laparoscope, a fiber-optic instrument that is inserted into the abdomen. Occasionally, open surgical biopsy is necessary.

Hepatocellular carcinoma is curable by surgery only if the tumor is small. Surgery may not be possible in individuals with advanced cirrhosis. If surgery is contemplated, extensive presurgical evaluation by CAT scanning, magnetic resonance scanning, and angiography (injection of dye into the hepatic artery followed by X-ray) is required. Some patients with cirrhosis and small hepatocellular carcinomas confined to the liver may be treated by liver transplantation. For large tumors, or cancer that has spread beyond the liver, chemotherapy, ligating (tying) or embolization (clotting) of the hepatic artery, alcohol injection into the tumor, or radiation may relieve symptoms and prolong life, though none is curative. Patients may also opt for enrollment in clinical trials utilizing these and other experimental procedures.

The prognosis after treatment of hepatocellular carcinoma depends upon the size of the tumor and the extent to which the liver has been already damaged by cirrhosis. For patients with hepatocellular carcinomas that are deemed to be surgically resectable, the five-year survival rate after surgery is 10 to 30 percent. Rare hepatocellular carcinomas, often discovered in young women without cirrhosis, are a fibrolamellar variant that has a better prognosis after surgical resection. Patients with advanced cirrhosis generally do poorly after surgical resection and should be considered for possible liver transplantation if the tumors are small and have not spread. At the present time, not much data are available regarding survival rates after liver transplantation for small tumors. For patients with hepatocellular carcinomas confined to the liver in whom complete surgical removal of the tumor is not possible, the five-year survival rate is about 1 percent. Virtually no patients with hepatocellular carcinoma that has spread beyond the liver survive for long; most die within a few months.

Cholangiocarcinomas can arise in both the liver and the bile ducts outside the liver. Cholangiocarcinomas are usually discovered first on radiological studies and diagnosed by biopsy. Carcinoembryonal antigen, or CEA, may be elevated in the blood of patients with this tumor. In some parts of the world, liver fluke (*Opisthorchis sinensis* or *Clonorchis sinensis*) infection is a predisposing risk for development of cholangiocarcinoma. Patients with primary sclerosing cholangitis are also at increased risk for development of cholangiocarcinomas.

The prognosis of cholangiocarcinoma is similar to that for hepatocellular carcinoma. Small tumors may be surgically resected in rare cases only; otherwise, the patient may undergo liver transplantation. Patients with cholangiocarcinomas that cannot be surgically resected, or have spread beyond the liver, have a poor prognosis.

Benign Tumors

A variety of benign tumors can be found in the liver. One, hemangioma, is common while most others are relatively rare.

Hemangioma

Hemangioma (more precisely, cavernous hemangioma) is the most common benign liver tumor found in adults. They are more commonly found in older persons and rarely identified in young children. For reasons that are unclear, hemangiomas are more common in women and estrogen may increase their size. Hemangiomas are composed of vascular channels that may contain clotted blood and fibrous tissue. They range in size and can be as large as several inches across.

Patients with hemangiomas are usually asymptomatic, and the condition is almost always diagnosed incidentally when ultrasound, CAT scan, or other imaging studies are undertaken for other reasons. In some instances, a patient with a hemangioma will come to the doctor with abdominal pain, nausea, vomiting, or a mass that can be felt in the upper abdomen. Very rarely, patients will come with anemia or low platelet counts resulting from red blood cells or platelets that are trapped and/or destroyed within the tumor. In extremely rare instances, a hemangioma can rupture, usually after abdominal trauma.

A diagnosis of hemangioma is made using special imaging studies. Routine ultrasound may be suggestive but is not always diagnostic. Definitive diagnosis can usually be made by a tagged red blood cell scan, MRI scan, or dynamic CAT scan performed after intravenous contrast dye is given.

Cavernous hemangioma causes much more worry and concern for patients than actual problems. Complications are extremely rare, and, in virtually all cases, nothing has to be done once a diagnosis is made. If a patient with a liver hemangioma exhibits none or only minimal symptoms, no treatment is necessary. In very rare cases, symptomatic hemangiomas may be treated by surgical resection.

Hemangioendothelioma is a rare tumor occurring only in infants and young children. It is sometimes associated with heart failure. Children with this type of hemangioma may die as a result of heart failure or rupture. If they survive, the tumor usually disappears as they grow.

Benign Nodular Lesions

Several nodular tumor-like lesions can affect the liver. They are often first suspected based on radiological scans with a biopsy required for definitive diagnosis. All of these conditions are rather rare.

Adenomas are benign tumors that rarely occur in the liver. Liver adenomas are much more common in women, and it is possible, but not conclusively proven, that they may be associated with long-term use of birth control pills. In many cases, they are first identified through radiological studies conducted for other indications. Sometimes patients come to their doctors with a mass or pain in the right upper abdomen. If an adenoma is suspected, a biopsy is usually done surgically because the tumor has a rich blood supply and needle biopsy can be dangerous. Because adenomas can rupture, surgical treatment is often recommended.

Focal nodular hyperplasia is characterized by benign nodules in the liver. Like hepatic adenomas, focal nodular hyperplasia occurs primarily in women. Birth control pills may predispose women to this condition. Most patients with focal nodular hyperplasia do not have symptoms, but a mass can sometimes be felt in the abdomen. Small lesions may have to be resected because of the chance of rupture.

Nodular regenerative hyperplasia is a condition characterized by nodules without scar tissue throughout the liver. Patients with nodular regenerative hyperplasia can sometimes develop portal hypertension and associated complications such as esophageal varices and ascites. Sometimes, liver transplantation may even be required to treat the complications of portal hypertension.

Partial nodular transformation is characterized by nodules surrounded by scar tissue in the liver. Patients with partial nodular transformation usually have portal hypertension.

Other Benign Liver Tumors

There are several other rare benign tumors and lesions that can arise in the liver. They are usually discovered by radiological scanning, sometimes in patients who complain of abdominal pain or other symptoms suggesting a liver mass. They usually do not require treatment. Definitive diagnosis may require biopsy.

Cysts

Cysts are cell-lined structures filled with fluid that occur within tissues. Many different types of cysts affect the liver. Most are benign and of little consequence. They are usually diagnosed by their characteristic appearance on radiological procedures. Some liver cysts can be quite large. Some inherited diseases, for example, Caroli disease, cause multiple cysts in the kidney and liver. In some forms of inherited polycystic kidney disease, liver cysts can also be seen. Very rarely, cystic lesions can be malignant. Whether or not a cyst needs to be worked up further after its discovery on a radiological test depends upon the radiological appearance and other factors. But they usually do not require further investigation.

An infectious disease that can cause cysts in the liver is echinococcosis or hydatid cyst disease. It is caused by small tapeworms of the genus *Echinococcus* that usually live in the intestines of dogs and other animals. *Echinococcus* is transmitted to humans by contact with animal feces. The disease is rare in the United States and is most common in sheep and cattle raising areas. Hydatid cysts are treated by surgery and/or the drug mebendazole.

Abscesses

Abscesses are walled-off areas of infection filled with pus. They can occur in the liver. Liver abscesses caused by bacteria usually occur after surgery or injury or as a result of blood infection. Liver abscesses can also be caused by parasites, including infection with an amoeba (*Entamoeba histolycia*). Patients with liver abscesses usually have signs and symptoms of infection, such as fever and chills. They may have pain in the right upper quadrant of the abdomen. Abscesses are treated with appropriate antibiotics. Surgical drainage may also be necessary.

Budd-Chiari Syndrome

Budd-Chiari syndrome is the obstruction of blood outflow from the liver, usually caused by thrombosis (clotting) of the hepatic vein. It can present as an acute or chronic illness. Most patients are ill for less than six months before seeking medical attention. The most common symptom in Budd-Chiari syndrome is ascites, which occurs in 70 to 90 percent of patients. Patients can also have abnormal blood tests that indicate liver disease. Some individuals with Budd-Chiari syndrome may be jaundiced.

Most patients with Budd-Chiari syndrome have an underlying condition that predisposes to blood clotting. About 10 percent have polycythemia vera, a condition in which abnormal amounts of red blood cells are produced, making the blood more likely to clot because it is too thick. Some cancers can also cause enhanced blood clotting. About

10 percent of patients with Budd-Chiari syndrome take birth control pills, which also may predispose them to blood clotting. It is not clear if these individuals also have blood clotting disorders that have not been diagnosed. Patients who suffer from Budd-Chiari syndrome without apparent predisposing conditions may have blood clotting disorders that have not been, or cannot yet be, diagnosed.

In a patient with Budd-Chiari syndrome, the examining doctors often first suspect cirrhosis as the primary cause of the symptoms. Budd-Chiari syndrome is then suggested based on findings on liver biopsy. Various radiological tests, such as ultrasound scan with Doppler studies, may also suggest the diagnosis. Hepatic venogram, which is direct catheterization of the hepatic vein with injection of dye followed by X-ray, is the definitive test to indicate that it is clotted. The hepatic vein also can be catheterized and the pressures measured to confirm the obstruction.

Patients with Budd-Chiari syndrome who have deteriorating liver function and/or complications of portal hypertension usually need to be treated by liver transplantation. In some cases, however, the underlying condition that caused the hepatic vein thrombosis excludes transplantation as a treatment option. Other surgical procedures have been used with varying degrees of success.

Congestive Heart Failure

In congestive heart failure, the heart fails to pump blood effectively. As a result, blood backs up in other tissues and organs, including the liver. Chronic congestion of blood in the liver can lead to fibrosis and cirrhosis. This condition is often referred to as *cardiac cirrhosis*. How this occurs is outlined in Figure 11.1.

The treatment approach for a patient with congestive heart failure is to treat the heart disease to prevent the cirrhosis from developing further. Congestive heart failure and constrictive pericarditis (inflammation of the lining around the heart leading to abnormal pumping) can cause ascites and edema prior to causing cirrhosis. On first impression, if poor heart function is not obvious, patients with congestive heart failure may be misdiagnosed as suffering from cirrhosis.

Figure 11.1 Congestive Heart Failure Causes Backup of Blood in the Liver

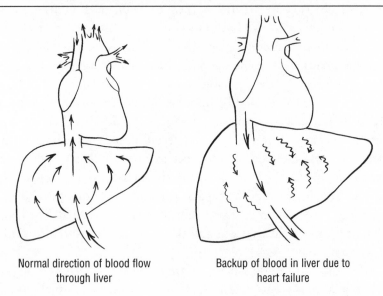

Normal direction of blood flow
through liver

Backup of blood in liver due to
heart failure

Backup of blood in the liver for long periods of time can lead to cardiac cirrhosis.

Shock Liver

Shock liver, or ischemic hepatitis, is caused by lack of oxygen delivery (ischemia) to liver cells. Causes of shock liver include heart failure, heatstroke, overwhelming infection (sepsis), burns, dehydration, and hemorrhage. In most cases, shock liver is accompanied by acute renal failure that similarly results from lack of blood flow and oxygen delivery to the kidneys. Although often present, low blood pressure (hypotension) is not present in all cases of shock liver.

In shock liver, numerous hepatocytes suddenly die and intracellular contents leak into the blood. As a result, blood alanine aminotransferase (ALT) and aspartate aminotransferase (AST) activities are usually massively elevated. The peak elevations in blood ALT and AST activities occur within two days after ischemic injury. This is followed by a return of the markedly abnormal laboratory values to normal or near-normal within seven to ten days.

Shock liver can cause fulminant hepatic failure. Treatment is directed at the underlying cause, for example, treating infection with antibiotics or treating hemorrhage with intravenous fluids and blood transfusions. Patients with shock liver die from either the underlying problem or fulminant hepatic failure, or they gradually recover if the underlying condition is reversible. Emergency liver transplantation can be performed in cases of fulminant hepatic failure where the underlying cause of shock liver is reversed.

Gallbladder and Bile Ducts

The smallest bile ducts within the liver merge into successively larger and larger ducts until they form the common hepatic duct that emerges from the liver. The common hepatic duct merges with the cystic duct, which is connected to the gallbladder, to form the common bile duct. The common bile duct then empties into the small intestine. The pancreatic duct, which drains the pancreas, also usually merges with the common bile duct at about the place where it empties into the small intestine. The anatomy of the gallbladder and bile ducts is shown in Figure 11.2.

Figure 11.2 Gallbladder and Bile Ducts

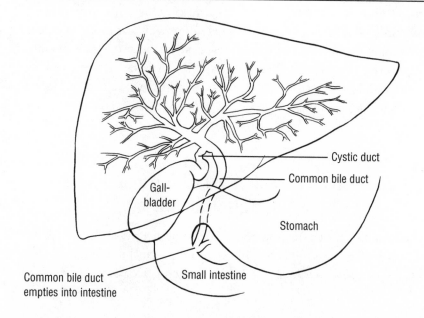

Disorders that affect the bile ducts and gallbladder may cause liver disease. Most important, bile duct obstruction resulting from gallstones, tumors, or improperly performed surgery can cause liver disease. In addition, disorders of the pancreas such as pancreatitis (pancreas inflammation) can also cause liver problems.

Acute total bile duct obstruction usually causes sudden-onset jaundice. For example, a common presentation of pancreatic cancer is jaundice because the tumor blocks the common bile duct. Complete obstruction of the common bile duct by a gallstone can cause sudden-onset pain, fever, and jaundice. The blood alkaline phosphatase and gamma-glutamyltranspeptidase (GGTP) activities will be elevated. Partial obstruction may not cause jaundice but will cause elevations in blood alkaline phosphatase and GGTP activities. Bile duct obstructions can lead to bacterial infections of the bile ducts (cholangitis) that can ascend into the liver (ascending cholangitis).

Long-standing obstruction of the external bile ducts will lead to biliary cirrhosis. Throughout the underdeveloped world, chronic complications of gallbladder surgery are a common cause of cirrhosis. Fortunately, this is very rare in the United States and other countries where high-quality medical care is available.

The management of liver complications due to bile duct obstruction is to treat the bile duct, gallbladder, or pancreatic problem causing it. This usually involves opening an obstruction or treating an infection. Obstructions can be corrected surgically, or more and more commonly by endoscopic procedures. Endoscopic retrograde cholangiopancreatography (ERCP) can be modified to extract stones from the common bile duct or place stents through obstructing tumors. If the problem is recurrent gallstones, the gallbladder can be removed.

Liver Diseases of Infants and Young Children

Children can suffer from many of the same liver diseases as adults. However, there are some liver diseases unique to children that do not affect adults. Kernicterus, or bilirubin toxicity, occurs in infants only.

Kernicterus

At very high blood concentrations, unconjugated bilirubin is toxic to the brain. Bilirubin toxicity is known as *kernicterus*, which occurs in newborn babies with very high unconjugated bilirubin concentrations, usually above 20 milligrams per deciliter of blood. In newborn babies, the unconjugated bilirubin can readily cross the undeveloped blood-brain barrier. In addition, the brain of a newborn is very sensitive to the toxic accumulation of bilirubin.

Kernicterus can occur in infants with genetic disorders of bilirubin metabolism. (See Table 10.1 in Chapter 10.) It can also occur in very premature babies and some mature babies with neonatal jaundice. The encephalopathy of kernicterus usually manifests as refusal to feed, high-pitched crying, and increased muscle tone. If severe, the baby can die. Babies who survive often have irreversible problems including mental retardation, deafness, and cerebral palsy.

Infants with highly elevated unconjugated blood bilirubin concentrations may be treated by phototherapy to prevent kernicterus. In phototherapy, the infant is placed under visible light that sometimes is greenish. Light induces subtle changes in the orientation of atoms around certain chemical bonds in the unconjugated bilirubin molecule. As a result, bilirubin becomes increasingly water soluble and is excreted in the kidneys. These more soluble forms of bilirubin are referred to as *photoisomers*.

Neonatal Jaundice

Many infants are born with mild elevations in their blood unconjugated bilirubin concentrations. In most cases, this is due to neonatal jaundice or neonatal hyperbilirubinemia. Neonatal jaundice occurs because enzymes and other cellular factors involved in bilirubin metabolism in the liver are not yet mature. The activity of UDP-glucuronosyltransferase, the enzyme that conjugates bilirubin, is decreased in newborn babies, especially those born premature. In addition, newborns usually have increased destruction of red blood cells leading to increased production of bilirubin.

In most cases, there are no untoward consequences of neonatal jaundice. The condition usually resolves soon after birth. Infants with

neonatal jaundice, usually those born premature, are at risk for kernicterus if the blood unconjugated bilirubin concentrations are very
high. These babies may be treated with phototherapy until they mature
to the point when their livers can adequately conjugate bilirubin and
secrete it into bile.

Biliary Atresia

Biliary atresia is defined as the lack of a lumen in part or all of the bile
ducts outside of the liver, causing complete obstruction of bile flow. In
reality, there may be some bile flow, but it is severely decreased. Newborn babies with biliary atresia present with jaundice, and the challenge for the pediatrician is to differentiate this condition from other,
less serious causes of jaundice.

Biliary atresia occurs in about one in ten to fifteen thousand live
births. In some cases, it is associated with other congenital malformations. Alagille syndrome is an inherited condition characterized by biliary atresia and decreased numbers of smaller bile ducts within the liver.
Children with Alagille syndrome suffer from associated conditions that
include abnormal pigmentation in the eyes, heart valve problems, bone
problems, and neurological changes. They also have characteristic physical features such as a broad forehead, pointed jaw, and bulbous tip of
the nose. There are also cases of biliary atresia with decreased bile ducts
in the liver without these syndromatic malformations.

Without treatment, the prognosis of babies with biliary atresia is
extremely poor. Most die within one year of diagnosis. Some surgical
procedures have been shown to prolong survival, such as the commonly
performed Kasai procedure. These surgical procedures attempt to
restore the flow of bile from the liver to the intestine. They are usually
of temporary benefit; in the long term, most children do not do well.
Liver transplantation provides the best overall option for children with
biliary atresia, even for those who have had previous Kasai operations.
Liver transplantation not only reestablishes bile flow but also replaces
an organ that may be damaged as a result of bile duct obstruction. The
long-term prognosis for most children who receive liver transplantation for biliary atresia is excellent.

Hepatoblastoma

Hepatoblastoma is a malignant primary liver cancer that essentially occurs only in children, usually within the first three years of life. Small, isolated tumors may be cured by surgical resection. Babies with large hepatoblastomas, or ones that have spread beyond the liver, have a very poor prognosis.

Liver Diseases and Pregnancy

Pregnant women can also suffer from the same liver disease as other adults. The most common liver disease that occurs during pregnancy is, in fact, viral hepatitis. However, there are several liver diseases unique to pregnancy, including:

- Liver involvement in hyperemesis gravidarum (morning sickness)
- Cholestasis of pregnancy
- Fatty liver of pregnancy
- Liver involvement in eclampsia and pre-eclampsia
- Hemolysis, elevated liver enzymes, and low platelet count (HELLP) syndrome

Liver Involvement in Hyperemesis Gravidarum (Morning Sickness)

Hyperemesis gravidarum is known by most people as *morning sickness*. It occurs during the first three months of pregnancy. In some cases, the vomiting due to morning sickness can be extremely severe, even requiring hospitalization. In such cases, liver problems are often manifested as elevations in blood ALT and AST activities and, sometimes, the bilirubin concentration. In severe cases the patient can become jaundiced.

Liver abnormalities associated with morning sickness are mild and of little clinical consequence. Patients who get seriously ill with this condition do so because of dehydration, not liver failure. Liver abnormalities rapidly resolve when the patient stops vomiting.

Cholestasis of Pregnancy

About 1 percent of pregnant women suffer from cholestasis of pregnancy, which is impaired bile flow within the liver during pregnancy. The cause of this condition is not understood, but it may be related to the effects of excess estrogens on bile flow within the liver (some of the same individuals may become jaundiced while taking birth control pills). Cholestasis of pregnancy usually occurs during the last three months of pregnancy but can sometimes occur earlier. The symptoms are pruritus (itching) in virtually all cases, and jaundice in about 25 percent. The blood bilirubin concentration and AST, ALT, alkaline phosphatase, and GGTP activities may be elevated to varying degrees.

Cholestasis of pregnancy may be unpleasant, but it is rarely serious and never fatal. Itching may respond to treatment with cholestyramine. Several studies have reported an increased incidence of premature labor in women with cholestasis of pregnancy. A woman with this condition, therefore, should be monitored closely by her obstetrician.

Fatty Liver of Pregnancy

Fatty liver of pregnancy is one of the most serious, and often fatal, complications of pregnant women. Fortunately, it is very rare and occurs in only about one in thirteen thousand deliveries. The cause is not known, but some recent studies have suggested an association with certain genetic defects in fat metabolism.

Fatty liver of pregnancy occurs during the last three months of pregnancy and is associated with sudden onset of severe liver disease. Patients may suffer from jaundice, edema, ascites, and fulminant hepatic failure. Blood tests reveal elevated aminotransferase activities. The blood bilirubin concentration is also usually elevated and prothrombin time prolonged.

Women with sudden-onset severe liver disease during the third trimester must have liver biopsies to diagnose or exclude fatty liver of pregnancy. The diagnosis is made by the finding of fat (microvesicular steatosis) in hepatocytes. About 50 percent of cases are fatal to both mother and fetus. There is no treatment except for immediate delivery by cesarean section. The condition resolves after pregnancy.

Liver Involvement in Eclampsia and Pre-Eclampsia

Eclampsia and pre-eclampsia are obstetrical conditions characterized by high blood pressure and other associated abnormalities. They most frequently occur in young women during their first pregnancies. Pre-eclampsia is new-onset high blood pressure during pregnancy with protein in the urine. Eclampsia is hypertension, protein in the urine, and seizures. Pre-eclampsia is a fairly common condition, and about 10 percent of women with it will have evidence of liver abnormalities in blood tests. About 5 percent will become jaundiced. Eclampsia is a rarer condition. Patients with eclampsia may develop serious liver disease. The exact causes of liver damage in pre-eclampsia and eclampsia are not known. Immediate delivery should be performed if the mother's life is in danger.

HELLP Syndrome

HELLP stands for *hemolysis* (destruction of red blood cells), *elevated liver* enzymes, and *low platelet* count. It is a relatively uncommon condition of pregnant women, usually occurring during the final three months of pregnancy. The diagnosis is made by finding the three characteristic features that define the disease (without another cause) in a pregnant woman. Mother and fetal mortality is high in HELLP syndrome. Patients should be carefully monitored and prompt delivery performed once diagnosis is made.

Pregnancy in Women with Chronic Liver Diseases

Should a woman with a chronic liver disease, who is able, become pregnant? This question goes beyond science and medicine, and I cannot tell all such women what to do in this regard. Some facts, however, should be considered when a woman with chronic liver disease decides to, or becomes, pregnant.

In advanced cirrhosis, pregnancy can be life-threatening to the mother and fetus. Most women with very advanced cirrhosis are infertile, so pregnancy is not an issue. But elective abortion should be considered as an option in cases where the lives of the mother and fetus are at high risk.

Most questions about pregnancy arise in women who have either chronic hepatitis B or chronic hepatitis C without cirrhosis or early cirrhosis. In chronic hepatitis B and C, the mother should realize that there is a small risk of passing on the disease to her children. This consideration aside, pregnancy is probably not high risk in patients with hepatitis B and hepatitis C who do not have cirrhosis. The risk increases in women with cirrhosis, even if they do not have clinical complications.

Autoimmune hepatitis generally affects young women of childbearing potential. In autoimmune hepatitis, the drugs used to treat the disease are one issue. Prednisone and prednisolone are probably relatively safe in pregnancy, but the effects of azathioprine (Imuran) on the unborn baby are not known. If a woman with autoimmune hepatitis desires to become pregnant, azathioprine should be stopped and only prednisone or prednisolone should be used to manage the disease. If a woman with autoimmune hepatitis becomes pregnant while taking azathioprine, elective abortion should be considered as an option. If the woman wants to carry the pregnancy to term, all attempts should be made to stop the azathioprine as soon as possible and manage the disease with only prednisone or prednisolone for the remainder of the pregnancy. Finally, a woman with autoimmune hepatitis must realize that if a flare-up in disease activity occurs during pregnancy, her condition could become quite complicated.

Other important issues related to pregnancy are the inherited liver diseases such as Wilson disease, hemochromatosis, and alpha-1-antitrypsin deficiency. (See Chapter 10.) These disorders can be passed on to the baby. Professional genetic counseling should be obtained in cases where the prospective parents have questions, including situations where the disease runs in the mother's and father's families but the parents are not affected. Hemochromatosis, Wilson disease, and alpha-1-antitrypsin deficiency can theoretically be detected in the fetus prior to birth, but fetal testing for these diseases is not routinely performed. If testing is performed, elective abortion is an option if a fetus is found to be affected.

A few women have become pregnant and delivered healthy babies after liver transplantation. Pregnancy in a liver transplant recipient is a very special case. Such patients require complex medical care by several different specialists.

12

Liver Transplantation

LIVER TRANSPLANTATION should be considered as a "life insurance policy" for individuals with chronic liver disease. Most individuals with chronic liver disease will not need liver transplantation. But if they do, it can save their lives. The vast majority of liver transplantation procedures are performed on patients with end-stage cirrhosis resulting from chronic liver diseases. Liver transplantation can also be lifesaving in patients with the acute condition fulminant hepatic failure.

Liver transplantation can be divided into three phases: (1) pretransplant, (2) transplant, and (3) posttransplant. The actual transplant phase is brief compared to the pre- and posttransplant phases. Generally, patients have the most anxiety and questions during the pretransplant phase. An exception is the patient with fulminant hepatic failure who may be never be conscious during this phase.

Pretransplant Phase

In many cases, the most important aspect of liver transplantation for a patient with chronic liver diseases is for his or her primary doctor to know when to refer to a transplantation center for evaluation. Good medical judgment is necessary, and the decision is not always easy. In babies, the pediatrician must readily recognize conditions such as biliary atresia that require referral to a liver specialist. In adults with chronic liver disease, deterioration is usually gradual, and during the many years of follow-up, the doctor must decide when referral to a transplantation center is indicated. In cases of fulminant hepatic failure, it must be recognized immediately.

When complications of cirrhosis cannot be controlled medically, referral to a liver transplantation center is clearly indicated. These complications include worsening hepatic encephalopathy, refractory ascites, and difficulty in controlling bleeding from gastric or esophageal varices. Cachexia, or generalized wasting, sometimes becomes an unstoppable complication of cirrhosis, and transplantation should be performed before such patients literally "waste away." Other important parameters to consider include blood albumin concentration, blood bilirubin concentration, and prothrombin time. A low blood albumin concentration, rising blood bilirubin concentration, and prolonged prothrombin time indicate deterioration in liver function. Deteriorating kidney function in someone with cirrhosis, most easily assessed by blood creatinine concentration, is another parameter.

There are a few reasons not to refer a patient with end-stage cirrhosis for liver transplantation. Virtually no center will transplant patients who are actively abusing or dependent upon alcohol or other drugs. Such patients should first, or at least concurrently, be referred to a rehabilitation facility. In addition, few centers will perform transplantation in patients over age seventy. Many centers will not transplant individuals with HIV infection; however, a few might. Patients with metastatic cancer or other terminal diseases are also usually ineligible for liver transplantation. If a doctor cannot determine if a patient is eligible for liver transplantation, he or she should contact a liver specialist at the nearest transplantation center to find out.

How to Select a Transplant Center

Liver transplantation is no longer a rare or esoteric procedure. More than six thousand liver transplants are performed in the United States each year at more than 120 different centers. In some regions of the country, there may be only one center within hundreds of miles where liver transplantation is performed. In metropolitan areas, there may be several liver transplant centers to choose from. How does one choose a liver transplant center and program?

The United Network of Organ Sharing (UNOS) "Transplant Living" website (transplantliving.org) recommends reviewing the following factors when selecting an organ transplant center:

- Experience of the transplant team and support personnel
- Cost of the procedure and related items
- Availability of insurance coverage
- Geographical proximity to the program
- Quality and availability of pre- and posttransplant services
- Commitment to keeping up with technologic advances
- Multicultural sensitivity
- Availability of friends and family for assistance

These factors make a lot of sense. For example, while patients may find that the experience of the transplant team and support personnel are similar among programs in a region, they may find out that their insurance company or health maintenance organization works only with one of the centers. A patient who does not speak English may feel more comfortable at a good transplant center with translators and/or staff who speak the same language. Just because a transplant center one thousand miles from home may have done a few more procedures, it may be unreasonable for a patient to go there because family and friends would not be able to visit and because posttransplant care would likely have to be transferred elsewhere. Other factors that may be important in some cases are the indication for transplantation, as some centers may have more experience with patients with unusual conditions or complications. Also, some centers may perform or have much more experience with living donor transplantation.

Patients can find out more about transplant centers in their regions from their doctors and from organizations such as the American Liver Foundation and UNOS. Most transplant centers and organizations have websites. A few minutes of working with a search engine will likely identify many sites with a lot of information.

Once the Patient Is Referred to a Center for Liver Transplantation

Usually, a hepatologist (medical liver specialist) will be the first type of doctor to see a patient at a liver transplant center. During the first visit, a transplant surgeon also may see the patient. The hepatologist will take a complete medical history, review all past medical records, and perform a physical examination. The hepatologist will also order a battery of blood tests, some routine, some appropriate for the particular case, and some especially relevant to the transplant evaluation such as blood typing. The hepatologist also will answer many of the patient's and family members' questions about the liver transplantation process.

At the initial evaluation visit, the patient and family members will likely meet a transplant nurse coordinator. Nurse coordinators specialize in the care of patients undergoing organ transplantation. Throughout the pretransplantation evaluation, the patient will probably get to know the nurse coordinators best compared to any member of the transplant team. A nurse coordinator is often the first person the patient will call with questions or problems. These nurses, as their name indicates, will coordinate the numerous tests, doctor visits, and special procedures that patients being evaluated for liver transplantation require.

At the initial consultation, the patient and/or family members may meet with a financial counselor. Liver transplantation is an expensive procedure, and the pretransplant evaluation, surgery, and hospital stay may add up to $250,000 or more. The financial counselor will need detailed information about the patient's insurance coverage. Many major insurance policies, as well as U.S. federal-state programs such as Medicaid and Medi-Cal, will cover the costs associated with organ transplantation. Problems about financial eligibility sometimes occur with uninsured patients who do not have Medicare or Medicaid. The financial counselor may help such patients apply for benefits or try to help arrange coverage for other expensive aspects of transplantation such as the costs of medicine after the procedure.

A patient undergoing a liver transplant evaluation will often require several radiological tests. A chest X-ray, liver ultrasound, and CAT scan will almost always be performed. The CAT scan will be done in a special way to measure the volume of the liver. This is important because a small person will need a small donor liver and a larger person a larger liver. Other radiological procedures or scans may also be performed as indicated.

As part of the transplant evaluation, the patient will also see several different doctors and health professionals. Many patients—especially older ones—will see a cardiologist for a heart evaluation. Cigarette smokers and patients with lung diseases will see a pulmonologist (lung specialist). Patients with kidney problems will be evaluated by a nephrologist (kidney specialist). Most patients will see a psychiatrist, especially those with a history of alcohol or drug use. All patients, and usually their family members, will see a social worker for help in coping with stress and other issues associated with transplantation. Patients may also have to see a dentist to remove teeth that are decaying, which could be a source of infection. Visits to other specialists or subspecialists may be scheduled as necessary.

At certain centers, the possibility of living donor transplantation may be discussed with the patient. A suitable living donor must be identified who is physically fit, psychologically stable, and willing to provide informed consent after obtaining a thorough understanding of the entire process and potential risks. The donor need not necessarily be a relative and, in terms of compatibility, must only have an appropriate blood type. The advantage of living donor transplantation is that the waiting time until surgery can be significantly reduced, as the patient need not wait for an available cadaveric organ. Hence, living donor transplantation may be appropriate for individuals who have identified a suitable donor and who are extremely sick at the time of their initial arrival at the transplant center.

Once the patient has undergone the necessary tests and has been evaluated, members of the transplant team and possibly other appropriate physicians discuss the case in a meeting. In living donor transplantation, the suitability of the living donor is also considered. Various doctors, nurse coordinators, financial counselors, and social workers may be asked to comment on their recommendations. Questionable test results will be discussed. After the discussion, the group as a whole makes the decision as to whether or not the patient is eligible for liver transplantation.

If the patient is deemed to be a candidate for liver transplantation, he or she is "listed"—or put on the waiting list—for a liver (or in the case of living donor transplantation, the surgery is approved). Sometimes, for various medical, psychological, or social reasons, the team decides that the patient is not a transplant candidate. In rare cases, patients are not approved for a liver transplant because they may not need the procedure. These patients will usually be followed by their primary doctors, sometimes in consultation with the transplant team, and reevaluated at a later date if their conditions deteriorate. Some patients are deemed ineligible for liver transplantation because other serious illnesses, such as cancer, AIDS, or heart disease, are identified during the pretransplant evaluation. Psychological and social exclusion criteria involve active drug or alcohol use in many cases. Patients actively using drugs may be turned down for transplantation but offered another chance in the future, usually if they demonstrate at least six months of abstinence and participation in programs such as Alcoholics Anonymous.

What Determines When a Patient on the Waiting List Gets a Liver?

Once a patient with liver disease is listed for transplantation, a waiting period begins. In the United States, the rules are established by UNOS under federal contract. Livers are *not* allocated on a first-come, first-served basis but based upon how sick the candidate is. Another factor is that the recipient and donor must be of compatible blood type. The waiting time on the list will vary from patient to patient and may also vary from one part of the country to another. Some patients who are not yet that sick may wait for a few years. Severely ill patients may receive livers within a few weeks.

Candidates waiting for liver transplantation are currently prioritized based on statistical formulas that predict who needs a new liver most urgently. The Model for End-Stage Liver Disease (MELD) is used for candidates twelve years old and older. The Pediatric End-Stage Liver Disease Model (PELD) is used for patients under twelve years of age.

MELD is a numerical scale, ranging from 6 to 40. It determines a score that predicts the chances that the patient will die within the next three months without a transplant. Three routine laboratory tests, the blood bilirubin concentration, the prothrombin time (reported as INR), and the blood creatinine, a test of kidney function, are used to calculate the MELD score. The equation to calculate the MELD score is:

MELD Score = 10{0.957 Ln[Creatinine] + 0.378 Ln[Total Bilirubin] + 1.12 Ln(INR) + 0.643}

Ln is the natural log or log base e. Values for blood creatinine and total bilirubin are entered into the equation in units of milligrams per deciliter. If values are less than 1, a value of 1 is used in the equation. For blood creatinine concentration, a maximum value of 4 is used (if the creatinine concentration is greater than 4, 4 is put into the equation). Similarly, if the patient is undergoing kidney dialysis, a value of 4 is used for creatinine. MELD scores around 6 are considered as less ill, and 40, the highest score, is considered extremely ill. The higher the score, the more urgently the patient needs a liver transplant.

PELD score for younger patients is calculated based on blood bilirubin concentration, prothrombin time, and blood albumin concentration. Age below one year when put on the waiting list and the presence of growth failure also factor into calculating the score. PELD score is calculated using the following equation:

PELD Score = 10{0.480Ln[Total Biliburin] + 1.857Ln[INR] − 0.687Ln[albumin] + 0.436 (if patient is less than 1 year old when listed and until the patient reaches the age of 24 months) + 0.667 [if the patient has growth failure determined by standardized charts]}

While studies have demonstrated that MELD and PELD are reasonably good predictors of three-month survival in patients with end-stage liver disease, they are not perfect. In addition, a patient's score may go up or down over time depending on the status of his or her liver disease and kidney function. For this reason, most liver transplant candidates will have their MELD score assessed many different times while they are on the waiting list. If the prothrombin time, blood bilirubin concentration, or blood creatinine change for reasons other than a deterioration in liver function—for example, as the result of taking a new medication or concurrent medical problems—the MELD score may change without a change in liver function. There are also some patients with potentially life-threatening liver diseases, such as small hepatocellular carcinomas, who may not have very high MELD scores but require transplantation before the tumors get too large. Another example would be a patient with primary sclerosing cholangitis with multiple episodes of life-threatening bacterial cholangitis but a fairly low MELD score.

How are livers allocated based on MELD and PELD? Donor livers are first offered to compatible patients in the donor's local area (usually a large metropolitan area or a state) and then to a larger region of the country determined by UNOS, and, finally, nationwide. Because patients with fulminant hepatic failure, which are classified as Status 1 candidates, usually need livers most urgently, each available donor liver is first offered to local and then to regional Status 1 candidates. After Status 1 candidates are considered, age is a factor. If the donor is younger than eighteen years old, the organ is considered first for children needing a liver before any adult candidates in similar need. Allocation is then based on MELD and PELD scores. Generally, listed candidates with a MELD or PELD score of 15 or higher are considered for a donor liver before any candidates in the same local, regional, or national area with scores of less than 15. Waiting time on the list only determines who comes first when there are two or more patients with the same blood type and the same MELD or PELD score.

The main point about using MELD and PELD scores to prioritize patients for receiving donor livers is that, in general, patients who have the highest chance of dying get donor organs first. Patients with higher MELD or PELD scores will be considered before those with lower scores, even if patients with lower scores have waited longer. Although there may be some exceptions, sicker patients who need a liver more urgently should get it sooner using MELD and PELD criteria.

Fulminant Hepatic Failure

The pretransplant phase is very different for someone with fulminant hepatic failure who does not show evidence of spontaneous recovery. As already discussed in Chapter 3, fulminant hepatic failure occurs in acute, not chronic, liver disease. In such cases, liver transplantation sometimes is the only hope for survival. Patients who have fulminant hepatic failure—who will die if not transplanted within a few days— are usually made the highest priority. These patients are known as *Status 1A* and *Status 1B*. MELD and PELD are not reliable in determining how sick a patient with acute liver failure is, and, therefore, they are not used in these cases.

Transplant Phase

When a suitable donor liver becomes available, the person "whose turn it is" to receive the liver is either called (or paged) or informed in his or her hospital bed that it is time for surgery. Liver transplantation is orthotopic in that the new liver is put in the same place as the old one. The trickiest part of the surgery is probably attaching the bile duct from the new liver to the part of the recipient's bile duct that remains in place. A major complication of liver transplant surgery is bleeding. Patients who undergo liver transplantation often have massive blood loss. Transfusion of many units of red blood cells, fresh frozen plasma, and platelets may be necessary.

After surgery, the patient is taken first to the recovery room and then the surgical intensive care unit. Most patients wake up within twenty-four hours after surgery while on a respirator. Some patients will need kidney dialysis for a few days after transplantation. The blood bilirubin concentration, alanine aminotransferase (ALT), and aspartate aminotransferase (AST) activities are followed carefully to establish if the new liver is functioning properly or damaged. Medications to prevent rejection of the transplanted liver are begun at surgery and continued afterward. The concentrations of some of these medications in the blood are monitored closely, and they may have to be adjusted frequently. If all goes well, a patient can leave the hospital less than two weeks after liver transplantation. Sometimes, complications arise that require longer hospital stays after surgery.

Posttransplant Phase

Complications from surgery can occur in the immediate posttransplant phase. These include bile leaks from newly sewn together bile ducts that must be treated by placement of drains by endoscopic retrograde cholangiopancreatography (ERCP). Local wound infections and systemic infections can also occur after surgery. Bleeding is also a common occurrence after any surgical procedure. Postoperative surgical complications are usually treated successfully, but they can sometimes require a return trip or two to the operating room for repair.

The major aspect of posttransplant care is to prevent organ rejection and infections. Rejection occurs because the recipient's immune system recognizes the grafted donor liver as foreign. A strong immune response against the organ occurs that causes it to be destroyed. Without medications to suppress the immune system, known as *immunosuppressive drugs*, the grafted liver would be rejected. Liver transplant recipients, therefore, need to take medications to prevent rejection for the rest of their lives. Some of the drugs that patients receiving organ transplants may receive are listed in Table 12.1.

Table 12.1 Immunosuppressive Drugs Commonly Used to Prevent Liver Transplant Rejection

Generic Name	Trade Name
Cyclosporin A	Sandimmune, Neoral
Tacrolimus (FK506)	Prograft
Sirolimus	Rapamune
Azathioprine	Imuran
Prednisone	almost always prescribed generically
Mycophenolate mofetil	CellCept
Muromonab-CD3	Orthoclone OKT3
Basiliximab	Simulect
Daclizumab	Zenapax

Virtually all patients receiving liver transplants will take either cyclosporin A (Sandimmune or Neoral) or tacrolimus (Prograft), which used to be called *FK506*. Others may take sirolimus (Rapamune), which is of the same general class. Most patients will also take prednisone and azathioprine (Imuran), which are agents that act by different mechanisms to suppress the immune system. Others may take mycophenolate mofetil (CellCept). These drugs are started immediately after transplant surgery. Each of these drugs has different side effects, and doctors may change the drugs and adjust their doses depending upon the patient's condition and adverse events experienced. These drugs are expensive, in most cases more than $10,000 a year. Most important, patients must take all of their immunosuppressive drugs as prescribed to prevent rejection. Failure to take these drugs can lead to severe rejection.

After discharge from the hospital, patients will generally return to see a doctor from the transplant team at least once a week for the first month or two. Laboratory tests will also be checked for evidence of rejection or liver graft dysfunction. Medications may be adjusted depending upon laboratory test results. If the patient's condition remains stable, the frequency of follow-up visits will be gradually decreased.

Rejection can usually be suspected according to blood test results. Most episodes of rejection will be detected by increases in blood ALT or AST activities. Rejection can be definitively diagnosed only by liver biopsy. If blood testing suggests rejection, liver biopsy will be performed. Most patients will experience some degree of rejection the first couple of weeks after liver transplantation. These rejection episodes are usually mild or moderate and respond to intravenous steroids (usually methylprednisolone) followed by a brief period of increased prednisone doses. Severe rejection episodes, or those not responding to steroids, are usually treated by intravenous administration of antibodies against lymphocytes, the white blood cells that attack the transplanted organ. These antibody drugs include muromonab-CD3 (Orthoclone OKT3), basiliximab (Simulect), and daclizumab (Zenapax). About 10 percent of patients who undergo liver transplantation develop chronic rejection that does not respond to drugs. For these patients, a second transplant is the only option.

Infection is another common complication after organ transplantation. Because the immune system is suppressed by drugs, posttransplant patients are at risk for infections that patients with normally functioning immune systems are not. These include infection with *Pneumocystis carinii*, which causes pneumonia, and cytomegalovirus (CMV), which causes many problems including hepatitis in the new liver. Patients may take trimethoprim/sulfamethoxazole (Bactrim or Septra) to prevent *Pneumocystis* pneumonia. Patients may also take ganciclovir (Cytovene) to prevent CMV infection. CMV infection can mimic rejection, and the two can usually be differentiated only by liver biopsy. Many other infections that do not normally cause problems in people with normal immune systems, including those by fungi, *Mycobacterium*, and other viruses such as herpes simplex and herpes zoster, can occur.

Another concern after liver transplantation is that the original disease will recur in the new organ. Autoimmune hepatitis, primary biliary cirrhosis, and primary sclerosing cholangitis generally do not recur. If a former alcoholic does not drink, alcoholic liver disease will not occur. However, I have seen a case of alcoholic hepatitis in a patient who continued to drink after transplantation (usually such individuals will probably stop taking their immunosuppressive drugs and suffer severe rejection first). Patients who had cirrhosis from viral hepatitis B or C are at risk for the new liver to again become infected. Although the new liver is almost always reinfected with the hepatitis C virus in recipients who suffered from this disease, the degree of posttransplant hepatitis is usually mild. Severe and rapidly progressive hepatitis due to hepatitis C virus infection sometimes occurs in the transplanted liver, however. Hepatitis B virus reinfection of the new liver often leads to severe hepatitis and destruction. Fortunately, this can be prevented by drugs. Patients transplanted for cirrhosis from hepatitis B usually receive hepatitis B immune globulin (HBIG) and/or lamivudine, adefovir, or entecavir after transplantation.

Immunosuppressive drugs to prevent rejection have many adverse events. Among them are kidney damage and nervous system problems. If adverse events related to these drugs arise, the doctors may adjust the doses or switch from one agent to another similar one, such as from tacrolimus to cyclosporin A. In the long term, patients chronically receiving immunosuppressive agents are at increased risk for developing some types of cancer and, therefore, require monitoring.

The five-year overall survival rate for patients who undergo liver transplantation at most centers is 80 to 90 percent. Many patients recover sufficiently to return to productive lives at home and work within a few months after surgery. These patients must always remember, however, to take their immunosuppressive drugs as prescribed and to follow up regularly with their doctors. They should also contact their doctors immediately should problems arise.

13

Living with Liver Disease

OVER THE YEARS, I have noticed that many patients with liver disease have similar questions about how to live their lives. Some of these common issues are discussed in this chapter.

Selecting the Right Doctor

Most patients with liver diseases do not immediately seek out a liver specialist. The diagnosis of liver disease in adults is generally made first by the patient's primary doctor, usually a family practitioner or internist. In the case of children, the primary doctor is usually a family practitioner or pediatrician. Most primary doctors know how to diagnose the most common liver diseases, or at least know how to recognize a liver disease and refer the patient to a specialist for further diagnosis. Internal medicine, pediatrics, and family practice have their respective specialty boards, and in order to receive board certification in these specialties, the doctor must undergo appropriate training and pass an examination. A first step in determining the qualifications of your primary doctor is to establish if he or she is board certified (having passed the specialty examination) or board eligible (having completed the necessary training to take the examination) in his or her specialty.

For further evaluation, specialized procedures, and possibly treatment, most primary doctors will refer a patient with a liver disease to a gastroenterologist. Gastroenterologists are internists or pediatricians who complete specialty training in internal medicine or pediatrics. After completing specialty training, they usually perform an additional three years of fellowship training in the subspecialty of gastroenterology. Most of this training focuses on diseases of the gastrointestinal tract, especially the esophagus, stomach, small intestine, colon, and rectum. Part of the training of all gastroenterology fellows is also focused on the diagnosis and treatment of liver diseases. There are subspecialty boards in gastroenterology, and although any doctor can call himself a "gastroenterologist," you can determine if he has actually had adequate training in this field, including some training in liver diseases, by asking if he is board certified (or board eligible) in gastroenterology. Board-certified or board-eligible pediatric or adult gastroenterologists who have trained in the United States have had at least some training in liver diseases.

In clinical practice, the majority of gastroenterologists devote most of their time to nonliver diseases. Some gastroenterologists take a special interest in liver diseases or hepatology (the study of liver diseases). Gastroenterologists who see a reasonable number of patients with liver diseases and who are skilled in diagnosis and treatment are often referred to as *hepatologists*. Some of these doctors will have devoted additional time during their gastroenterology fellowship training—sometimes an additional year—studying liver diseases. Others who never formally trained in gastroenterology (myself included) study liver diseases sometime in their careers and become hepatologists. Internists and pediatricians who subspecialize in hepatology only (not gastroenterology) are usually found at academic medical centers that are closely affiliated with medical schools.

There is no official subspecialty board in hepatology. Therefore, it is sometimes difficult to determine if doctors who call themselves hepatologists are actually experts in liver diseases. A doctor who is a full-time faculty member at a major medical school and considered to be a liver specialist or hepatologist is probably a legitimate one. Many such doctors will have published papers in peer-reviewed journals concerning some area of liver diseases. I do not mean articles on the Internet, in "throwaway" medical journals, or even perhaps a book like this, but scholarly articles in medical journals that have been peer reviewed before publication. In the United States, membership in the American Association for the Study of Liver Diseases (AASLD), a professional society, usually indicates some degree of expertise in hepatology (non-physician scientists may also be AASLD members).

A patient with immediately life-threatening or end-stage liver disease may need referral to a center where liver transplantation is performed (unless, of course, the patient is too sick, is too old, or has a concurrent condition that excludes liver transplantation). Currently, there are more than 120 liver transplant centers in the United States, providing coverage in almost every region of the country and several choices in some regions. Tips on choosing a liver transplant center were given in Chapter 12. Liver transplantation centers have medical or pediatric liver specialists with special expertise in the treatment of patients with end-stage cirrhosis or fulminant hepatic failure. Liver transplantation centers also obviously have surgeons who subspecialize in performing liver transplantation and other aspects of liver surgery. In addition, such centers will have doctors in a wide range of subspecialties who can handle problems that may occur in patients with end-stage liver disease, for example, kidney specialists and infectious disease specialists.

How to Find a Liver Specialist

How does a patient find a liver specialist? Usually, the best source for referrals is the patient's primary doctor. It is likely that the patient's primary doctor knows local specialists and subspecialists in most areas of medicine. Most primary doctors will at least know a good gastroenterologist knowledgeable in the diagnosis and treatment of liver diseases.

What if your primary doctor really does not know a liver specialist? Or what if you just do not like the specialist recommended by your primary doctor? Some organizations keep track of medical specialists. Several publications that can be found in many public libraries also list board-certified medical specialists. The American Liver Foundation has several local chapters that maintain lists of liver specialists in their regions. You can reach the American Liver Foundation at:

American Liver Foundation
75 Maiden Lane, Suite 603
New York, NY 10038
(800) GO LIVER (465-4837)
liverfoundation.org

Some patients want to see an expert in liver diseases. Usually, the leading researchers and doctors in a particular field are full-time faculty members at medical schools. Before seeing such a doctor, the patient should ask if seeing one is really necessary. In most cases, the special expertise of doctors at an academic medical center is not always necessary. Also, some "experts" at leading medical schools spend most of their time doing research and do not see very many patients, or will see patients only for a onetime consultation or as part of a study.

At medical centers with active liver disease research programs, there will usually be several specialists who devote most of their time to caring for patients with liver diseases. If you are fortunate enough to live near a leading medical school, and your health insurance will cover the cost, you can usually call a medical center directly for referral to a specialist. Some academic medical centers will have toll-free phone numbers for referral services. Many patients do not know this, but the best way to find a medical subspecialist is often to call the appropriate academic division directly. For example, if you are an adult with a liver disease, you can find the phone number for the office for the Division of Gastroenterology (or its equivalent, such as the Division of Digestive Diseases, Division of Liver Diseases, or Division of Hepatology) in the Department of Medicine at the nearby medical school. For a child, a similar division in the Department of Pediatrics can be contacted. You will very likely find someone there who can direct you to a specialist for your problem. Many academic medical centers and medical schools also have direct referral lines to call to obtain help in finding an appropriate specialist.

Academic divisions and departments at medical schools often have websites with doctor referral information. These websites are frequently very informative. But use caution on the Internet: Any doctor can advertise his or her practice to make it appear as a world-renowned medical research institution. For this reason, I generally recommend using the Internet only to search websites of reputable medical schools or major medical centers for referrals. Some HMOs and preferred provider organizations (PPOs) will also have websites with lists of specialists who participate in the plans or accept the patient's insurance.

Problems with HMOs

I hear many complaints from patients along the lines of: "My HMO doctor does not know enough about hepatitis C or whatever." Similarly, I hear many people say, "My HMO will not let me see a specialist." In my experience, the validity of these complaints often depends upon the HMO. Some HMOs allow access to excellent specialists who provide state-of-the-art medical care. Some, frankly, do not. I do not know exactly how to help a patient who perceives that his or her HMO doctor is not qualified to make the correct diagnosis or provide adequate treatment. The bottom line is that life comes before money, and, in some cases, a patient's only option may be to pay cash for a one-time, second opinion consultation with a liver specialist that will not be covered by insurance. In many cases, the patient will be relieved to hear that their current doctor is doing everything correctly (this will probably be worth the cost of one visit). If by chance you discover your current doctor cannot handle the problem, a letter from a noted liver specialist at an academic institution explaining why you need specialized care may help in convincing your HMO to change its mind about covering the cost of outside care. If all else fails, one possibility is to explore legal options if you feel that your HMO or insurance provider is prohibiting a second opinion by an appropriate specialist.

Clinical Trials

Many patients with liver diseases, especially those with chronic viral hepatitis B and C, want to be enrolled in clinical trials. Clinical trials are studies of new drugs or procedures in groups of patients. In good clinical trials, some of the patients will receive a new or experimental treatment and others will receive either no treatment (placebo or dummy drug) or the currently available treatment. Who gets which is determined randomly. Clinical trials sometimes provide patients with access to new and promising drugs before the U.S. FDA has approved them for the market. In addition, study investigators frequently, but not always, have more expertise regarding the disease being studied.

Much of the recent desire for patients with liver diseases to enroll in clinical trials has been driven by the newly available treatments for hepatitis B and C. Most of these are very serious clinical trials designed by academic investigators or major pharmaceutical companies. Unfortunately, some of these have been driven by "marketing" efforts by pharmaceutical companies to get doctors to use their products. Many of these are not really valid clinical trials at all but merely programs in which pharmaceutical companies pay doctors to prescribe their products to a group of patients. Some pharmaceutical sponsors will go through elaborate efforts to set up "studies" or "clinical trials" in which the companies will pay doctors to prescribe their drugs. Studies of this kind are often poorly designed, and their results will never be published. In recent years, this practice has proliferated in many areas of medicine. Fortunately, it has started to slow, in part as a result of stories published in the press, including ones about doctors being paid to participate in "clinical trials" of interferon alpha-based treatment for hepatitis C.

There are several questions patients should ask before enrolling in a clinical trial for the treatment of a liver (or any) disease. These include:

1. Where is the study taking place? Most studies that take place at medical schools or academic medical centers are probably legitimate. At these institutions, trials must be approved by an Institutional Review Board (IRB) that assures they are safe and ethical. Greater caution should be exercised when enrolling in studies in private doctor's offices. Some are completely legitimate, but some use so-called central IRBs that are essentially private companies that approve studies. It is not always clear if these IRBs impose the same standards as those at medical schools or hospitals. Ask to see proof of IRB approval before enrolling in a study.

2. Who is the study sponsor? The National Institutes of Health (NIH) or other government agencies fund many of the best studies, but these are few and far between. Many studies are sponsored and

supported by pharmaceutical companies and can either be investigator initiated or sponsor initiated. The distinction usually depends upon who designs the study. Some of the company designed and initiated clinical trials may be marketing "pseudo-studies" that merely pay doctors to prescribe particular drugs. On the other hand, many of them are the first and best-designed trials to test new drugs. Be more suspicious of clinical trials designed by pharmaceutical companies if a drug is already approved for the indication being studied. Those that involve unapproved drugs may be the best studies to offer patients potentially promising new drugs.

3. Who is the principal investigator of the study? A clinical trial with a full-time faculty member at a medical school as principal investigator is more likely (but not always) a better choice than a study conducted in the office of a doctor who does not have a medical school affiliation.

4. What does your doctor think? Never enroll in a clinical trial without discussing it first with your doctor.

Most studies will not involve new drugs conducted by professors at the best medical schools. On the other hand, most studies will not be poorly designed marketing efforts designed to induce doctors to prescribe an already approved drug. They are usually something in between. Just remember to make certain beforehand that the study is IRB approved. Do some homework and find out the reputations of the sponsor and principal investigator. And check with your doctor before enrolling.

Keeping the Right Attitude

People with liver diseases must live with their illnesses. This is sometimes difficult for their doctors to realize, and it is often difficult for family members and friends to realize. It is also sometimes difficult for patients to accept. Perhaps the most important advice for most people with chronic liver diseases is to keep the right attitude. Remain positive toward your day-to-day life and about your future.

Beyond keeping a positive attitude, it is impossible to give any specific recommendations that will help all patients with liver diseases live happily. First of all, there are many different chronic liver diseases, and the outlook for each is different. The prognosis for different patients with the same disease can also vary tremendously. Most patients with chronic hepatitis B or chronic hepatitis C will live full and essentially normal lives while a minority will develop cirrhosis and possibly liver cancer. Perhaps scariest of all is that you often cannot be sure what will happen to you. However, in many cases, the odds will be in your favor.

In an attempt to provide some general rules about living with liver disease, it is important to realize that some patients have very special needs. Most important to consider are patients with liver diseases who are actively abusing alcohol or other drugs or who are dependent upon alcohol or other substances. The social and psychological issues of patients who are substance abusers make their priorities quite different. Another small group of patients having special considerations are those with advanced cancer involving the liver. Such patients should probably seek out cancer support groups and foundations such as the American Cancer Society for information. Finally, young children have special needs that are different from adults. There are several support groups devoted to children with liver disease, and pediatricians should also prove helpful in these instances.

Some people with chronic liver diseases need help keeping the right attitude and understanding their situation. For them, I discuss some general guidelines that will help many people with liver diseases. Then I discuss the special needs of patients actively using alcohol or drugs. At the end of this section is a list of some patient organizations that provide access to support groups and information.

Living with Liver Disease

Many patients live with their liver disease appropriately and need very little outside support. Others are terrified. What seems to terrify most patients are:

- **Uncertainty.** Most patients do not know if they will develop serious complications from their disease or if it will shorten their lives.
- **Fear.** Many patients fear that liver disease will kill them.

- **Lack of information.** Many patients are not well informed about their disease and do not understand it.
- **Misinformation.** Many patients hear things about liver diseases (often on the Internet) that are not true or relevant to their cases.

Uncertainty

Most patients with chronic liver disease live full and normal lives. Some, such as those with primary biliary cirrhosis, will invariably progress, albeit slowly, perhaps so slowly it will not affect their life expectancy. Most patients with chronic viral hepatitis B or hepatitis C will not have their condition progress to cirrhosis, but some will. The problem is that rarely can a doctor tell a patient with chronic liver disease with certainty whether the disease will progress to end-stage cirrhosis, or whether the patient will develop other serious complications.

Although an individual patient's long-term outcome may be uncertain, those with chronic liver disease should not fixate on the worst outcomes. In fact, the worst outcomes are usually realized in only a minority of cases. Patients with chronic liver diseases should live and plan for full and exciting lives. They should follow up regularly with a knowledgeable doctor and discuss all their problems and concerns. And just in case things do worsen, patients with chronic liver diseases should realize that liver transplantation is a "life insurance policy," keeping this in the back of their minds.

Fear

Most patients with a chronic liver disease will not die from it. However, the uncertainty just discussed often breeds fear. It is easy for a doctor to tell a patient not to be scared, but that does not always help the problem. Sometimes fear is difficult to overcome, and patients should discuss their feelings with their doctor. If fear is excessive, they should consider consultation with a health professional, such as a psychiatrist, psychologist, or social worker. Finally, there are many legitimate support groups for patients with liver disease, a few of which are mentioned in this chapter and in Resources at the end of this book.

Lack of Information

Ask your doctor! Ask your doctor! Ask your doctor! Don't be afraid. I cannot believe that people regularly send me e-mail messages after finding my website asking about specific problems and adding, "I don't want to call my doctor" or "I can't talk to my doctor until next week." Why are they comfortable asking a doctor they've never met but not their own doctor? Clearly, something is wrong. Ask your doctor anything that concerns you. Expect your doctor to return your calls within a reasonable time frame. If he or she does not, find another doctor.

If you want to confirm what your doctor is telling you, see another doctor for a second opinion. Despite all of the patient information currently available, including this book, other books, and a plethora of websites, only a doctor who obtains a complete history and examines the patient can answer specific questions regarding diagnosis, treatment, and prognosis in a specific case. Use books such as this one, reliable Internet resources, and information from patient organizations to help understand your disease. Never use these resources as a substitute for good medical care.

Misinformation

Be careful of misinformation, especially on the Internet. On the Web, anyone can appear to be an expert. Be leery of websites, books, "doctors," and other sources claiming "new" or "miracle" cures for liver diseases.

Don't believe what you hear about alternative, herbal, or holistic remedies. If such remedies or methods had been subjected to rigorous scientific testing, mainstream physicians and scientists would take note. None of these remedies has yet been subjected to scientific scrutiny or tested in controlled clinical trials. Milk thistle and its supposedly "active ingredient" silymarin have been promoted by fans of alternative medicine—and even some mainstream doctors—as compounds for "good liver health." They also have been promoted as cures for virtually every known liver disease. Despite the hype, milk thistle or silymarin has never been shown to be effective in a controlled clinical trial for any liver disease. Furthermore, these and many other "herbal" or "alternative" remedies have not even been proven safe for patients with liver disorders. So be careful about what you hear without doing further research on your own and asking your doctor!

In most cases, you can trust what you hear from your doctor or legitimate patient organizations such as the American Liver Foundation. Take any other information with a grain of salt. If you want to research something, go to the library and search the medical literature or conduct a search on the Internet (try Pub Med at ncbi.nlm.nih.gov/entrez/query.fcgi?db=PubMed). Bring articles to your doctor and seek help when trying to understand complex medical issues.

Overcoming uncertainty, fear, and poor information should help a patient with chronic liver disease maintain the right attitude toward life. Some people, perhaps with the help of their doctors, can do it themselves. Others could benefit from legitimate support groups. Perhaps the best organization to start with regarding information about support groups is the American Liver Foundation, which has local chapters in most regions of the United States.

Special Situations: Patients Actively Abusing Alcohol or Other Substances

Alcohol is the number one cause of liver disease in the Western world. Intravenous drug use is also a major risk factor for hepatitis B and hepatitis C. For these reasons, a large number of patients with liver disease have substance abuse or substance dependence disorders.

For patients with active substance use disorders, the number one priority is to deal with the substance disorder. I cannot emphasize this enough. It applies to the patient with alcoholic hepatitis who is finally discharged from the hospital, the alcoholic with cirrhosis who cannot be considered for liver transplantation while drinking, or the heroin addict with chronic hepatitis C who wants treatment. Even for those with cirrhosis and end-stage liver disease, treating their substance use is paramount. Individuals who need liver transplantation to survive will almost never receive a transplant if they are actively abusing drugs or alcohol.

All of the information for patients not actively abusing alcohol or drugs also applies to the person with liver disease who is actively using these substances. However, dealing with the substance disorder is always the number one priority and must be emphasized separately from everything else. Some general guidelines for alcohol or substance users with liver diseases are discussed next.

Rehabilitation

Many individuals with drug or alcohol abuse or dependency disorders require inpatient rehabilitation—usually a one-month voluntary stay in a facility where intensive treatment is directed at the substance disorder.

Alcoholics Anonymous and Narcotics Anonymous

Alcoholics Anonymous (AA) is an informal society of more than two million recovered alcoholics in the United States, Canada, and other countries. These men and women meet in local groups ranging in size from a handful of people in some localities to many hundreds in larger communities. Narcotics Anonymous (NA) is a similar society for individuals with other drug abuse or dependency disorders. Individuals with liver diseases and alcohol or other substance abuse disorders should participate in AA or NA, respectively. Anyone can contact AA or NA. You may contact their world headquarters at:

Alcoholics Anonymous
Grand Central Station
P.O. Box 459
New York, NY 10163
alcoholics-anonymous.org

Narcotics Anonymous World Services
P.O. Box 9999
Van Nuys, CA 91409
(818) 773-9999
na.org

Concurrent Medical Care

The sick person with a drug or alcohol abuse or dependence disorder may also require medical care while in a rehabilitation program or attending AA or NA meetings. The patient should follow up with a

doctor regularly who understands their treatment needs. Many rehabilitation programs also offer medical services. Some patients with substance abuse disorders may also benefit from psychiatric care, and
patients should discuss referral to a psychiatrist, perhaps one special-
izing in substance abuse disorders, with their primary care physician
or liver specialist.

Family Support

Family members and friends should be supportive of an individual's
commitment to treat a substance abuse disorder. Sometimes it can be
incredibly stressful, especially if a loved one refuses treatment and continues to abuse alcohol or drugs. If family members or friends are having a difficult time with a loved one who abuses alcohol, they can
contact Al-Anon, a worldwide organization that offers a self-help
recovery program for families and friends of alcoholics whether or not
the alcoholic seeks help or even recognizes the existence of a drinking
problem. Al-Anon also has a division for younger members, Alateen.
In the United States, call 1-888-425-2666 for the location of an
Al-Anon or Alateen meeting near you. Al-Anon also maintains a website (Al-Anon-Alateen.org) with information in numerous languages
and contact information for many countries.

The patient with liver disease and a substance abuse or dependence
disorder has two problems to deal with. The special needs of these
patients require medical care, frequently psychiatric treatment, self-
help, and participation in programs such as AA or NA. In addition, the
advice for patients not abusing alcohol or other substances is relevant
to these individuals. Most important, individuals with substance abuse
disorders, as well as their doctors, family members, and friends, must
realize that treatment of these disorders is every bit as serious an
issue—and sometimes more serious—as treatment of the liver disease.

Children

Depending on their age and sophistication, children will have different
degrees of insight into their medical conditions. What is most important for parents to understand is that their children with chronic liver
disease should, in most cases, be treated like all other kids! Most can
go to school, play, and participate in sports. Most will lead long and

normal lives and probably not suffer from complications of liver disease.

I receive many inquiries from parents whose children have liver problems. A very common concern comes from parents whose child is chronically infected with the hepatitis B virus. These parents often think that it is the end of the world for their child. However, the parents should realize that most children with liver disease will do well. Most important, they should plan for their children to lead full and normal lives and remember that liver transplantation is an "insurance policy" if needed. For children who are very ill or who need transplantation, several support groups are available.

Maintaining Relationships with Others

Many patients with liver diseases are very concerned about their relationships with others. Some of these concerns are reasonable and others are exaggerated or unrealistic. Many patients with chronic liver diseases will live normal lives. Some have contagious diseases, which potentially put household contacts and sexual partners at risk. Others may be very sick and have shortened life expectancies. Some patients and their family members will experience major medical events, such as liver transplantation or a major surgery. Because of the variations in diseases and conditions, it is not possible to come up with specific recommendations about relationships that would apply to all patients with chronic liver disease—except that patients and relevant family members and friends should be well-informed about the reality of the patient's illness. *Patients with chronic liver diseases should have happy and fulfilling relationships with their family and friends.*

Summarized in this section are a few aspects regarding relationships that are of concern to many patients.

Giving the Illness to a Family Member or Friend

Many patients are concerned when they have contagious liver diseases that they will pass it on to their close contacts. Some patients are inappropriately concerned about this when the disease is not contagious.

Many people associate the term *hepatitis* with contagious disease. I've sometimes even been asked if autoimmune hepatitis and alcoholic hepatitis are contagious. These are not contagious diseases, and the patient's doctor should clearly explain this. However, viral hepatitis is contagious, and there are things these patients and their relations should know.

The main concerns about transmitting liver disease from one person to others involve chronic hepatitis B and chronic hepatitis C. Fortunately, these are not transmitted by casual contact but by blood and sex. For hepatitis B, the solution is relatively simple: household contacts and sexual partners of an infected individual should be vaccinated. In addition, caution should be used to avoid exposure to blood. Items such as razors or toothbrushes should not be shared, for instance.

There is no vaccine for hepatitis C. Fortunately, the risk of transmission appears to be rather low among people who do not share needles for injecting drugs. Although real, the risk of sexual transmission is also low. In a long-term monogamous relationship, usual sexual activities can be continued; however, the partner should be aware and the option to use condoms is available if there is concern about the low risk of sexual transmission (probably less than 1 percent). Sexually promiscuous individuals are at higher risk and they or their partner should use condoms. Similar to chronic hepatitis B, household contacts should avoid contact with items that can transmit blood, such as razors.

Individuals with hepatitis B and hepatitis C should be realistically cautious but not overly concerned about passing on the virus to their friends and loved ones. Avoiding exposure to blood is the most important thing to remember. For hepatitis B, vaccination is key.

Potential mothers are also concerned about passing on hepatitis B or hepatitis C to their babies. Pregnant women in the United States are tested for hepatitis B. If they are infected, treatment of the newborn with hepatitis B immune globulin (HBIG) and vaccination soon after birth is very effective in stopping transmission. Fortunately, transmission of the hepatitis C virus from mother to newborn is low (probably 1 to 2 percent). The newborn's pediatrician should know that the mother has chronic hepatitis C, and the baby should be tested as appropriate after birth.

Inherited Diseases

Patients with liver diseases are also concerned about the inheritance of their diseases and passing their diseases on to a child. Or they are concerned that a sibling may develop the same disease. Liver diseases that are inherited are discussed in Chapter 10. The patient should understand the real odds of family members being affected with the disease. Unfortunately, many doctors do not even know this and referral to a genetic counselor is sometimes prudent. This is particularly important if a patient is considering having children, in which case the potential mother and father should learn about the possibilities for prenatal diagnosis and the options for elective abortion if a fetus is affected.

Patients with diseases such as autoimmune hepatitis, primary biliary cirrhosis, and primary sclerosing cholangitis often ask me if these diseases are inherited. While autoimmune conditions such as these may tend to run in families, the chances of siblings or children having the condition are still extremely low. These are not inherited diseases in the strict sense of the term and should not be factored as such if a patient affected with one is considering having a child. The important factor in such situations is the health of the potential mother.

Substance Abusers with Liver Disease

The patient with an alcohol or other substance use disorder may be the most difficult in terms of relationships. Many individuals with substance use disorders have complex pathological interactions with their families, friends, and coworkers. In many of these situations, professional help and/or support groups are needed. Consider Al-Anon and Alateen.

It is important for loved ones and friends of people with substance use disorders to understand that they cannot fix the problem or cure the patient. It is mostly beyond their control. Usually, the best a loved one can do is to help the patient get medical attention or counseling, but often they cannot succeed at this. It is important for family members and friends to remember that substance abuse is an illness that is even difficult for professionals to treat. It is also important for them to know that treatment of substance use disorders is as important, and sometimes more important, than treating the liver disease the patient may have.

The Seriously Ill

Patients with cirrhosis and complications and with end-stage liver disease are seriously ill. These individuals may have realistic concerns about disability and dying in the near future. Treatment approaches for such patients are similar to those for others with any serious or terminal illness. The doctor should keep the patient and appropriate family members or friends realistically informed about the prognosis. If liver transplantation is an option, the entire family and certain close friends may also become very involved in the process.

Family members and friends of patients with terminal illnesses requiring tremendous attention must remember something important: they have lives, too. I am not being callous, but people with close relationships to very sick individuals must get on with their own lives. People who have a difficult time dealing with the complex medical needs of a loved one and of the sad feelings about the person should seek out help. This may be from support groups, clergy, close friends, other family members, or health professionals such as social workers, psychologists, or psychiatrists. Help your sick loved one as much as you can, but do not let it completely ruin your own life. This is sometimes hard to accept. However, it may be critical for your own health and what your sick loved one wants for you, too.

Nutrition and Exercise

Many patients have lots of questions about nutrition and exercise, including questions about fad diets or nutritional programs that are not based on medical or scientific data. Here are a few important points about nutrition and exercise for people with liver disorders.

Diet for Individuals with Chronic Liver Disease

Fortunately, in America we have a free press. For the most part, people can write what they want. Publishers can publish what they like. There is a book called *The Liver-Cleansing Diet*. I must admit I have not read more than the first few pages of this book. But the title alone cracks me up. On the first page of the book, the author, who is a medical doctor, writes: "excessive weight is a symptom of liver dysfunction." She then claims to have treated more than one thousand patients "to improve liver function." For all I know, the rest of the book goes on to describe a general healthy diet that may be good for all people. But "liver cleansing" has no medical or scientific meaning. And after reading the preceding chapters of this book, I hope you now understand a little about what liver dysfunction is and that "cleansing" is not a treatment. The point here is to beware of claims not based on science, even when the source has a medical degree.

Beliefs about diets to clean the liver or promote liver health probably derive from so-called alternative or holistic medical practices. Many alternative or holistic products include preparations for a healthy liver, healthy heart, healthy kidney, or other organs. Milk thistle or silymarin is considered by many to be a natural product that "strengthens" the liver or keeps it healthy. These diets or products have not been shown to be effective in any scientifically valid studies.

While there are appropriate dietary interventions for some patients with certain liver diseases, particularly those with complications of cirrhosis, there is no general "liver diet" or any diet to keep the liver "clean" or "healthy." For the most part, diet and a lifestyle that is conducive to general good health are probably good for the liver. All individuals, including those with chronic liver disease, should minimize fat intake and maintain ideal weights by watching what they eat and exercising.

What about vitamins? Excessive consumption of some vitamins, vitamin A in particular, can actually damage the liver. Some elements, such as excessive iron, are also probably not a good idea for people with chronic liver disease. My recommendation is that most people with chronic liver diseases—and most people without liver disease—should take a regular multivitamin each day (individuals with chronic liver diseases should probably take ones without iron). Excessive vitamins should be avoided.

Naturally, all individuals should use common sense and avoid substances and actions that can potentially damage the liver or other parts of the body. These include excessive alcohol consumption, use of illicit injected drugs, and use of herbs or "remedies" that may be toxic. Ask your doctor about herbs and nonprescribed "remedies" if you really want to take one.

Alcohol consumption in moderation will not hurt the liver. Perhaps it is even good to drink alcohol in moderation. Some studies suggest that one or two drinks of red wine a day decrease the risk of developing coronary heart disease. Using common sense about alcohol consumption is probably fine for one's liver, assuming of course the individual has common sense.

What do I tell patients with chronic liver diseases, other than alcoholic liver disease, who ask about drinking alcohol? While there is no good scientific study on which to base a decision, except to say that *excessive* drinking *is* dangerous, and some liver specialists believe that patients with any liver disease should not drink alcohol, I tell such patients that *reasonable* alcohol intake is not harmful. The late Dr. Fenton Schaffner, who was a very distinguished liver specialist and my teacher, used to tell his patients with liver diseases not caused by alcohol abuse that it was OK to drink as long as they drank "only the good stuff." His point was that responsible drinking in moderation is probably not harmful. A couple of glasses of wine with a nice dinner, a beer at a sporting event, a glass of champagne at a party, or an occasional cocktail will probably do no harm.

I can't provide exact numbers on how individuals with liver disease should limit their drinking. Probably no more than one or two drinks a day on a regular basis is reasonable. My general recommendation is that moderate alcohol intake is safe for most individuals with chronic liver disease (again, other specialists may have different opinions). Patients with nonalcoholic fatty liver disease, especially nonalcoholic steatohepatitis (NASH), may want to limit their consumption a bit more because alcohol can cause fat to accumulate in the liver. It is also a source of excess calories. One absolute exception to being allowed to drink alcohol is the person with an alcohol or substance use disorder. *People with alcohol use disorders should not drink, whether or not they have liver disease.*

Diets for Special Situations

Having discussed diets in general for most people with chronic liver disease, there are, however, some conditions where special diets may be indicated.

Cirrhosis and Complications

Individuals with cirrhosis and complications may need special diets. They should obtain advice about an appropriate diet from their doctor or a registered dietician. In general, patients with ascites and/or edema will require a low-salt diet. Those with hepatic encephalopathy may need a low-protein diet. Patients with hyponatremia (low blood sodium) may need to restrict fluid intake.

The salt restriction necessary for patients with significant ascites is rather severe—virtually no canned foods, no processed foods, and only small portions of meat, as meat has sodium in it. Such patients will usually need to obtain their diets from a doctor or dietician.

Fatty Liver

Although there is no specific diet for fatty liver, low-fat diets and weight loss are likely to be beneficial. Patients with nonalcoholic fatty liver disease, especially those with NASH, should probably limit alcohol intake, as heavy alcohol consumption can also cause fat accumulation. Many individuals with fatty liver will have diabetes mellitus, and diets recommended for their diabetes will likely help their fatty liver, too. Specific diabetic diets appropriate for an individual should be obtained from a doctor or registered dietician. Exercise also may be extremely helpful for patients with fatty liver.

Exercise and Liver Disease

Chronic liver disease is generally not a contraindication to exercise. I once had a patient with chronic hepatitis C who ran the New York City marathon in under four hours while taking interferon alpha! Exercise is important to overall health and will help avoid access adiposity, insulin resistance, and fatty liver. Exercise will also reduce the risk of developing heart disease and may have numerous other beneficial effects. People should exercise as much as they can. In particular, aerobic exercise such as running, jogging, rapid walking, riding a moving or stationary bicycle, running on a treadmill, using an elliptical trainer, or using a stair master is important. Ideally, a person should get thirty minutes of aerobic exercise a day. If that is not possible, one should aim for at least thirty minutes several days a week.

Patients, especially older ones, who routinely see doctors should ask what degree and types of exercise are safe for them. Exercise may have to be limited not because of chronic liver disease but possibly because of other nonrelated problems, such as heart disease or joint disease. Some people have a hard time initiating an exercise program on their own, especially as they age. Advice from a doctor could help. If their doctors agree, working out with a certified athletic trainer may be extremely helpful. (I am forty-six years old and have a personal trainer.) There are also good exercise classes at many gyms and health clubs.

Patients with cirrhosis and complications or end-stage liver disease may have limitations on the amount of exercise they can do. Complications of cirrhosis that could limit exercise include ascites, edema, muscle wasting, or hepatic encephalopathy. But even these individuals should have some exercise as recommended by their doctors. They also may benefit from a referral to physical or occupational therapists who can design appropriate exercise programs.

Exercise may be a good therapy for some liver diseases and may help some of the associated symptoms. Aerobic exercise, in particular, will help with weight loss, which may improve fatty liver and NASH. A combination of diet and exercise is probably important for individuals with these conditions, benefiting them not only by reducing fat in the liver but also by helping the heart and improving insulin resistance. For patients with chronic liver disease who suffer from fatigue, exercise may help them overcome their fatigue. Last, but not least, exercise helps people "feel good." Regular exercise will help people with chronic liver diseases keep a positive attitude, which is so important.

Work and Play

There is not much I can say regarding work and play except to do what you want—or have to do at work—and not think twice. Chronic liver disease without complications of cirrhosis should rarely limit one's activities. There are almost no jobs or recreational activities that most patients with chronic liver disease should not do, so long as they can tolerate it. If they cannot tolerate work or a favorite recreational activity, they should consult their doctor to find out why. In many cases, it may not be the liver disease but another medical or psychiatric problem.

However, cirrhosis and its complications may limit work and play activities. Complications of cirrhosis can lead to severe disability and perhaps allow for disability insurance benefits. Rarely, other complications of liver disease such as severe pruritus (itching) or problems such as arthritis in patients with primary biliary cirrhosis (PBC) could cause disability. Patients with complications of cirrhosis or rare symptoms of other chronic liver diseases should discuss these symptoms with their doctors.

Patients with chronic hepatitis B or chronic hepatitis C treated with an interferon alpha may sometimes experience side effects of the medications that limit work or play. Treatment can lead to irritability, depression, and other psychiatric problems. It can also sometimes cause intolerable flu-like symptoms and fatigue. Patients who encounter problems working or playing while being treated for chronic viral hepatitis should discuss the symptoms and problems with their doctors. In some cases, treatment may have to be stopped or postponed (e.g., if it is interfering with a particularly important year of work or family activities). The symptoms and limitations will resolve when treatment is discontinued or completed.

People with liver disease caused by alcohol use or drug use disorders may have difficulties at work. These patients need treatment for their substance use disorders. After they have been successfully treated, the contribution of liver disease, if any, to work or play limitations can be better established and dealt with.

14

Research and the Future

PERHAPS THE MOST exciting aspect of modern medicine is that basic scientific advances made in the laboratory will lead to new diagnostic methods and treatments of diseases. Since the revolution in molecular biology and the emergent discipline of biotechnology that was built upon it, the amount of time it takes for discoveries in the laboratory to be translated to a patient's bedside has decreased. One of the best examples of how the biotechnology industry has had a tremendous impact on a human disease, in fact, concerns a liver disease. This disease is hepatitis C.

Scientists at Chiron, a biotechnology company, discovered the hepatitis C virus in 1989. Before that time, it could not be diagnosed and the blood supply could not be adequately screened. Recombinant interferon alphas, made by cloning their genes and inserting them into cultured animal cells or microorganisms for protein expression, are used for treatment of this disease. While these interferons are now manufactured and marketed by different pharmaceutical companies, they were originally developed by the biotechnology industry. So the diagnosis and treatment of chronic hepatitis C has derived almost entirely from the biotechnology industry. However, the currently available treatments for chronic hepatitis are far from optimal, and much better ones are needed. A preventive vaccine also appears to be a long way off. Hopefully, the biotechnology and larger pharmaceutical industry will make progress on this as well as treating other diseases.

Surveying the different liver diseases, it is unlikely that the fight against all of them will progress at equal rates. I am optimistic that, in the near future, more effective treatments will exist for several liver diseases. Top on my list for major advances in the next decade is the development of specific medications to treat chronic hepatitis C. Despite my current optimism, I must admit that since I wrote the first edition of *The Liver Disorders Sourcebook* in 1999, the advances in the treatment of chronic viral hepatitis C have sadly been relatively minor. They have merely been the development of modified versions of already available drugs or the development of similar imperfect drugs in the same class. Truly novel drugs have not been introduced into clinical practice since prior to the publication of that book. However, they now seem to be closer on the horizon.

I also think that better treatments may evolve for genetic diseases, such as hemochromatosis and Wilson disease, now that the genes for these disorders have been identified and they can be understood at the molecular level. It is also probable that transplant immunology will advance, making liver transplantation safer and more effective. However, major advances in these areas will probably not see the clinic for several years to come.

While still optimistic, I believe that the understanding of some liver diseases and the development of treatments will be slow. The autoimmune liver diseases are poorly understood and will probably remain a major challenge, without significant breakthroughs in treatment during the next several years. I also think that significant advances in slowing the liver's response to chronic injury, namely the scarring and abnormal regeneration of the liver that leads to development of cirrhosis, are a long way off.

In some instances, socioeconomic factors and not science will slow the progress in our fight against liver diseases. An example is hepatitis B. At the present time, there are effective vaccines that could theoretically eradicate this virus. However, if cheap and easy-to-administer vaccines are not distributed to the underdeveloped countries of the world where hepatitis B virus infection is endemic, eradicating this disease will remain a dream.

I would like to provide some of my views on research and the near future for patients with liver diseases. I do not have a crystal ball, and basic scientific discoveries that are made today may change my opinions tomorrow. Based upon what I know now, however, I will speculate on where some of the most promising breakthroughs will occur during the next decade and also some of the most exciting areas of research for the more distant future.

Treatment for Viral Hepatitis

Until relatively recently, there were no specific drugs to treat viral infections. When a virus infects a host cell, it must use some of the host cell's own machinery to replicate. For this reason, drugs that attack viruses and do not simultaneously harm the host cells have been very difficult to design.

One of the first breakthroughs in designing specific antiviral drugs came against the human immunodeficiency virus (HIV). HIV causes AIDS. At the time the virus was discovered in 1980, progression of HIV infection to AIDS was almost a certainty with a life expectancy of about eighteen months once HIV was diagnosed. In the fifteen years or so since HIV was discovered, however, major strides have been made to allow people infected with this virus to live long and productive lives.

The development of HIV protease inhibitors and DNA polymerase inhibitors has led to highly active antiretroviral therapy (HAART). This has revolutionized the treatment of HIV-infected individuals. HAART utilizes drugs having different mechanisms of action at the same time. If the virus develops resistance to one drug by mutation, the other drugs will theoretically remain effective. Furthermore, a combination of drugs working at two distinct targets may be more effective in inhibiting viral replication than any one drug against any one target. Combination therapy is not a new idea in medicine; it has been used for some time in cancer chemotherapy and treatment of bacterial infections such as tuberculosis. The explosion in research on HIV made this the first virus against which so many different drugs are active and have been successfully utilized together. By taking combinations of polymerase and protease inhibitors, many patients with HIV infection are now living long lives and not developing AIDS.

I predict that in the next several years combination therapy with *specific* drugs will be available to treat hepatitis C. Interferon alpha and ribavirin are partially effective drugs for hepatitis C and result in "cures" in some people, but they are *not* specifically directed at the virus. Interferon alpha is a natural product made by your body that stimulates the immune system to fight viral infections. The theory behind giving excessive amounts of interferon is that it helps your own body attack the hepatitis C virus. Unfortunately, interferon alpha has other effects, which are readily apparent from the unpleasant symptoms that many individuals suffer while taking it. Ribavirin is a nonspecific drug that looks like a molecular building block essential to viral metabolism. Combined with interferon, it helps fight the hepatitis C virus but it does not *specifically* attack any viral proteins.

The good news is *drugs that specifically attack the hepatitis C virus are already being tested in early-stage clinical trials*. These drugs inhibit the NS3 protease and NS5B RNA polymerase of the virus. These proteins carry out specific functions necessary for virus replication, and if the functions of these viral proteins are inhibited, the virus cannot replicate.

Crystal structures of these proteins, and also the RNA helicase domain of NS3, have provided chemists with pictures of these molecules. By looking at these pictures, chemists can design drugs that may bind to and inhibit these molecules. This method is considered rational drug design because, rather than trying millions of compounds in potluck fashion, drugs can be synthesized based upon knowledge of the target's structure. Rational drug design can be combined with another type of methodology, combinatorial chemistry, in which thousands of structurally similar molecules are synthesized and tested against the target. High throughput screening can be performed in part by robots to speed the screening process. By combining rational drug design and combinatorial chemistry, inhibitors of these viral proteins can be rapidly identified. Many pharmaceutical and biotechnology companies are currently doing exactly this to develop drugs against hepatitis C virus. In addition to the NS3 protease inhibitors and NS5B polymerase inhibitors already being tested in early clinical trials, more are likely to make it out of the laboratory and into human subjects in the next few years. Hopefully by the end of the decade, one or more will be shown to be safe and effective and approved for routine clinical use.

The future treatment of chronic hepatitis C virus infection will probably be combination therapy with protease inhibitors, RNA polymerase inhibitors, and, possibly, other novel drugs. Using drugs that attack multiple viral targets, or two or more drugs that inhibit the same target by different mechanisms, will help avoid the development of resistance. Interferon alpha, possibly at lower doses, may be used along with these more specific compounds to fight the virus in another manner. Oral compounds are also being studied that stimulate the immune response, including the release of interferon alpha from the patient's own cells. Because hepatitis C is a slowly progressive chronic disease, people with this disorder who do not respond to currently available treatments should be optimistic that more specific and more powerful treatments will be available during their lifetimes. Some are already being tested in humans.

Specific drugs that attack viral targets are already approved to treat hepatitis B. Lamivudine, adefovir, and entecavir are nucleoside analogues that inhibit the hepatitis B viral DNA polymerase. Several other compounds that similarly inhibit the hepatitis B virus DNA polymerase are also under investigation and some that are already in clinical trials are likely to be approved in the near future. The problem with taking only one inhibitor of the hepatitis B virus DNA polymerase is that the virus can develop resistance by mutation. Combination therapy with two or more protease inhibitors may be more effective in the treatment of chronic hepatitis B. One challenge is designing the proper clinical trials to test these combinations and come up with the best ones. I hope that in the next several years, good clinical trials of more than one drug to treat chronic hepatitis B will be carried out. This may take some collaborative efforts between different manufacturers or support from nonindustry sources. So far, the only conclusive trials of more than one drug to fight hepatitis B have examined the use of an interferon alpha plus lamivudine. These trials were negative. In the longer term, I also hope that there will be new drugs with novel mechanisms of action against hepatitis B.

Vaccination for Chronic Viral Hepatitis

Effective vaccines for hepatitis A and hepatitis B already exist. Universal vaccination with hepatitis B virus has already been shown to decrease the incidence of liver cancer in Taiwan. This sounds revolutionary, but it is true. There is a vaccine that prevents cancer. It is a shame that hepatitis B vaccination is least available in the parts of the world where it is needed most. Universal vaccination, such as that for smallpox, could eradicate hepatitis B completely. Unfortunately, socioeconomic and not scientific factors will make this unlikely in the near future.

A vaccine against hepatitis C virus may be difficult to develop as there are several different genotypes and the virus can mutate into quasispecies that are not recognized by the immune system. However, novel scientific research may lead to a vaccine by the end of the next decade. Unfortunately, if realized, a hepatitis C vaccine may remain a commodity for citizens of wealthy nations only—and not be available in other parts of the world where it is needed.

Impact of Genomics

Genomics has become a household word. The entire human genome's DNA has been sequenced. Concerning liver diseases, the impact of genomic research has already been realized. The genes responsible for Wilson disease and hereditary hemochromatosis have been identified since the development of routine methods of gene mapping and DNA sequencing. Screening tests for these diseases are now possible. Furthermore, the proteins encoded by these genes are now known and their functions are being studied in the laboratory. Such studies should lead to drugs or other methods of treatment, such as gene therapy, for these genetic disorders. For example, studies have shown how the gene mutated in hereditary hemochromatosis encodes a protein that regulates uptake of iron by cells. Better knowledge of the mechanisms can lead to the development of drugs having the same functions in patients with the disease who lack normally functioning protein.

One aspect of genomics investigates changes in DNA sequences that associate with susceptibility to certain diseases or disease progression. Phamacogenomics investigates differences in DNA sequences that predict responses to drugs. Genomic and pharmacogenomic stud-ies are becoming cheaper to carry out as techniques for rapidly sequencing DNA improve and more powerful computer programs to analyze the data are developed. Careful genomic studies could poten-tially identify which patients with chronic hepatitis C, or other chronic liver diseases, will develop cirrhosis and which ones will not. A pow-erful and accurate predictive test of this nature may make treatment of most patients unnecessary. Pharmacogenomic studies could be carried out to predict who will respond to interferon alpha-based therapies or newer drugs in development for chronic hepatitis C. They could also theoretically determine who will suffer serious adverse events. Much of the technology to do these types of studies is already here. Design-ing the studies appropriately and obtaining the funding to do them are critical issues.

The rapidly growing discipline of genomics may impact on autoim-mune liver diseases. While these diseases are not inherited in the tra-ditional sense, individuals probably inherit many different genes that predispose them to acquiring them. Genomic studies could potentially identify which genes predispose people to these autoimmune diseases. Gene identification may lead to breakthroughs in understanding what goes wrong with the immune system in individuals who have them and could also lead to the development of novel treatments.

Transplant Immunology

Liver transplantation is a lifesaving procedure for those with end-stage cirrhosis or fulminant hepatic failure. The major problem most patients face after liver or other organ transplantation is that their own immune systems recognize the transplanted tissues as foreign and reject them. At the present time, this problem is solved using drugs that suppress parts of the immune system. These drugs not only prevent transplant rejection but also suppress the immune system so that it is less able to fight off certain types of infections that are of little or no consequence to an otherwise healthy person. Long-term suppression of the immune system by these drugs also makes that patient susceptible to certain types of cancer as the anticancer surveillance of the immune system is partially disabled.

Over the past few decades, an explosion of knowledge has taken place concerning our fundamental understanding of the immune system. Over the next several years, specific drugs that prevent the immune system from attacking the transplanted organ may be developed. For example, drugs that specifically block the foreign molecules on the transplanted organ from being recognized by the host's immune system could prevent organ rejection but not inhibit the immune system's ability to fight infection or cancer. These drugs may not be available tomorrow but perhaps in the next decade.

Another possibility in the area of organ transplantation is xenotransplantation—the transplantation of organs between species. If xenotransplantation is ever widely employed (ethical and scientific issues remain to be resolved), it is likely to have a major impact on liver transplantation because donor organs are at a shortage in many parts of the world. Xenotransplantation is most often discussed concerning the organs of pigs and humans. A pig liver is instantly rejected when transplanted into a human because the immune system detects certain proteins on the surface of pig cells as extremely foreign. Current immunosuppressive drugs cannot stop this intense reaction against such foreign proteins. However, advances in genetic engineering and cloning large animals (like the late Dolly the sheep and other animals) will theoretically make it possible to block the expression of foreign proteins on cells and, consequently, clone large numbers of pigs that lack these proteins. Thus, huge farms could be established where cloned pigs are raised to provide organs for human transplantation. While this may sound like something out of a futuristic science fiction novel, scientifically it likely will be possible in the next few years.

In addition to the ethical issues of breeding pigs to produce organs for humans, there are concerns that pig pathogens may gain access to the human population by transplantation and mutate to new forms that will then become human pathogens. For example, if a pig virus is transplanted to a human host, and the host is receiving immunosuppressive drugs to prevent rejection of the transplanted liver, that pig virus may replicate in the host and mutate to a form that can infect human cells. The concern is that this may allow for the evolution of novel viruses that can cause disease in humans, becoming widespread in the population. At present, many scientists believe that there should be a moratorium on xenotransplantation until these possibilities are excluded. Others feel that the risk is small. In fact, some biotechnology companies are already gearing up to produce animal organs for transplantation into humans.

Even more exciting than xenotransplantation is the tremendous promise of stem cell research. Nuclear transfer into embryonic stem cells and propagating the cells in culture (cloning) provides tremendous hope for the treatment of human disease. For example, the nucleus containing the DNA from a skin cell of a patient can theoretically be transferred to a cultured human embryonic stem cell. These cells can be coaxed to grow into hepatocytes in the culture dish. These haptocytes, or pre-hepatocytes, could possibly be injected into the portal vein if the patient has liver failure and start dividing to generate normal liver cells to replace damaged ones. As the cloned cells would have the identical genetic make-up as the patient, there would be no rejection. An even more exciting possibility in the distant future could involve tissue engineering, in which a genetically identical liver is created in the laboratory and then transplanted into the patient.

Supporting Research

Compared to funding for research in other areas, funding for liver diseases is low in the United States. Despite its fundraising efforts, the American Liver Foundation can fund only a little more than $1 million worth of research projects per year. By contrast, the average one-year budget of a single grant funded by the American Cancer Society is more than $100,000. It is true that cancer and heart disease kill more Americans than liver disease, but liver disease research remains poorly funded by any measure. Many people with liver disease or their family members are interested in supporting relevant research. There are a few things that everyone should realize when considering how to support liver disease research:

1. Most academic medical research in the United States is supported by the National Institutes of Health (NIH), a component of the Public Health Service of the Department of Health and Human Services. The money comes from tax dollars. Most NIH-funded research, despite being called "cancer research," "heart research," or

whatever, is basic and will have implications for all human diseases. To support broad, basic medical research, call, write, or e-mail your congressional representative and senators asking for increased funding for the NIH.

2. If you are very ambitious, and have a lot of money, you may want to do your own investigation and find out who is doing exciting research at universities or medical centers. Many universities or medical centers may allow you to make a donation to directly support that individual's research. However, unless you are qualified to judge a scientist's ability, or you obtain help from people who can, choices about supporting specific investigators may be best left to funding organizations with professional staffs and peer reviewers.

3. If you donate money to a legitimate foundation such as the American Liver Foundation, do not worry about it being targeted to a specific disease or scientist. This decision is better left to scientists on foundation advisory boards who make these decisions and know which areas of research, and which investigators, are likely to benefit most from funding.

4. More money is needed for basic laboratory research. Pharmaceutical companies spend billions of dollars every year developing drugs. They also spend billions supporting clinical trials. Relatively speaking, basic research—that with the most promise for the future—is poorly funded. You will get much more bang for your buck by supporting basic, fundamental research. Donations to universities, medical schools, and foundations such as the American Liver Foundation generally support basic research.

If you, a family member, or a friend suffers from a liver disease, you will benefit from basic research that is taking place now. Stay optimistic about the future. The best treatments for liver disease are yet to come.

15

Frequently Asked Questions

As a LIVER SPECIALIST and researcher with a website on liver diseases, through the years I have received tens of thousands of e-mails with questions from patients. During this time, I have noticed several similar or identical questions that are asked by many individuals. Hopefully, the answers to most of these questions will be obvious to those who have already read this book. Nonetheless, to emphasize and clarify these issues of common concern, here is a list of fifteen of the questions that people most often ask me about liver diseases along with my answers.

I was just denied insurance because my "liver enzymes" are elevated. What does this mean?

There are several laboratory blood tests that are commonly referred to as "liver enzymes." These include the alanine aminotransferase (ALT), aspartate aminotransferase (AST), alkaline phosphatase, and gamma-glutamyltranspeptidase (GGTP) activities. There are *many* causes of elevations of these enzyme activities in the blood, and *only a doctor who knows the complete history and examines the patient can make a diagnosis*. In *general*, however, elevations in the blood ALT and AST activities indicate inflammation of the liver (hepatitis) or destruction of liver cells from other causes. The most common liver disorders that cause the ALT and AST activities to be elevated are alcohol-related liver disease, chronic hepatitis C, chronic hepatitis B, prescription drugs, and fatty liver. However, there are other possible causes. In *general*, elevations in the alkaline phosphatase and GGTP activities indicate bile duct diseases; however, they may be elevated in other liver diseases, too. The blood GGTP activity alone may be elevated from heavy alcohol drinking, consumption of other drugs, or for no apparent reason in some normal individuals. The blood alkaline phosphatase activity also may be elevated in bone disorders in the absence of liver disease. Elevations in any of these enzymes are not diseases *per se*, but indicate that something may be wrong. An individual finding out about "abnormal liver function tests" or "liver enzymes" should *see a doctor* for a diagnosis.

What do you think of milk thistle (silymarin) for my liver disease?

In the worlds of alternative or herbal medicine, silymarin, which is present in milk thistle, has become the substance that is supposed to help anyone with any liver disease. Some individuals even advocate taking this to "keep the liver healthy." In short, however, there is no scientific evidence that silymarin, or milk thistle, is an effective treatment or preventative agent for any liver disease.

First, there should be a sound scientific basis for the effectiveness of any substance to treat a disease or condition. This usually results from laboratory studies or studies on animals. To the best of my knowledge, there is no reproducible laboratory research showing that silymarin does anything to protect the liver or improve any disease. Next, before any compound can be considered effective in humans, it must also be tested in clinical trials. The gold standard clinical trial is randomized, double-blinded, placebo-controlled. In such a trial, many subjects are randomly assigned to receive either an investigational new drug, a placebo (dummy drug), or an older, established therapy if one exists. Neither the treating doctors nor the patients know which treatment they are receiving (this is what "double-blind" means). All patients are monitored for adverse events and responses to treatment. (Responses must be defined before the study begins in order to prevent looking backward for apparently effective results.) At the end of the study, it is disclosed which individuals received the new drug and which did not. Adverse events and responses to treatment are then compared between the two groups. A statistical analysis is then performed to establish with the highest degree of probability that any detected differences are real and not a result of chance. Results from studies such as these are what the U.S. FDA usually wants to see before approving a drug. To the best of my knowledge, there are *no* randomized, double-blind, placebo-control studies of silymarin for any liver disease. Therefore, the effectiveness of this compound or, for that matter, its potential dangers, have not been established.

My relative (or friend) drinks excessively. He (or she) has symptoms of liver disease (or has once been told by a doctor about liver disease) but refuses to get help. What can I do?

This is an unfortunate and common situation. A relative or friend can suggest, even insist, that a patient seek medical help for any disease, including substance dependence, but cannot force the individual to seek help. The best approach to take is probably to suggest that the sick individual see a doctor to help make him or her feel better. Regarding alcohol abuse, the friend or family member can also suggest that the individual go to an Alcoholics Anonymous meeting. Unfortunately, these approaches often do not work, especially with substance dependence.

Al-Anon (and Alateen for younger individuals) is a worldwide organization offering self-help programs for families and friends of alcoholics whether or not the alcoholic seeks help or even recognizes the existence of a drinking problem. If a friend or family member of an individual with alcohol abuse or alcohol dependence needs help and support, he or she should contact Al-Anon or Alateen.

My doctor told me I have chronic hepatitis C. Do I need a liver biopsy?

Individuals who are newly diagnosed with chronic hepatitis C almost always ask if they need a liver biopsy. There is no absolute right or wrong answer to this question, but I'll try to explain the reason why *most* liver specialists will recommend a liver biopsy for *most* patients with chronic hepatitis C. Let's first deal with the issue of patients in whom liver biopsy may not change things that much. For example, per-cutaneous liver biopsy is high risk in someone with cirrhosis, a low platelet count, and an elevated prothrombin time. When the presence of cirrhosis is already obvious, liver biopsy should probably be per-formed in such patients if the information obtained will somehow influ-ence the outcome. In such cases, liver biopsy would probably have to be performed by an alternative approach such as by a transjugular approach or with a laprascope. If such a patient has strong evidence of hepatitis C (history of a risk factor and positive laboratory tests), biopsy is not necessary to confirm the diagnosis. Since it is already obvi-ous that the patient has cirrhosis, biopsy is not necessary to establish the presence of fibrosis or cirrhosis or how the degree of inflammation will influence prognosis. Biopsy may only be necessary in such a patient if a different diagnosis is possible or if a tumor is suspected.

Liver biopsy also may not be necessary in individuals in which liver disease is not a primary problem. For example, there is probably no need to assess the prognosis of a patient with hepatitis C if he or she has a more serious concurrent disease. The prognostic information obtained by liver biopsy may also not be useful in an elderly individ-ual. (Why do a liver biopsy in an eighty-year-old with hepatitis C?)

But what about most patients with a clinical and laboratory diag-nosis of hepatitis C and no other medical contraindications to the pro-cedure? In almost all such cases, liver biopsy provides essential data that cannot be obtained by any other test. *Most* liver specialists would advo-cate liver biopsy in such individuals. First of all, in relatively healthy individuals without complications of cirrhosis, known bleeding disor-ders, or other medical problems, the risk of complications from liver biopsy are very small. In exchange for this very small risk, the biopsy will provide critical information, especially regarding prognosis and pos-sible response to treatment. Only liver biopsy can establish for certain if most patients with chronic hepatitis C have cirrhosis. The degree of inflammation and fibrosis on biopsy also provides important prognos-tic information. No fibrosis and minimal inflammation correlate with a good prognosis. The absence of cirrhosis, significant scarring, and min-imal inflammation also correlate with a better response to treatment. Hence, the information obtained by liver biopsy is extremely useful in most individuals with chronic hepatitis C.

How does someone get "on the list" for a liver transplantation, and how long is the list?

Patients, and even their primary doctors, do *not* decide who is eligible for liver transplantation (at least in the United States). This decision can only be made at medical centers where transplantation is performed and depends upon a comprehensive evaluation by hepatologists, surgeons, psychiatrists, social workers, and, sometimes, other medical subspecialists. The decision is then made by consensus after considering the findings of each of these specialists. So the only way a patient can become a candidate for liver transplantation is to be evaluated at a center where liver transplantation is performed.

Once the patient is approved, he or she is put on a waiting list for transplantation. This list includes all individuals who have been deemed eligible for transplantation at a particular center. Several factors are taken into account when assigning a priority to a patient to receive an available donor liver, with the most important factor being how sick the patient is determined using the Model for End-Stage Liver Disease (MELD) or Pediatric End-Stage Liver Disease Model (PELD) statistical formulas.

Liver donor transplantation may be an alternative for some patients depending upon the particular case, potential availability of a donor, and the center.

What can I do to keep my liver healthy?

Many people seem to believe that there is some sort of "healthy liver diet" or "healthy liver lifestyle." Such beliefs probably derive from alternative or holistic medicine practices. Many alternative or holistic products include preparations for a healthy liver, healthy heart, healthy kidney, and so on. Milk thistle or silymarin (see the second question) is sometimes considered as a product that "strengthens" the liver or keeps it healthy.

In truth, there are no substances or diets for a "healthy liver." In general, a lifestyle that is conducive to general good health is also good for the liver. All individuals should minimize fat in their diets and try to maintain ideal weights by watching what they eat and exercising. This will avoid the accumulation of fat in the liver, just as it will in all other parts of the body. Alcohol consumption *in moderation* will *not* hurt the healthy liver; common sense should be used when it comes to drinking. Finally, risk factors for conditions that can damage the liver should be avoided. These risk factors include excessive alcohol consumption, injection drug use, and use of drugs, herbs, or "remedies" that may be toxic.

I have pain in the right side of my abdomen—can it be my liver?

Pain in the abdomen can come from many sources; only a doctor who examines the patient can determine the cause. Usually, individuals with chronic liver diseases do not have pain in the area of the liver. However, acute liver inflammation, tumors, and other mass lesions can cause pain if they irritate the capsule of the liver. Pain in the right upper portion of the abdomen is more often caused by disorders of the gallbladder, colon, or even the diaphragm than by liver diseases.

My ultrasound (CT scan/biopsy/etc.) shows _____. What does this mean?

Many patients with liver diseases are deeply concerned about one particular test result. It is usually what they consider the "big" test or test that is not routine. Most frequently, people are concerned about a pathologist's report of a liver biopsy or a radiologist's report about a CAT scan or ultrasound scan. All I can say is that in most cases, the results of one individual test are meaningless without knowing the complete case history and examining the patient. Concerns about a specific test must be directed to a doctor who has examined the patient and knows the entire case history.

I've just been diagnosed with a chronic liver disease. Will I die (or will I get cirrhosis)?

Most individuals with chronic liver diseases live full and normal lives. *Most* individuals with alcoholic liver disease who do not yet have advanced cirrhosis get better *if* they stop drinking. Even without treatment, *most* individuals with chronic hepatitis B and chronic hepatitis C do not develop cirrhosis in their lifetimes. Some chronic liver diseases, such as primary biliary cirrhosis, invariably lead to cirrhosis. However, progression may be slow and patients may have normal life spans and die of other natural causes before developing complications of liver disease. Unfortunately, it is often difficult to predict which patients with chronic liver disease will progress to cirrhosis and which ones will not. Perhaps most important, measures can be taken to prevent the chance of progression of chronic liver diseases in *most* patients.

Individuals with alcoholic liver disease must stop drinking. Chronic hepatitis B or hepatitis C can be treated with alpha-interferons and other drugs. Autoimmune hepatitis responds to treatment with steroids and azathioprine. Ursodiol may slow the progression of primary biliary cirrhosis. Effective treatments are also available for hemochromatosis and Wilson disease. Finally, liver transplantation can be considered an "insurance policy"—a lifesaving treatment of last resort for patients with chronic liver diseases that progress to end-stage cirrhosis. All things considered, *most* patients with chronic liver diseases should *not* die from them.

What are "lesions (spots) on the liver"?

For some reason, lots of people ask me about "lesions (or spots) on the liver." My guess is that these questions stem from abnormal ultrasound or CAT scans that detect a mass, a cyst, or other abnormality in the liver. Radiologists and other doctors often call these "lesions" and frequently tell patients that "lesions" were found in the liver on the test that was performed. These "lesions" can be *many* different things, some benign and some very serious. So "lesions on the liver" is *not* a diagnosis but merely a statement that something was detected in the liver, usually on a radiological test, that normally should not be there. Further tests, frequently biopsy, may be required to determine what the "lesions" are.

A friend has cancer of the liver. What can he (or she) do now?

Liver cancer is not a specific term. First, the type of liver cancer must be determined. *Hepatocellular carcinoma* is primary liver cancer, or a cancer that arises in the liver. The cell of origin appears to be the hepatocyte. Hepatocellular carcinoma is rather rare in the United States, but it is a leading cause of cancer death in the world. It almost always occurs in the United States in individuals with cirrhosis. Around the world, chronic infection with hepatitis B virus is the major risk factor. Cancers can also arise in the liver from the bile duct cells and are called *cholangiocarcinomas.*

Most "liver cancers" in the United States and other Western countries are *metastatic* carcinomas, or carcinomas that arise in solid organs from cells of the epithelial type. Carcinomas that arise in almost any other organ, common examples being the colon, rectum, pancreas, lung, breast, and prostate, can spread to the liver. Lymphomas and sometimes leukemias can also involve the liver.

The treatment option depends upon the type of cancer. Patients with cancers that arise in the liver, namely hepatocellular carcinomas or cholangiocarcinomas, generally have bad outcomes. Very small tumors of these types may be able to be resected surgically or treated by liver transplantation with a chance of cure. Usually, however, the cancer is fairly large at the time of diagnosis. Various treatment options do exist, such as alcohol injection and a technique known as *emoblization* that results in disruption of the tumor's blood supply. These treatments usually do not cure the patient but may alleviate symptoms and prolong life.

Patients with carcinomas from other organs that have spread to the liver almost always have a bad prognosis. Once a carcinoma has spread to the liver from another organ, it is likely disseminated throughout the body. However some tumors may respond to chemotherapy and rare ones (e.g., testicular) are curable. Other tumors may respond to direct infusion of chemotherapy into the liver. In general, chemotherapy may prolong life or quality of life but not cure the patient with metastatic liver cancer. A notable exception is testicular cancer that can be cured. Lymphoma or leukemia involving the liver may also respond to chemotherapy and be cured.

The bottom line is that patients with "liver cancer" need an extensive workup to establish the type of cancer and its extent throughout the body. Treatment options can then be considered. Unfortunately, the prognosis is not good for *most* types of cancer that involve the liver. Patients with liver cancers should generally be evaluated by an oncologist or medical cancer specialist to determine appropriate treatment options.

I have fatty liver. How can I make the fat go away?

Fat most frequently infiltrates the livers of individuals who drink alcohol, individuals with diabetes mellitus, and individuals who are obese. Some drugs can also cause fat in the liver. Occasionally, fat can be seen in the liver of otherwise apparently healthy individuals. The diagnosis is usually *suspected* when the ALT and/or AST activities are elevated on blood testing and there is no other obvious cause of liver disease. The diagnosis of fatty liver can only be made by liver biopsy. There are two major forms of fatty liver distinguished on liver biopsy. One, called *steatosis*, is only the presence of fat within the liver. The other, more severe form, is called *steatohepatitis* and is characterized by fat plus a particular type of inflammation. Steatosis generally has a good prognosis, but steatohepatitis can progress to cirrhosis. If the cause of steatohepatitis is not alcohol, it is called *nonalcoholic steatohepatitis*, or *NASH*.

If alcohol is the cause of fatty liver, the patient should stop drinking and the fatty liver will reverse. If a drug is suspected, the drug should be discontinued. Although there are no large, well-controlled studies, clinical experience and common sense suggest that fatty liver will resolve in obese individuals who lose weight. A healthy, low-fat diet and exercise may also help nonobese individuals with fatty liver. In diabetics who have fatty liver, better control of blood sugar may help it resolve. So, less alcohol, a low-fat diet, exercise, weight loss in overweight individuals, and better control of blood sugar in diabetics may make the fat go away in those with fatty liver.

I have a liver disease not related to alcohol. Can I drink?

There is no definite right or wrong answer and no scientific data on which to base a decision (except to say that *excessive* drinking *is* dangerous). Some liver specialists strongly believe that patients with any liver disease should *never* drink alcohol. Others, myself included, feel that *reasonable* alcohol intake is most likely not harmful. (However, I very strongly believe, and scientific data support this belief, that patients with alcoholic liver disease, or those with alcohol abuse or dependency disorders, should *never* drink alcohol.)

My teacher, the late Dr. Fenton Schaffner, a distinguished liver specialist, used to tell his patients with *nonalcoholic* liver diseases that it was OK to drink as long as they drank "only the good stuff." His point was that responsible drinking in moderation is probably not harmful. A couple of glasses of wine with dinner, a beer at the baseball game, or an occasional cocktail will probably do no harm. I can't provide exact numbers on how many drinks individuals with liver disease should limit themselves to (probably no more than two drinks a day on a regular basis). But my general recommendation is that mild alcohol intake is probably safe for most individuals with liver diseases, *except of course for the person with alcoholic liver disease or a substance use disorder, who should not drink*. Again, not all liver specialists agree, and some say that patients with liver disease should never drink.

I have a liver problem, and my doctor or HMO refuses to send me to a specialist. Can you please help me?

Most general internists, pediatricians, and family doctors should be able to diagnosis the most common liver diseases. If you really think that your doctor cannot, it is an unfortunate situation and I can only recommend seeing another doctor. I don't know what to say if your HMO or insurance provider does not allow you to see another doctor, except to suggest that you pay out of pocket or perhaps explore legal options about referrals by contacting a state medical board, a state insurance board, or an attorney.

Problems sometimes arise with specialized treatments, the diagnosis of rare diseases, and liver transplantation. Sometimes, a small HMO may really not have a doctor who knows how to diagnose, treat, and manage patients with rarer liver disorders such as primary biliary cirrhosis, autoimmune hepatitis, or Wilson disease. Sometimes, doctors in HMOs or in rural communities really do not know when to refer patients for liver transplantation (although these days, I hope that most do). I do not know exactly how to help except to recommend that you explore legal options if your HMO or insurance provider prohibits a second opinion by a specialist. The bottom line is that life comes before money, and in some cases a patient's only option may be to pay for a second opinion consultation with a liver specialist that will not be covered by his or her insurance. In many cases, you will be relieved to hear that your current doctor is doing things right. If by chance you find out that your current doctor cannot handle the problem, a letter from an outside expert explaining why you need specialized treatment not available in your "network" *may* help convince your HMO to change its mind about covering outside care.

What can I do to "lower my liver enzymes"?

The goal in a patient with a liver disease is *not* to treat laboratory values. The goal is to make a diagnosis to determine the cause of the laboratory abnormality. Then specific treatments or interventions aimed at the disease and *not* the laboratory abnormality can be prescribed. Absolute values of so-called "liver enzymes" (generally blood ALT, AST, alkaline phosphatase, and GGTP activities) are not the major issue. Identification and treatment of the diseases is.

Glossary

THIS GLOSSARY DEFINES words used throughout this book as well as frequently used words related to the liver and its diseases. The names of specific liver diseases are not included. For information on these, see the Index for the chapters where they are discussed.

Activity: A unit of measurement used by biochemists that is proportional to the amount of an enzyme at a given temperature, concentration, and other conditions. Various blood tests used to assess liver function are measured in units of activity.

Adefovir: An orally administered drug approved for the treatment of chronic hepatitis B. It belongs to the class of drugs known as nucleoside analogues.

Albumin: The most abundant protein in the blood that is synthesized in the liver. Its concentration in the blood may be low when liver function is compromised.

Alcoholic: An ill-defined term applied to a person with either an alcohol abuse or alcohol dependency disorder.

Alcohol use disorders: Conditions, precisely defined in the American Psychiatric Association's *Diagnostic and Statistical Manual of Mental Disorders*, that describe people with chronic problems related to alcohol consumption. The chronic alcohol use disorders are alcohol abuse and alcohol dependency.

Alkaline phosphatase: An enzyme present in the bile ducts as well as other organs such as bone, kidney, and placenta. Its activity is frequently measured in the blood; elevations may indicate bile duct or liver disease.

ALT: See *Aminotransferases.*

Aminotransferases: Enzymes present in hepatocytes (and other tissues). The activities of two aminotransferases, alanine aminotransferase (ALT) and aspartate aminotransferase (AST), are frequently measured in the blood. These enzymes leak out of hepatocytes when they are damaged or die. Their blood activities are often elevated in liver diseases such as hepatitis.

Antibodies: Proteins in the blood that are produced by cells of the immune system and recognize components of infecting organisms such as viruses or bacteria. In abnormal circumstances, the immune system may make antibodies against the body's own components. These antibodies are called autoantibodies.

Antigen: A protein or other type of chemical compound recognized by an antibody. See also *Antibodies.*

Antimitochondrial antibodies: A type of autoantibody found in the large majority of patients with primary biliary cirrhosis. See also *Autoantibodies.*

Antinuclear antibodies: Types of autoantibodies found in patients with various autoimmune liver diseases such as primary biliary cirrhosis, primary sclerosing cholangitis, and autoimmune hepatitis. See also *Autoantibodies.*

Ascites: Abnormal accumulation of edema fluid in the abdomen. See also *Edema.*

AST: See *Aminotransferases.*

Autoantibodies: Antibodies against components of an individual's own body. See also *Antibodies.*

Autoimmune: A state in which the body's immune system attacks and damages the body's tissues and organs. Primary biliary cirrhosis, primary sclerosing cholangitis, and autoimmune hepatitis are thought to be autoimmune liver diseases.

Autosomal recessive disorder: Genetic diseases in which two abnormal copies of a gene must be inherited for the disease to be manifested. The liver diseases hereditary hemochromatosis, alpha-1-antitrypsin deficiency, and Wilson disease are autosomal recessive disorders.

bDNA: A type of blood test sometimes used to measure the amount of hepatitis C viral RNA in the blood.

Bilirubin: A chemical compound produced in the human body primarily from the breakdown of old red blood cells. It is taken up by the liver, changed to a more soluble form, and then secreted into the bile. The blood bilirubin concentration is often measured in the clinical laboratory and may be elevated in various liver diseases as well as in some conditions in which red blood cells are destroyed at an abnormal rate. If the blood bilirubin concentration is higher than about 2 milligrams per deciliter, the person will appear jaundiced.

Cachexia: A generalized wasting, especially of muscle mass, that can be seen in advanced cirrhosis as well as other chronic diseases.

CAT scan: Computerized axial tomography; an X-ray test used to obtain cross-sectional images of the body. It may be useful in evaluating the liver and gallbladder, especially in searching for tumors, gallstones, or evidence of bile duct obstruction.

Cholestasis: Stagnation of bile flow in the liver.

Conjugation: The chemical reaction in bilirubin metabolism in which glucuronic acid moieties are coupled to bilirubin to make it soluble so that it can be secreted into the bile. Conjugation takes place in hepatocytes of the liver and is catalyzed by the enzyme UDP-glucuronosyltransferase. Other substances, such as drugs and toxins, may also be conjugated in the liver to make them more soluble for elimination in either the bile or by the kidneys.

CT scan: See *CAT scan.*

Edema: Abnormal accumulation of fluids in the tissues of the body.

Encephalopathy: Abnormal mental functioning secondary to organic causes. See also *Hepatic encephalopathy.*

Endoscope: A fiber optic tube that is used to directly visualize the inside of body cavities, including the upper and lower gastrointestinal tract. In patients with liver diseases, endoscopy may be necessary to visualize the esophagus, stomach, or proximal small intestine. These tubes may be modified so that procedures can be performed through them under direct visualization.

Endoscopic retrograde cholangiopancreatography: Abbreviated ERCP, a procedure in which a small tube is inserted into the bile via an endoscope and dye is injected. Then an X-ray image can be obtained of the bile ducts inside and outside of the liver as well as the pancreatic duct because X-rays cannot pass through the injected dye. This procedure also can be modified to do procedures such as remove gallstones trapped in a large bile duct.

Endoscopic rubber band ligation: A procedure in which esophageal, or possibly gastric, varices are tied off through a fiber optic tube (endoscope) under direct visualization.

Endoscopic sclerotherapy: A procedure in which esophageal varices are treated with a caustic chemical to occlude them. This procedure is performed via a fiber optic tube (endoscope) under direct visualization.

Enlarged liver: See *Hepatomegaly.*

Entecavir: An orally administered drug approved for the treatment of chronic hepatitis B. It belongs to the class of drugs known as nucleoside analogues.

Enzyme: A protein that catalyzes (speeds up) a chemical reaction.

ERCP: See *Endoscopic retrograde cholangiopancreatography.*

Esophageal varices: Varicose veins in the esophagus.

Fibrosis: Scar tissue.

First pass metabolism: A term used for the chemical reactions many drugs and toxins undergo in the liver before reaching the systemic circulation (things absorbed in the gut first go to the liver before the heart).

Gamma-glutamyltranspeptidase: Often abbreviated GGTP, an enzyme present in the bile ducts. Its activity in the blood is frequently measured in the clinical laboratory. Elevations can indicate a wide variety of liver diseases and may be high in some individuals without any significant disease. It may be elevated in patients who consume excess alcohol or are taking certain drugs. It may also indicate bile duct disease.

Gastric varices: Varicose veins in the stomach.

Gastroenterologist: A doctor who specializes in diseases of the digestive system, including the liver. Some gastroenterologists, however, prefer to primarily care for patients with diseases of the esophagus, stomach, intestines, and rectum and do not devote much time to liver diseases.

Genotypes: Slightly different groups of the hepatitis C virus classified based on the sequences of their genetic material.

GGTP: See *Gamma-glutamyltranspeptidase.*

Gynecomastia: Breast enlargement in men that can occur as a result of cirrhosis and poor metabolism of circulating estrogens in the blood.

HBIG: See *Immune globulin.*

Hepatic artery: A blood vessel that delivers oxygen-rich blood to the liver directly from the heart.

Hepatic encephalopathy: A change in mental state caused by the inability of the liver to metabolize ammonia and other nitrogen-containing toxins that are absorbed from the gut and are toxic to the brain. Clinically, hepatic encephalopathy can range from subtle changes in the ability to concentrate to deep coma.

Hepatic vein: The major vein via which blood exits the liver.

Hepatitis: A general term for inflammation of the liver. There are many causes of hepatitis including alcohol, drugs, toxins, viruses, and metabolic disorders.

Hepatocyte: The primary cell type of the liver. Many different biochemical reactions essential for whole body metabolism and health take place in hepatocytes.

Hepatologist: A doctor who specializes in diseases of the liver.

Hepatology: The study of liver diseases.

Hepatomegaly: Enlarged liver. It is not specific for any one liver disease. There are many causes, including some diseases of the liver.

Hepatorenal syndrome: A type of kidney failure that is seen only in patients with liver failure. It is virtually always fatal unless liver transplantation is performed.

Heterozygote: Regarding genetic diseases, this term is used to refer to a person who has inherited one copy of an abnormal gene. In autosomal recessive disorders, a heterozygote will not have the disease but will be a carrier.

Homozygote: Regarding genetic diseases, this term is used to refer to a person who has inherited two copies of an abnormal gene. In autosomal recessive disorders, a homozygote will have the disease.

Hyperbilirubinemia: Elevated bilirubin concentration in the blood.

Hypoalbuminemia: Low albumin concentration in the blood.

Immune globulin: A preparation of antibodies against a particular organism. Hepatitis B immune globulin (HBIG) contains antibodies against the hepatitis B virus and may be given to people with known exposure. Immune globulin in general almost always has antibodies against the hepatitis A virus and may be given to people who are exposed to this virus or traveling to high-risk areas before having time to be vaccinated.

Immunosuppressive drugs: A class of drugs used to suppress the immune system and prevent organ transplant rejection. Some are also used to treat autoimmune hepatitis.

Interferon: Naturally occurring substances that have many functions in the body, including helping to fight off viral infections. Synthetic types of interferon, administered by injection, are used in the treatment of hepatitis B and hepatitis C.

Jaundice: Yellowing of the skin, whites of the eyes, and mucous membranes secondary to high bilirubin concentrations in the blood.

Kayser-Fleischer rings: Abnormalities seen in the eye in most patients with Wilson disease.

Lamivudine: An orally administered drug approved for the treatment of chronic hepatitis B. It belongs to the class of drugs known as nucleoside analogues.

Liver enzymes: A term used for various blood tests that are related to the liver. Generally it refers to the aminotransferases, but it may also be used to refer to alkaline phosphatase and gamma-glutamyltranspeptidase.

Liver palms: Reddish palms (called palmar erythema by doctors) that may be seen in individuals with various liver diseases.

Liver-spleen scan: A nuclear medicine test that can sometimes detect cirrhosis.

MELD: An abbreviation for Model for End-Stage Liver Disease, a statistical formula that provides a score used to prioritize individuals age twelve years and older waiting for liver transplantation.

MRI: Magnetic resonance imaging; an imaging study of the part of the body that uses the phenomenon known as nuclear magnetic resonance. It is sometimes used to visualize the liver and may be useful in searching for certain types of tumors.

Paracentesis: A procedure in which fluid (ascites) is removed from the abdominal cavity by inserting a needle through the abdominal wall. A small amount of fluid may be removed for diagnostic purposes or a large amount for therapeutic reasons.

PCR: See *Polymerase chain reaction.*

Peginterferon: Interferon modified by attaching a polyethylene glycol molecule, which increases its half-life.

Pegylated interferon: See *Peginterferon.*

PELD: An abbreviation for Pediatric End-Stage Liver Disease Model, a statistical formula that calculates a score used to prioritize children under twelve years old who are waiting for liver transplantation.

Platelets: The smallest blood cells that play a role in blood clotting.

Polymerase chain reaction: A type of chemical reaction used to amplify small amounts of DNA of a specific sequence. This type of chemical reaction, combined with reverse transcription or copying of RNA to DNA, can be used to detect hepatitis C virus RNA in the blood.

Portal gastropathy: Diffusely dilated veins in the stomach that result from portal hypertension.

Portal hypertension: Usually caused by cirrhosis, it is high pressure in the portal vein and connected veins. Portal hypertension can lead to many problems, including the development of gastric and esophageal varices and splenomegaly.

Portal vein: The major blood vessel that supplies blood to the liver. Blood in the portal vein contains substances absorbed from the stomach and gut.

Prothrombin time: A blood test used to assess the amounts or activities of certain clotting factors in the blood. It may be prolonged if liver function is abnormal. It may also be prolonged in other disorders.

Pruritus: Itching, which is a symptom of some liver diseases.

Quasispecies: Slightly different variants of the hepatitis C virus that arise by mutations in the viral RNA.

Red blood cells: Cells that circulate in the blood whose function is to carry oxygen.

Ribavirin: An orally administered drug that is used in combination with an interferon alpha in the treatment of chronic hepatitis C.

Shunt: A type of surgical procedure in which a vein of the portal circulation is connected to a blood vein of the systemic circulation to relieve portal hypertension. Besides being performed at surgery, these days it is a type of shunt performed by radiologists. See also *Transjugular intrahepatic portosystemic shunt*.

Sonogram: See *Ultrasound*.

Spenomegaly: An enlarged spleen that can be caused by portal hypertension.

Spider angiomata: Small marks on the skin that have central red areas and "legs" that radiate out from the center, making them look like spiders. If pressure is applied, they blanch and turn red again when pressure is released. They are seen in patients with chronic liver diseases and sometimes in pregnant women.

Steatosis: A pathologist's term for fatty liver.

Thrombocytopenia: Low platelet count.

TIPS: See *Transjugular intrahepatic portosystemic shunt*.

Transjugular intrahepatic portosystemic shunt: Abbreviated TIPS, a procedure performed by radiologists in which a tube is passed through the liver to connect the portal and hepatic veins and reduce portal hypertension. It is indicated to stop bleeding from gastric and esophageal varices.

Ultrasound: An imaging study that uses sound waves to obtain an image of internal organs. Often used to image the liver and gallbladder, it's an excellent test to look for liver tumors, gallstones, and bile duct obstructions.

Vena cava: The largest vein of the body that returns blood to the heart. The hepatic vein via which blood exits the liver empties directly into the vena cava.

Resources

MANY PATIENTS WANT disease-related information that goes far beyond this book. Some even want to read medical textbooks or stay up to date with the latest medical literature. Major television networks and news services will likely report major breakthroughs in medicine related to liver disease. Newspapers such as the *New York Times* or the *Wall Street Journal* will frequently report major findings. Medical news regarding new drug treatments that influence pharmaceutical companies is often reported in the business sections of major American newspapers. Various websites devoted to business news are often loaded with press releases about new drugs and "new" studies of old drugs, including those for liver diseases.

For patients who want to learn about liver diseases in depth or keep up with the most current literature, I have provided here the names of relevant major medical journals. Since more and more people are surfing the Web for medical information, also provided are some Internet resources I think are reputable. Please note that these lists are not complete, merely my personal recommendations.

Medical and Scientific Journals

Basic discoveries that will ultimately be important in liver diseases may be published in highly technical journals. These papers are usually incomprehensible to the nonspecialist and even most practicing physicians. However, some scientific journals will publish papers that may be of immediate impact on clinical liver disease, for example, the cloning of a gene that causes a particular genetic disease or the discovery of a new hepatitis virus. The most significant clinical papers related to liver diseases that impact clinical practice are usually published in the most important general medical and scientific journals. There are also several specialized journals that publish papers on both clinical hepatology and science related to liver diseases. Some of the medical and scientific journals that frequently publish important papers related to the liver and liver diseases are listed in Table A. There are many more, but I consider the ones in this table to be some of the better ones.

Reputable Internet Resources

Many patients, friends and family members are turning to the Internet for medical information and even advice. When using the Internet, *be careful.* Anyone can put up an impressive looking website and make ridiculous or misleading information look important. Many also try to sell miracle cures or wonder treatments that the medical profession have ignored or tried to suppress (really watch out for these!). People can masquerade as doctors and professors and provide medical advice. My strongest recommendation is *never accept medical advice from anyone except a doctor who has taken a complete history and examined you.*

There are thousands of medical websites. A comprehensive and complete analysis of them is beyond the scope of this book (perhaps any book). Most can be found using general Internet search engines. I will provide only a *brief* list of a few websites that are good starting points to obtain reputable information on liver diseases. Many other websites also provide outstanding information. I apologize to the excellent websites that I have omitted, but you will likely find them as you surf.

Table A Reputable Scientific and Medical Journals Publishing Papers on or Related to Liver Disease

General Medical Journals	Medical Journals Focused on Liver Diseases	Scientific Journals
Annals of Internal Medicine	American Journal of Gastroenterology	AJP—Gastrointestinal and Liver Physiology (physiology of liver/diseases)
Lancet	Clinical Gastroenterology and Hepatology	American Journal of Human Genetics (genetic diseases)
New England Journal of Medicine	Gastroenterology	American Journal of Pathology (pathology of liver/diseases)
	Gut	Biochemistry (biochemistry of liver/diseases)
	Hepatogastroenterology	Cell (general)
	Hepatology	Genomics (genetic diseases)
	Journal of Hepatology	Human Molecular Genetics (genetic diseases)
	Journal of Viral Hepatitis	Immunity (immune/autoimmune system)
	Liver	Journal of Biological Chemistry (biochemistry of liver/diseases)
	Liver Transplantation	Journal of Cell Biology (cell biology of liver/diseases)
		Journal of Cell Science (cell biology of liver/diseases)
		Journal of Clinical Investigation (general)
		Journal of Experimental Medicine (mostly immune/autoimmune system)
		Journal of Immunology (immune/autoimmune diseases)
		Journal of Virology (hepatitis viruses)
		Nature (general)
		Nature Genetics (genetic diseases)
		Nature Medicine (general)
		Proceedings of the National Academy of Sciences USA (general)
		Science (general)

General Liver Disease Information

American Association for the Study of Liver Diseases
aasld.org

This is the homepage of the predominant American organization for physicians and biomedical scientists with an interest in the liver and its diseases.

American Liver Foundation
liverfoundation.org

The American Liver Foundation is a national, voluntary health agency dedicated to preventing, treating, and curing hepatitis and all liver diseases.

Diseases of the Liver
http://cpmcnet.columbia.edu/dept/gi/disliv.html

This is my own site. I won't comment more.

National Institute of Diabetes and Digestive and Kidney Diseases
   (NIDDK)
niddk.nih.gov

NIDDK is the institute of the National Institutes of Health of the Department of Health and Human Services devoted to most issues regarding digestive diseases. This site contains information on digestive diseases, research funding, and NIDDK's own intramural research programs and clinical trials. It may take some exploring of the site to find the information you're looking for.

Viral Hepatitis

Centers for Disease Control and Prevention (CDC)
cdc.gov/ncidod/diseases/hepatitis/index.htm

The CDC is one of the thirteen major operating components of the Department of Health and Human Services. It is devoted to public health efforts to prevent and control infectious and chronic diseases, injuries, workplace hazards, disabilities, and environmental health threats. This is their page with information on viral hepatitis.

Metabolic Liver Diseases

Online Mendelian Inheritance in Man (OMIM)
ncbi.nlm.nih.gov/entrez/query.fcgi?db=OMIM&itool=toolbar

OMIM is a comprehensive database of human genes and genetic disorders authored and edited by Dr. Victor A. McKusick at Johns Hopkins University and his colleagues and developed for the Web by the National Center for Biotechnology Information (NCBI). It is arguably the best online resource on inherited liver diseases such as Wilson disease, familial hemochromatosis, and alpha-1-antitrypsin deficiency.

Liver Transplantation

United Network for Organ Sharing (UNOS)
unos.org

UNOS administers the national Organ Procurement and Transplantation Network and the Scientific Registry on Organ Transplantation under contracts with the Department of Health and Human Services. This site, and their related site Transplant Living (transplantliving.org/), contains information and statistics on organ transplantation, including liver transplantation.

Alcohol-Related

Alcoholics Anonymous
alcoholics-anonymous.org

This website contains information about AA and how individuals with alcohol use disorders can obtain additional materials.

Al-Anon and Alateen
Al-Anon-Alateen.org

This website is the work of Al-Anon member volunteers in various countries. It provides information about the organization for family members and friends of individuals with alcohol use disorders.

Searching the Medical Literature

National Center for Biotechnology Information Pub Med
ncbi.nlm.nih.gov

This website provides the user with access to free searches of primary literature, with abstracts available for many articles. It also provides access to many biomedical databases and references, mostly for health professionals.

Index